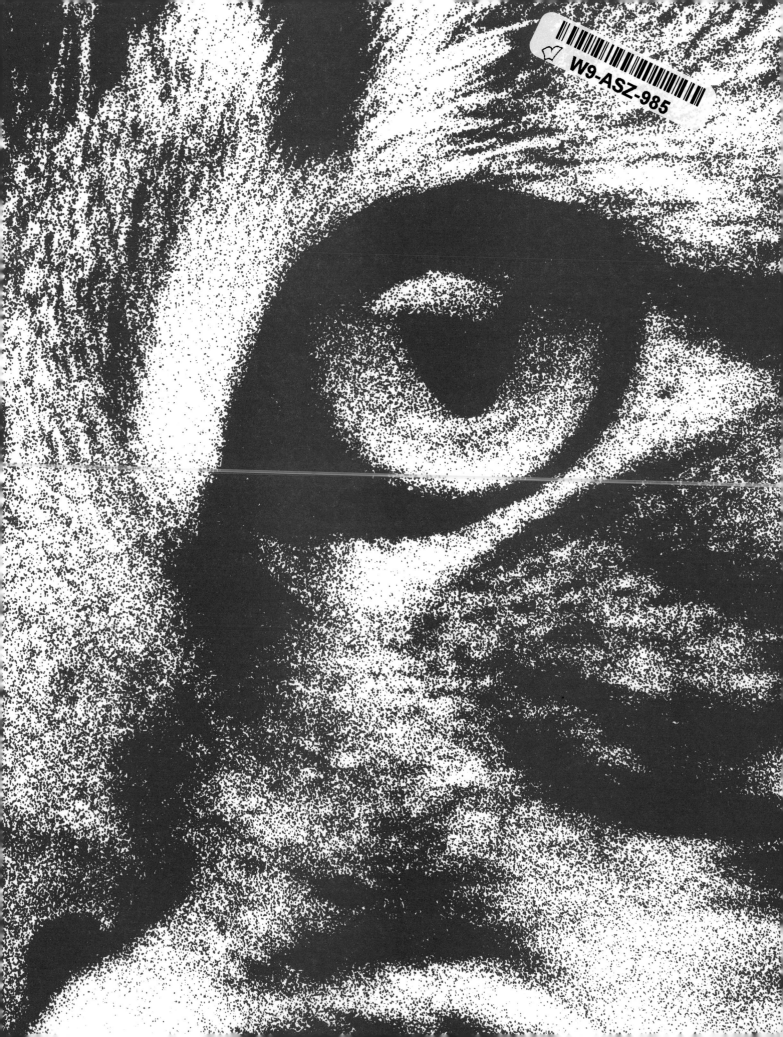

COMPLETE ILLUSTRATED
Guide to
CAT CARE

COMPLETE ILLUSTRATED
Guide to
CAT
CARE

THUNDER BAY
P·R·E·S·S

A DK PUBLISHING BOOK
www.dk.com

SECTION ONE
Project Editor Liza Bruml
Art Editor Clair Watson
Production Controller Hilary Stephens

SECTION TWO
Project Editor Alison Melvin
Art Editor Lee Griffiths
Production Controller Antony Heller
US Editor Mary Ann Lynch
ASPCA Consultant Stephen Zawistowski

Published by Thunder Bay Press
5880 Oberlin Drive, Suite 400
San Diego, CA 92121-4794
1-800-284-3580
http://advmkt.com

1 2 3 4 5 99 00 01 02 03

Library of Congress Cataloging-in-Publication Data

Fogle, Bruce.
   The complete illustrated guide to cat care and behavior / Bruce
Fogle & Andrew Edney : foreword by Roger Caras.
       p.   cm.
   Rev. ed. of: ASPCA complete cat care manual / Andrew Edney. 1st
American ed. 1992. And Know your cat : an owner's guide to cat behavior /
Bruce Fogle. 1st American ed. 1991.
   Includes index.
   ISBN 1-57145-184-6
   1. Cats.   2. Cats—Health.   3. Cats—Behavior.   I. Edney, A. T. B.
II. Edney, A. T. B.   ASPCA complete cat care manual
III. Title.
SF447.F63   1999
636.8—dc21   99–13542
                                                                  CIP

CONTENTS

Do we really know cats?

CATS ARE ABSOLUTELY magnificent. They control their emotions far better than we do. They are much more agile than dogs. They are self-sufficient, independent, strong, and well-built. However we frequently misunderstand them and we do so because, unlike dogs, cats are in many ways quite different from us.

Dogs, like humans, are pack animals. Both have developed a reliance upon and enjoyment of the companionship of their own kind. In the process of doing so, a dynamic range of welcoming body language has evolved. But cats come from a different beginning. They evolved or, to be more accurate, are in the process of evolving from solitary hunters to a more sociable species. They moved into human society later than any other domesticated animal but, in this century, have become extremely popular pets. In the United States, there are more than 50 million cats; they are already more popular than dogs. Add the estimated 50 million in Europe and countless other millions worldwide, and there are over 200 million domestic cats – the most successful feline that has ever existed.

Domestic cats are divided into two main groups: domestic pet cats and feral cats. Domestic pet cats live with human company. Usually raised by us, they are content to live in our homes and share our food and affection. In fact for cats, humans often make better companions than other cats.

Body language
With arched back and erect fur, this kitten is sending out a "go away" signal.

Seeking security
Although magnificent predators, cats are prey to many larger animals and hiding is a natural behavior.

Making friends
This cat was handled when a young kitten, so she now enjoys being stroked by her owner.

Stimulating play
Playing with objects improves the young cat's mental and physical dexterity.

Choosing a partner
This female will probably mate with several toms. Until recently, cat breeding was left to nature.

Feral cats are domestic cats born in the wild and raised outside human communities. The only difference between ferals and pet cats is in their early upbringing. If they are denied human contact during the important first seven weeks of life, they will always retain a timid fear of us. Early contact with humans is vital.

The North African wild cat, from which our pets evolved, was a hunter. Even today, domestic cats retain a strong urge to hunt. In the wild, kittens stop playing with each other when the need to hunt for food, protect themselves, mark out territories and find mates become dominant factors. Pet cats, with all their daily needs taken care of, remain often playful when mature, as they never have to grow up.

Slowing down
In old age the cat's reaction time is reduced, but with improved health care and diet cats are living longer than ever.

Mutual grooming
Although cats are independent creatures, they still enjoy some sociable behaviors.

Do cats really think? Of course they do. Do cats have emotions? The answer is yes. And it is not anthropomorphic to credit cats with emotions, for both humans and cats have identical regions in the brain responsible for emotion. Through the book I am going to emphasize this point and put thoughts into the cat's mind.

Every day, on the examining table at my animal hospital, cats are telling me something. In most instances, it would probably not be suitable for publication, but my point is that through their body language and demeanor cats are skilled communicators. I hope I am acting as a good interpreter for them.

Quiet temperament
Flat-faced breeds are often calmer and more retiring than lithe oriental cats.

KNOW YOUR CAT

A GUIDE TO CAT BEHAVIOR

UNDERSTANDING YOUR PET

Reading faces
A relaxed expression can communicate happiness, contentment or curiosity.

Cats have a **magnificent variety** of ways of communicating with each other. Some of their methods are so subtle that we human beings are not sensitive enough to understand what they are saying. Their use of body language is most often quiet, controlled and dignified. A mere flick of the tail, the slightest movement of the ears, the mildest dilation of the pupils – these messages are worth a thousand words to another cat. Because their body language is so restrained, and because we find it so difficult to understand, we make mistakes interpreting it.

The curious consequence of misunderstanding on our part is that we sometimes think that cats are deceitful. We believe they are lying to us with their bodies. In fact, they are telling us what they *really*

Voicing complaints
A demand meow and an erect tail emphasize the urgency of this kitten's request.

Threatening signals
Issuing a forceful hiss and staring with dilated pupils, this cat adopts a threatening, but defensive, posture.

Patrolling territory
With concentrated expression and alert ears, the cat patrols his territory daily, leaving visual and odor signals.

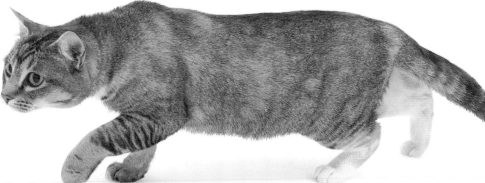

think, but in such subtle ways that we often fail to understand. It is easier for us to comprehend what cats are saying when they use their voices. Here, too, the range of sounds, from the purr to the happy "chirp," and the variety of meows, hisses, shrieks and spits, is gloriously extensive. Learning to make sense of the feline vocal range is a vital part of successful communication between cats and humans.

Cats indicate their territories with visual signs or with scent. Using their waste products as well as the scent-producing glands located on different parts of the skin, cats mark out humans and their environment. Unburied droppings or scratched fence posts and tree trunks silently communicate ownership of territory. Yards are perfect places to leave both scent and visual signals to neighborhood cats.

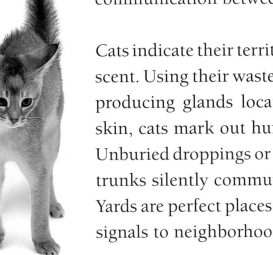

Increasing bulk
By arching his back, standing sideways and stiffening his body fur, this cat is trying to appear larger than he actually is.

Telling tails
A flicking tail usually indicates ambivalence, but also developing anger or annoyance.

Interpreting Cat Personality

ALTHOUGH ALL CATS share some behavior patterns with all other cats, each individual has its own personality. Some are friendly, assertive and bold; others are nervous, timid and shy. Personality differences originate in the genes – female blue-eyed white cats, for example, are likely to be timid. But early experience at kitten stage is also very important in creating personalities. Kittens that are stroked and played with are more likely to develop into confident cats.

Definitions applied to human personalities can also be used to describe your cat. The extrovert or outgoing cat is sociable, lively, assertive and adventurous; the neurotic or reserved type is shy, moody, emotional, tense and anxious. Some cats are antisocial, giving no warmth to humans.

I am as much an individual as you are.

Paw-swipe rehearses conflict

Relaxed head-to-head contact is part of normal development

Physical contact is an important social activity

Playful personality
Kittens cuddle and jostle with one another, often touching heads, as part of their normal social development. If they grow up without the opportunity of playing with other kittens, they do not develop a complete repertoire of cat behavior.

Outgoing individual
Playful batting and teasing is common between lively kittens. This sort of extrovert behavior during kittenhood often leads to similar behavior later in life, but it is not always possible to predict what type of personality a cat will develop.

Flicking tail
is tentative

Introverts and extroverts

Detailed experiments have shown that simply talking softly to kittens soon after they are born results in their growing up into more confident and independent adults. Such kittens even finish nursing sooner. Active kittens grow up to be high-energy individuals, while reserved kittens often mature into more retiring cats.

Facial expression
shows worry

Apprehensive adult

(ABOVE) *The introvert personality usually develops when the kitten lacks social contact. Although slow, quiet and less responsive than an extrovert, the cautious cat learns faster and is easier to train.*

Dominant hind-
quarters stance

Timid face
reveals
apprehension

Dominant kitten

Physically dextrous, this extrovert kitten is paw-fighting with her sibling. The outgoing character is accentuated by gregarious play activity. Dominant kittens grow to become dominant cats as the personality trait is already present in the genes.

Shy puss

Watchful, tense and solitary, the introvert peeps out from behind an object. Lacking self-confidence and often fearful of or hostile toward people and other cats, the introvert type of character is established in the first weeks of life.

Reading Your Cat's Face

Watch my face closely and you might be able to tell my mood.

Ears and eyes

There are over 20 muscles that control the position of the ears. When a cat is relaxed, greeting or exploring, the ears are held forward. Ears down indicate aggression; ears pinned back signal either fear or aggression, or both. Some cats, such as the Maine Coon, have extra ear tufts that accentuate ear position.

A cat's eyes also reveal mood. When your cat is completely relaxed, the eyes will shut. If frightened, the "fight-or-flight" response is automatically activated. The adrenalin then secreted causes the pupils to dilate.

TO HUMAN EYES the cat's face is often inscrutable, but to other cats the slightest change in expression can mean many things. Cats are not a sociable species, so they have little need for cooperative signals. The position of the ears will usually give you the most accurate clue to your cat's mood. Unlike humans or dogs, the cat has not developed a facial expression or gesture, such as a friendly wave or a tail-wag, that is universally recognized as a greeting. A cat's face simply maintains a relaxed and alert look, even when truthfully pleased to see you. On the other hand, the cat's face is exquisitely expressive at telling you "Goodbye." Ears, eyes, whiskers and mouth leave you in no doubt as to the intended message.

The contented cat
(LEFT) *Cats reveal their pleasure by half-closing their eyes in a reverie of contentment. This expression, with ears forward, is often accompanied by purring and is the ultimate sign of relaxation. The cat is free from any fear or worry.*

The relaxed and alert cat
(ABOVE) *This is the most common facial expression. It gives no "go away" signal and is used when cats greet us, when they demand attention, lie down, sit, stand, walk or trot. It communicates no danger to other cats.*

Ears move
back slightly

Pupils remain
constricted

Ears draw
back for
protection

Pupils dilate
in agitation

The ambivalent cat
*Twitching ears mean your cat is uncertain of how
she feels. Her mood can develop in any direction.*

The fearful cat
*When your cat is afraid, her ears fold down.
In extreme fear, her ears will flatten completely.*

Ear postion
upright
and alert

Position of scent
receptor above
roof of mouth

Ears moved
forward to
pick·up noises

Dilated pupils
indicate
excitement

The "flehming" cat
*This sneering expression occurs when a male
picks up the scent of urine of a female in heat.*

The curious cat
*The inquisitive cat perks his ears forward to
funnel in sounds. The pupils are slightly dilated.*

Erect, furled
back ears
show anger

Swept forward
whiskers indicate
bad temper

Dilated pupils
signal fearful
aggression

Teeth bared
as fierce
weapons

The angry cat
*When a dominantly aggressive cat gets
annoyed, the pupils remain constricted.*

The aggressive cat
*The pupils are dilated in fear. The cat opens
her mouth wide to hiss, spit and show sharp teeth.*

Cat Talk

YOUR CAT USES his voice to welcome you home, beg for food, demand attention, call for a mate, complain, threaten and protest. The mood your cat is in – angry, indignant, anxious, content – is also revealed in the voice. By the time kittens are 12 weeks old they have mastered the full range of adult cat vocabulary, which we know includes at least 16 different sounds. Cats can probably distinguish many more. Some individuals and some breeds, especially the Siamese, are more vocal than others.

I can say much more than you think I can.

Mouth open in distress

Motherly purr
(ABOVE) *Her kittens busy suckling, the mother is in a relaxed position and purrs rhythmically with contentment. Exactly how a cat* purrs is not yet fully understood, but it is thought to be a sound transferred from somewhere deep in the chest. As the voice box is not used, she can chirp at the same time.

Anxiety attack
The young kitten calls in distress. She makes this anxious cry, which is similar to a baby's, when she is hungry, cold or away from mother.

Extensive vocabulary

Cat language can be divided into three general sound categories: murmurs, vowels and high-intensity sounds. Murmurs include purring and the gentle chirping used in greeting or to express contentment. A mother cat will chirrup to beckon her kittens. Vowel sounds such as "meow," "mew," "MEE-ow" and "meOW" are made when the cat is demanding, complaining or bewildered. High-intensity sounds include the growl, angry wail, snarl, shriek of pain or fear, hiss, spit and the mating cry of the female.

Hissing and spitting
This cat arches her tongue in fear or anger to force out a jet of hot breath. Used to intimidate, the feel and smell of the hiss are just as important as the sound.

Lips curl to make vowel sounds

Mouth is shut tight

The demand meow

This hungry cat is meowing plaintively, asking to be fed. The inflection and intonation of the meow can express a range of feelings. However, sometimes it is only from your cat's begging posture that you can tell he is meowing as he may make a high-pitched meow, which is out of our range of hearing.

Purring in bliss

Sprawled at ease on a cushion, this cat is purring with pleasure. Such murmurs are normally a sign of a contented and secure cat. Paradoxically, a cat that is upset will also purr as a way of reducing his level of distress.

Rumbling growl

(ABOVE) This irritated cat growls with discontent. Her protest begins with clamped jaw and low rumble. She will then start to hiss or spit if she is in pain or trying to intimidate intruders. Although issuing from the voice box, the growl can be made with a closed mouth as it is not a vowel sound.

Source of the purr is deep in the chest

Being Defensive

Y OUR CAT IS more concerned with defending her personal territory than with forming lasting friendships with other cats. Compared to a dog, she is a far less sociable creature and is remarkably adept at giving "go away" signals. When your cat feels that she has lost control of the situation or that she is under threat, the "fight-or-flight" response is usually triggered and adrenalin is released. Your cat will stand her ground and make a show of aggression. Her hackles rise, her back arches, her tail bristles, her pupils dilate, and she may hiss and spit. Even a terrified cat will put on a convincing display of defensive body language, although in many cases such behavior masks fear rather than genuine aggression.

Sideways stance creates illusion of greater size

Acting tough
(RIGHT) *With bristling tail, arched back, and hair standing on end, this cat is very scared but is trying to hide her fear with a display of* *aggressive body language. Presenting herself sideways for maximum impact, she appears to be considering an attack on the opposition.*

Body position low to ground

Ears flatten back for protection

Pupils dilate in fear

Tail wrapped securely around body

Paws firmly on the ground, prepared for immediate flight

Weapons ready
(ABOVE) *Even though she is actually very frightened, this cat prepares to act* *aggressively. Hissing, she starts to roll over so that teeth and claws are bared, ready to defend herself.*

18

> *I'm hoping my tough-guy act will scare you away.*

Tail fur
stands up
slightly

Arched back
appears to
increase size

Poised for action

(RIGHT) *This terrified
cat is attempting
to hold her ground.
Stimulated by
adrenalin, her pupils
have dilated and
she gives a direct
stare to intimidate.
Puffed up to a larger
size, she is staging
a dramatic display
of bravado.*

Defensive display

(RIGHT) *With dilated
pupils, flattened ears,
bristling whiskers and
thumping tail, this cat
threatens with his
voice, and is prepared
for an attack.*

On the Offensive

THE ABILITY TO BLUFF with confidence is an absolute necessity for the cat that takes an offensive stance. There is no fixed pecking order in the cat world, so the tendency to act offensively or defensively varies according to the circumstance in which your cat finds himself. A cat in its own territory or holding the higher ground over an adversary – perhaps on a rooftop – will display offensive body language. Feeling confident, he is able to maintain full control of himself. Since, in this instance, the cat feels genuinely secure, the pupils do not dilate because the "fight-or-flight" response is not activated, as it would be in a frightened, defensive cat.

Secure at the top
While this cat sits on the roof he dominates all others below him. Exuding confidence with his head, *whiskers, perked ears and smooth coat, the cat keeps a lookout for intruders. He may use his height advantage to ambush or attack.*

Natural response
Crouched forward to hold her ground, the mother protects her young. The forward ear position and undilated pupils show that she is in control.

Ears perked forward show confidence

Thick cheek ruffs make the tomcat appear larger

Forelimbs prepared for a forward spring

Maternal anger
The mother's display of aggression frightens even the boldest of tomcats. She will not back off, and threatens him by hissing and spitting offensively. If he does not retreat, she will spring forward.

Look out! I'm in charge around here.

Dominant stance
Although obviously about to enter a confrontation, this cat is not frightened. With his well-developed sense of balance, he leans confidently over the post. Glaring down at the cat on the fence without worrying about falling off, he warns his adversary not to come any closer.

Smooth body fur signals confidence

Forward ears look assertive

Taut face muscles prepared for attack

Fighting spirit
(ABOVE) *With ears slightly furled, the confident but angry cat opens her mouth wide to hiss or spit. The tongue is folded to funnel out a shot of hot breath. The lips curl back revealing sharp teeth, emphasizing the snarl.*

Sweeping tail shows who is the boss

Pricked, furled-back ears display determination to stand ground

Direct eye contact indicates bravery

Facing a rival
By putting her head forward, this bold cat refuses to be intimidated by the cat on the high ground. However, the erect fur on the tail is a sure sign that she is a little frightened.

Tail fur begins to bristle in fear

Braced forepaws ready for action

Marking Territory

THE FELINE LANDOWNER routinely leaves messages to tell other cats who owns the territory. This involves making regular patrols of his home ground and marking important hunting, feeding and resting places. The marks he leaves can be either seen or smelled. The cat that rubs himself up against you is not simply showing affection. He is transferring his body odor, claiming you as part of his territory. When a cat has the freedom of the garden, he will scratch fence posts and tree trunks. Indoors, the cat may claw at sofas and chairs to make his mark visible. Both males and females can spray urine, even if they have been neutered, and a dominant tomcat will leave his droppings unburied as a combined visual and scent marker.

Staking a claim

(LEFT) *Urine spraying is a marking behavior and is completely different than emptying the bladder. The cat backs up to the object it intends to mark and, with a quivering tail, squirts urine straight out backward.*

The indoor cat

(ABOVE) *Most females and neutered cats are content with a small indoor territory, but they still make marks. This neutered female has a chair that she stoutly defends.*

The face rub

The cat rubs her face against the fence to mark it. Scent from the cheek glands is transferred to the wood.

Male cat's tail brushes its scent on to bushes

Urine is sprayed to mark. Anal gland squirts secretion on to droppings

Ears flatten back

Tail provides balance

It smells as if my neighbor has been here today. I'd better mark it as mine again.

Scratching posts

The ears fold back and an almost trancelike gaze comes over the cat as she reaches up to claw at the highest point possible. Wood is a favorite surface because it is not slippery. The scratches, which can be seen from a distance, are usually made in prominent sites.

Glands on cheeks, chin and around lips produce a distinctive odor

Sebaceous glands at the base of the hair follicles secrete an oily substance with a distinct smell

The routine patrol

The cat must make fresh markings every day using bodily secretions. The marks left do not frighten away other cats. Rather, they tell intruders on the territory how recently the owner passed through.

Paw is source of scented trail of sweat

23

Patrolling the Home Beat

MOST PET CATS adopt their owners' fences as their own territorial boundaries. Because cats are so successful at adapting to human ways, surprisingly few problems arise from this arrangement. The size of a territory depends upon the cat's age, sexual status and personality. Females and neutered cats are usually content with fairly small land rights, whereas tomcats feel the need to patrol and defend much larger territories – often ten times the area of a female's. Feral tomcats and cats without owners also establish a hunting range connected to their home territory by specific boundary lines and pathways.

Time to survey my domain.

Creating land rights

If your cat does not have sufficient room to maneuver, he will remedy the situation by appropriating a neighbor's lawn. He will stake it out with strategic droppings. Neutering dramatically reduces a cat's territorial demand because the sex hormone is one of the factors that drives the cat to create and defend territory.

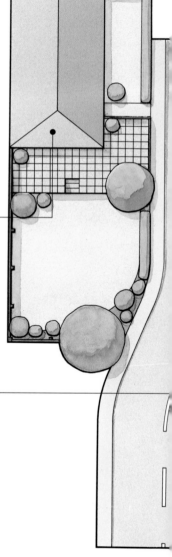

Holding the high ground
(*ABOVE*) *Regardless of which is the most dominant when two cats meet, the one that holds the highest ground has a distinct advantage. This is one reason why cats enjoy patrolling rooftops. From a height, your cat can survey his territory and shout insults at intruders.*

Patrolling from above
(*RIGHT*) *Cats live in both the vertical and the horizontal world. Tomcats tend to spend more time policing their territory than females.*

Preserving land

(LEFT) *Taking their cue from human territory markers, cats are often content to remain within one back yard but will vigorously defend that patch against other feline intruders. However, your cat's range may extend to more than one human territory.*

Adapting to human lifestyle

Many cats are content to live their lives indoors with us where there is no need to forage for food and where we "protect" the home territory. Even so, indoor cats will still assume ownership and defend a favorite spot, such as a chair.

Protecting the ideal home

(ABOVE) *A perfect home territory provides a reliable food supply and safe resting areas that are always accessible. The cat flap ensures your cat's independence, so he can come and go at will.*

CAT RELATIONSHIPS

Vital contact
Daily stroking ensures that young kittens will develop into adults that enjoy the company of human beings.

Cats are ideal companions. They are quiet, reliable, self-cleaning and independent. They always make good listeners, are perfect creatures for cuddling and have low maintenance costs. Breeding practices have not led to a dramatically altered cat anatomy, as is often the case with many new dog breeds, and so cats have comparatively few physical problems.

Cats satisfy a deep-seated human need to nurture and care for living things, and at the same time they are content to depend entirely upon us for their own survival. Cats are happy to remain dependants, permitting us to act as their surrogate mothers, providing them with food, protection, warmth and security. In many ways, cats and humans have the perfect symbiotic relationship.

Freedom to move
A cat flap gives your cat security while satisfying his need to explore outdoors.

Making friends
These three unrelated kittens will be lifelong friends because they were introduced to each other before the age of seven weeks.

Playing with toys
This cat needs the stimulation that playing with toys gives her. It encourages her to investigate the environment or capture prey.

However, a home designed for human habitation is an artificial environment for a cat. If we misunderstand a cat's needs, we may unintentionally create behavioral problems. In order to adapt successfully, cats must be exposed to our environment from the earliest possible age.

Treating problems
A squirt from a plant sprayer can break your cat of bad habits, such as scratching your furniture or clawing the curtains.

The desire to define and possess territory exists in all cats, whether they live in an urban apartment or in a remote rural area. When a cat has limited access to the great outdoors, we should provide him with articles that can be scratched and a toilet area that is appropriate, private and suitably placed. Cats are, of course, highly adaptable creatures, but we should still repay their friendship by providing them with a safe and comforting home that caters to every conceivable cat requirement.

Comfort behaviors
These Siamese kittens are wool-suckers. The problem is much more common in Siamese than in other cats and is probably caused by selective breeding.

Your Best Friend

Under my chin is my favorite place for a tickle.

THE SATISFACTION WE derive from caring for living things is at the root of our survival as a species. It is also the reason why so many of us find such pleasure in sharing our homes with cats. Curiously, cats may be even better than children in fulfilling our need to nurture: they never grow up and are always dependent on us. Stroking them indulges our desire for closeness. Talking, touching and eye-to-eye contact create an intimacy that is sometimes easier to maintain with a cat than with another person. Cats provide us with a reassuring constancy in our lives, which we like to interpret as loyalty.

Tongue leaves territorial saliva on human skin

Kitten is stimulated by gentle tickling

Mutual satisfaction
Feeling secure, the mother cat licks your hand as she would her own kittens. In return, you take pleasure from stroking the fur under her chin. Children, too, benefit from the affection engendered within a family for a pet cat.

Intimate relationship
Stroking your cat is very relaxing. Lying on your chest, enjoying the caresses, he makes a perfect listener. He sees you as a mother substitute, displaying none of the competitive behavior that normally occurs between two cats.

Direct eye contact demonstrates trust

Learning to socialize
(RIGHT) Kittens are "socialized" when they are handled and played with. The child also learns that there is a limit to the length of time during which they enjoy being handled.

Kitten sniffs hair
to pick up scent

Kitten feels
insecure and
tries to jump off

Secure footing
(ABOVE) *The kittens feel most secure
on the ground and are happy to be
petted. Stroking the chin satisfies the
kitten's need to leave her scent.*

Cat is relaxed
and trusts in
her companion

Lap of luxury
(ABOVE) *Lying on your
warm lap, your cat's
state of arousal is
diminished. She kneads
your leg with her*
*claws, which is a
comfort behavior, and
shows her appreciation
by arching her neck
back to try to give you
a friendly "head rub."*

Your Cat's Best Friend

FOR A CAT, humans make good cat substitutes. In many ways cats enjoy warmer, more convivial relations with us than they do with other felines. Humans are almost ideal social companions as they do not represent any kind of threat to a cat. We do not compete for food, territory or sexual supremacy – factors that interfere in the relationships between cats. When raised in close proximity to us, cats look upon humans as being "feline" enough to be treated as fellow cats while being sufficiently different not to be a danger. A lasting dependency and friendship can develop between a cat and a human being, with the cat regarding its owner as an all-powerful, all-providing mother.

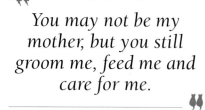

You may not be my mother, but you still groom me, feed me and care for me.

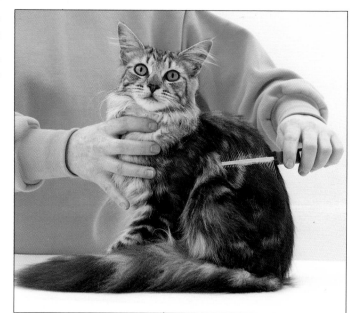

Grooming time
(RIGHT) *Long-haired breeds may need help to keep their coats in condition and to prevent them from becoming matted and tangled. This Maine Coon sits still while she is groomed with a comb. Most cats enjoy grooming as the sensation is similar to that experienced as kittens, when their mother licked their fur.*

Nose activated by smell of food

Meal time
The mother cat reaches up to ask for her food and smells it curiously. The begging action is also displayed by a kitten when the mother returns to the litter with a mouse.

Parent power
Cats are inherently lazy, always taking the easy option. When we provide food and shelter for our pet cat, we create a dependency that is similar to a kitten's total reliance on his mother. An adult feral cat is preoccupied with concerns of territory, competition and mating. Your pet cat does not have these worries and so retains a certain youthfulness, looking to you to provide for him just like a mother. Selective breeding has increased this dependency. Cats with long coats, for example, would not survive without help with grooming. Breeders are even selecting for temperament. For example, by choosing the aesthetic comforter in preference to the mouser, the floppy and affectionate Ragdoll breed has been created.

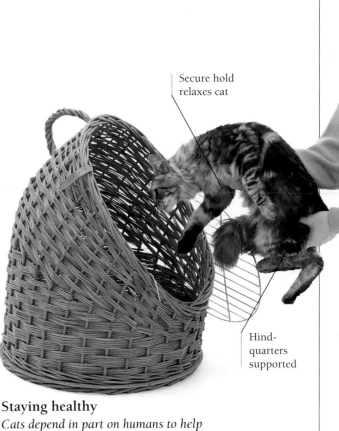

Secure hold relaxes cat

Hind-quarters supported

The cat scents and head rubs the hand in friendliness

Staying healthy

Cats depend in part on humans to help them maintain their health, so visiting the vet is an occasional necessity. Train your cat from an early age to travel in a cat basket. Always grasp your cat firmly when putting her into the basket.

The dependent feline

Reaching up, the cat sniffs your hand in greeting. She tries to get as close as possible to give you a "head rub," the cat's natural way of saying hello. Human interaction has perpetuated the dependency of the kitten on its mother. The result is a domestic cat that actively seeks out human companionship, relying on us for fundamental needs.

Hindleg stance allows full stretch

This kitten is relaxed because it is correctly supported

Being Handled

YOUR CAT IS not instinctively gregarious and can resent incorrect handling. She is a graceful, dignified, clean, independent, sensuous creature, so it is natural to respect her and often impossible to resist touching her. A cat unfamiliar with the sensation of being picked up will allow you to do this only if she feels relaxed, comfortable and secure. A cat that was not stroked as a kitten will fiercely resist any attempts at handling.

Hold me correctly and I'll be relaxed.

Correct handling

(ABOVE) *Support the kitten's hind-quarters with the palm of one hand while cradling the forelimbs and head with the other. Never pick up a kitten by the scruff of the neck as its mother does, because this can damage her fragile body. A kitten must be handled frequently to ensure that she enjoys being stroked later in life.*

Cat shows pleasure at being rubbed firmly behind the ears

The head rub

(LEFT) *By rubbing her head against your hand, the cat leaves her marking scent. Unable to groom behind the ears with her tongue, the cat likes being caressed here. Your strokes are similar to the licks her mother once gave her.*

Medicine time

(ABOVE) *A cat will try to swat or bite you when you give it a pill. Hold the head firmly with one hand and flex it back to open the mouth. Drop the pill in and then shut the mouth. Rub the throat to encourage the cat to swallow the pill.*

Stroking a cat

Your cat finds stroking pleasurable because the sensation is similar to that of grooming. However, this type of physical contact is not a natural adult cat behavior, so it must be included in your kitten's socialization period.

Handling time

Kittens should be handled for at least 40 minutes each day from two weeks of age onward. The more handling they receive when they are young, the more they will actively enjoy future handling. However, constant petting may produce mixed emotions. Cats can reveal their ambivalence by suddenly biting your hand and then coming back to ask for more affection. An aggressive response is most likely to occur when you rub the cat's belly because it is the least protected part of a cat's body and never mutually groomed.

Sitting comfortably

For a cat, being cradled is unnatural and unfamiliar. Preferring to be upright, the cat will tolerate being held like this only when it feels completely secure and relaxed with the girl.

Supporting hands

Pick the cat up with one hand on its chest behind the forepaws and the other under the hindquarters. This supports the full weight and avoids any discomfort to the legs or rib cage.

Correctly handled, the young cat remains relaxed

The handover

(RIGHT) *The limp tail and hanging paws show that the cat is relaxed as it is handed over to the girl. The child must have the cat firmly in both hands before you release your hold.*

Sheathed claws mean kitten is not alarmed

Crooked arm provides security

Limp tail shows cat is at ease

Roaming Freely

ALTHOUGH YOUR CAT is among the world's most prolific sleepers, he also needs frequent activity. One of his favorite natural pastimes is to make rounds of his territory. He will instinctively practice his hunting skills and leave marks to stake out his domain. If he is denied access to the outdoors, he may spend hours at the window watching the world go by. When he sees something that excites or distresses him, he might back up to the furniture, raise his tail and quiver. Spraying urine inside your home is the way he demonstrates his frustration when he is cooped up. This behavioral problem almost always occurs when your cat's access to the outside is limited, or if there are too many cats sharing your home.

Living indoors
(ABOVE) *This indoor cat concentrates on the outside world through the window. If he spots a bird, he may chatter his teeth and swish his tail. He could become agitated if his natural activity is restricted too much.*

Tail maintains balance

Using a litter box

If you cannot give your cat access to the great outdoors, you need to provide litter in a box in a secluded place. Part of your cat's natural behavior is to bury her droppings, so she is already receptive to the principle of using a litter box. She will become accustomed to the odor of the litter and the texture of it under foot and may object, refusing to use it, if you change the type of litter.

Perked ears
indicate
curiosity

Sensitive
whiskers
gauge width

Venturing abroad

Your cat is most active at dawn and dusk. He will frequently want to go out early in the morning while you are still asleep. A cat flap gives him independence, although initially you may need to help him learn to use it. Try tempting him through with morsels of food at first. However, it is wise to be wary of neighborhood cats following your pet back into your home and staking it out as theirs.

> " Time to get a little exercise and do some exploring. "

Leg stretches
out confidently

Walking purposefully

(LEFT) *Striding along the wall in your yard, your cat marks out his territory. He often chooses to adopt human boundaries, such as walls or fences, as his own. Unless the weather keeps him indoors, your cat will make daily patrols, leaving his territorial scents. This keeps him trim, exercises his sense of balance and stimulates his mind.*

Stalking prey

(ABOVE) *An insect is the prey for this hunter. With his ears perked forward in the alert position, he is pouncing on his prey. An indoor cat should always be encouraged to play in order to keep in good shape. He will thrive on any opportunity you give him to flex his muscles and practice his instinctive hunting behavior.*

Being Sociable

YOUR CAT CAN get along with a wide variety of other animals, as well as those of her own species. Provided a young kitten is introduced between two and seven weeks old, a lasting friendship with another cat or a different species can be established successfully. We always tend to think of the stereotype of dog chasing cat, but in reality many dogs are intimidated by cats. Make sure the first few meetings between a young kitten and potential soulmate are sensitively handled, taking care not to trespass on an existing pet's territory, and the kitten will enjoy the companionship later in life. The resulting friendship is a unique behavioral feature of domestic rather than feral cats.

Agitated
expression
shows insecurity

*Who goes there –
friend or foe?*

First encounters
(*ABOVE*) *Introduced to a dog
for the first time, this kitten
is terrified. Her fur stands
on end and she adopts a*

*defensive stance. Provided
that the meeting is not
provocative, the next time
they see each other the
kitten should be less scared.*

Well-socialized kitten
*Not at all inhibited by the dog,
this kitten met dogs frequently
when she was young so her
fear of larger animals is
diminished. If you want your
pets to be friends, make sure
that the kitten mixes with
dogs when between the ages
of two and seven weeks.*

Naturally fluffy tail
is relaxed and limp

Ear tilted forward
in dominant
position

Intimidating the stranger
This dominant adult cat defends her home from the new kitten. Hissing and spitting, her paw is raised, *about to swat the youngster. Nervous, he pulls back, too inexperienced to understand what is happening. His muted response is confused.*

Paw closed
in show of
dominance,
not to injure

Making friends
(LEFT) *These kittens amuse themselves, playing with the wool and each other. As the period during which kittens can bond starts early and is over so quickly, it is best to acquire several kittens at once if you plan to become a multicat family.*

Playing with humans
(BELOW) *Chewing and pulling on shoelaces, these kittens discover that humans make very good playmates. Neither kitten is fearful, but the one lying on his side, with his tail up, shows the beginnings of defensive behavior as he grabs with his forepaws and kicks with his hindlegs.*

Learning to share territory

Initially, a resident pet may not be willing to share territory with a new kitten. To make the introduction as smooth as possible, let the resident dog or cat sniff the sleeping newcomer.

Back legs
ready to
strike out

If you are getting a kitten from a breeder, make sure that he or she has already experienced social contact with other species. After seven weeks of age, the kitten can no longer make social bonds, so it will be very difficult for the cat ever to be friends with other pets. It is important to remember that a kitten that is not scared of your dog may be at risk from strange dogs.

Exercising Mind and Body

UNLESS YOUR CAT'S energy can be channeled in a positive way, he may become destructive. After all, he never has to worry about where his next meal is coming from, so there is no need for any real hunting or stalking. The frustrated cat that has excess energy to burn will chew your plants, scratch your furniture, tear your carpets and climb the curtains.

He may even go berserk for half an hour, running maniacally back and forth across the room or round the perimeter, doing the "wall of death" – strange behavior for a cat, normally so lazy a creature! Some cats develop the annoying habit of sucking wool, usually a sign of premature weaning. In order to prevent these problems occurring, ensure that your cat is always mentally stimulated and has plenty of opportunity for exercise.

Watch out – I'm going to create havoc!

Sharp claws scratch the bark

Gnawing problem
(LEFT) *The myth that cats only eat grass when they are unwell is just that. Although they are carnivores, many cats often nibble grass. Inside, this cat tears at a house plant instead. Make sure that none of your plants are poisonous.*

Wool sucking
(ABOVE) *If your young kittens suck wool, or even you, they could have been weaned too soon from their mothers. Siamese may start sucking after they are around six months old, but this is usually a genetically linked behavioral problem.*

Stimulating your cat

Toys provide a practical outlet through which cats can exhaust themselves. They need not imitate prey specifically, but should encourage activities such as scratching, chasing and batting. Toys that move erratically are often favored as they arouse the cat's curiosity.

Scratching posts

(LEFT) *Your cat needs to be able to scratch. Very often after waking, a cat has the urge to claw something, just as we like to stretch. Providing a good post will prevent damage to furniture.*

Loose claw is removed as the rope is scratched

With his paw, the cat tries to catch the ball

Paws bat as they would at a bird

Claws embedded in carpet for secure purchase

Stance is kangaroo-like for balance

Moving target

Standing up on his hind legs, with his tail straight out for balance, this cat is inquisitive about the toy. He will investigate it by feeling, sniffing, tasting and poking. As it swings back and forth, it will provide him with endless hours of amusement.

Training Your Cat

ALTHOUGH WE SELDOM notice it, cats are constantly training themselves. If, for example, your cat raids the garbage can successfully, he learns this is rewarding. However, rewards such as food or affection do not work well when training cats out of bad habits. Surprise, never involving pain, is the best way to overcome most of your feline's behavioral problems.

Bean bag
Throw a small bean bag near your cat if he attempts, for example, to climb the curtains.

Aluminum foil
(ABOVE) *If your cat defecates outside the litter box, spread aluminum foil on the area. Cats do not like the feel of it under their feet and will learn to prefer the litter box.*

Mothballs
(ABOVE) *To prevent your cat from digging up the houseplants, spread mothballs (cats hate the smell) on the soil. Make sure the mothballs are kept away from children.*

Plant sprayer
Cats dislike jets of water. Use a small sprayer or water gun to squirt your cat if she claws at the carpet or curtains.

Noisemakers
A noisemaker is an alternative surprise tactic. The clanging frightens the cat.

Select nozzle for an intensive jet of water

Punishing routine
When you see your cat misbehaving and the spray bottle is handy, simply fire the water the moment the cat claws the plant. Do not shout; the cat may begin to associate the punishment with you.

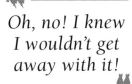

Gentle tap disciplines your cat

Correcting directly
(RIGHT) *If your cat uses you as a scratching post, or sucks at your clothes, gently tap him on the nose, but never inflict pain. Dominant cats often pat other cats if they step out of line. Admonish your cat in this way only when he has misbehaved directly toward you.*

" *Oh, no! I knew I wouldn't get away with it!* "

Retaliating first
(LEFT) *You may be absent when your cat decides to misbehave. In this instance, it is necessary to create "traps" that will discipline him instantly. For example, cover the kitchen work surface with pots and pans that are bound to be knocked over when he jumps onto it, or set mousetraps under paper around the base of chewable plants.*

Springing the trap
(BELOW) *In order to approach the foliage, this cat must step onto the surrounding paper. This provides enough pressure to spring the mousetrap.*

Trap will cause paper to explode in the air but cat will not be injured

41

Caring for Your Cat

THE DOMESTIC CAT is a highly adaptable African carnivore that has found living with humans to its liking. We may find some of its natural behaviors, such as territory-marking and toilet habits, socially unacceptable, but when offered the right equipment and given correct training, most cats can channel their natural habits into more domesticated directions. They will readily learn to use litter trays, scratch on special posts and eat food prepared by us.

PREPARING THE TRAY

TYPES OF LITTER

Litter

Liner

Scoop

Fuller's earth

Chalk

Compressed wood chips

Choosing litter
(LEFT) *Line the tray with a plastic bag before filling it with litter. For your cat, the most important quality of litter is how it feels under foot. Your cat may often develop a preference for one texture over another and may be unwilling to switch to a new type of litter.*

Granting freedom
(ABOVE) *Your cat's natural desire to climb and wander is so powerful that most want to venture outdoors. They can crawl through tight spaces and have no qualms about learning to squeeze through a cat flap once it is understood that the flap leads outside.*

Dry, crunchy morsels

Moist, canned food

Creating privacy
Cats are innately litter-box trained and most prefer quiet and private areas. Covered litter boxes will meet your cat's requirements for security. Some come with built-in odor filters.

Selecting a diet
Although soft food might seem to be a more natural option, many cats prefer crunchy food. Eating the bones of their rodent prey is normal, and chewing on dry, pellets of food might simply duplicate that eating pattern. Although many cats seem to obtain sufficient water from the food they eat, it is advisable to supply your cat with a handy source of fresh water.

Simple rewards

The desired end result of training your cat is to redirect his natural behaviors into habits more suited to your home environment. Praise works with dogs, but cats do not respond well to it. Caring for your cat means providing him with the necessities of life – for him, these are rewards in themselves.

Rope excellent for scratching off loose claw

Fur mouse simulates natural prey

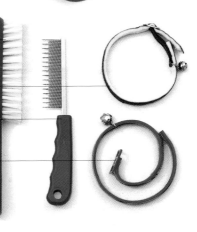

Traveling baskets

(*ABOVE*) *Your cat may learn to associate a traveling basket with a trip to the veterinarian. Using the basket as a warm, secluded bed at home helps to train your cat to associate the carrier with pleasant experiences.*

Exhilarating activity

(*RIGHT*) *Toys provide mental and physical stimulation. Lightweight balls will be batted; mouse-shaped toys encourage stalking and hunting activities. More sophisticated toys stimulate the senses of hearing and touch as well as sight.*

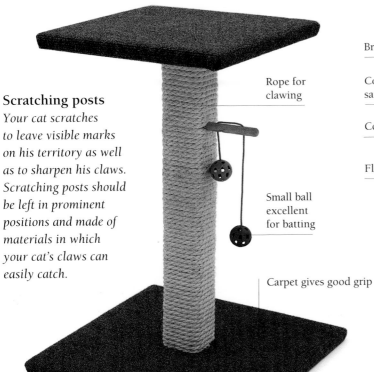

Scratching posts

Your cat scratches to leave visible marks on his territory as well as to sharpen his claws. Scratching posts should be left in prominent positions and made of materials in which your cat's claws can easily catch.

Rope for clawing

Small ball excellent for batting

Carpet gives good grip

Brush

Collar with elasticized safety section

Comb

Flea collar

Brushes, combs and collars

Domestic cats, particularly longhairs, need extra grooming from you in addition to the grooming they give themselves and each other. If your cat's coat gets very dirty, you may need to give him a wet or dry bath. Also, ask your vet to show you how to trim claws.

Having a Family

Feeling relaxed
Her distended abdomen indicates that this calm mother-to-be is close to delivering her kittens.

Total dependency
Licked dry, this kitten relies solely on mother for all his needs.

T RANQUILLITY, SERENITY AND dignified calm surround the mother cat before, during and after the birth of her kittens. From the moment she appears pregnant a few weeks after mating until the time she weans her kittens when they are around eight weeks old, her temperament and behavior are strongly influenced by progesterone, the hormone of pregnancy and lactation. She becomes calmer, is less likely to fight, appears more relaxed and may show greater affection toward humans. As birth approaches, and then for several weeks after the birth, she does not wander far from home, preferring to stay close to her nest.

Breathing space
Giving birth is a tiring process. This cat pants with exhaustion between deliveries.

Progesterone suppresses her fears and relaxes her, making her feel more secure. At the same time, however, it allows the unique maternal type

Rapid development
Although the senses develop quickly, this kitten needs his mother to stimulate his body functions.

Huddling together
The kittens snuggle together for warmth as their mother goes off in search of food.

First breaths
The mother's raspy tongue removes all birth fluids and stimulates the newborn into breathing.

of aggression to develop. If a nursing mother thinks that her kittens are at risk from an intruder, she will first threaten, then launch, a terrifying attack. Unlike other forays, there is no bluff involved in maternal aggression. The attack is maintained until the cause of her anxiety leaves the vicinity of her nest. Even the most powerful tomcat has a healthy respect for the ferocity of a female protecting her young.

Maternal care is overwhelmingly important in the life cycle of the cat. In fact, cats could be classified as a truly matriarchal species. The survival of each kitten depends solely upon females. Although the natural mother is primarily responsible for the care of her young, other females will feed and protect the kittens in her absence. Neither the father of the litter nor any other males assist in looking after the newborn.

Sole provider
For the first three weeks of life, this mother will furnish her kittens with milk, warmth, contact and comfort.

Expecting Kittens

Y OUR PREGNANT CAT should be allowed to lead a normal life. During the early stages of pregnancy, it is safe for her to venture out and hunt. Climbing can be dangerous when she is greatly distended because the weight of the unborn kittens alters her center of gravity and affects her balance. She will be innately more careful, but the experienced mother adapts better to changes caused by pregnancy. An increased level of progesterone brings on "maternal behavior," and the expectant mother spends more time relaxing. Near full-term her estrogen level rises and she will begin searching for a nesting site.

Lying comfortably
(BELOW) *The expectant mother adopts a prone position. Stretched out like this, the load in her abdomen is more evenly distributed and is supported by the floor. Although cautious, she remains normally active until the weight of the litter and the hormonal changes in her body gradually cause her to slow down and rest more of the time.*

Showing signs
The large belly shows up very clearly on the characteristically healthy but gaunt body of this oriental mother-to-be. The average number of kittens in a litter is four, but oriental cats tend to have larger litters than do other breeds.

Constricted pupils indicate she is relaxed

The unborn kitten

If you suspect your cat is pregnant, you can confirm the pregnancy by checking whether the nipples are pink and the belly is increasing in size. Between four to five weeks after conception you should be able to feel golf-ball-sized swellings. Prodding or poking can damage the embryo or even induce a miscarriage, so any manual examination should be gentle. Your cat should also start to behave maternally. The pregnancy lasts for nine weeks. Halfway through gestation, the embryo is already a perfectly formed miniature kitten. It then develops rapidly, weighing around 3½ ounces (100 grams) at birth.

Sixteen days
The embryo (a) is surrounded by fluid (b) and is attached to the wall of the uterus (c).

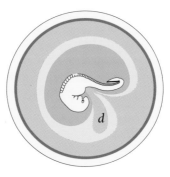

Eighteen days
Head, backbone and tail are obvious. The embryo feeds off nutrients in the yolk sac (d).

Behaving maternally

Even before your cat starts gaining weight and looking obviously pregnant, her appetite will increase and she will become less active. Closer to term, she will groom herself more frequently, especially her abdomen and genital areas. As birth approaches she will spend more time in her chosen nest, impregnating it with her scent. This will help her soon-to-be-born kittens in their orientation towards home.

I just don't seem to be able to get comfortable.

Large tummy makes her pear-shaped

Leg stretches out to find a relaxed position

Nipples are pink and obvious, in preparation for suckling

Preserving strength

(*ABOVE*) *To conserve the energy she will need to give birth, the expectant mother becomes less active. She tends to sit and lie down more of the time. An increase in the level of progesterone, the pregnancy hormone, causes this relaxed, maternal behavior.*

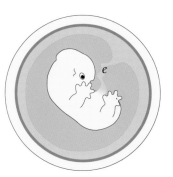   

Twenty-one days
The limbs are visibly forming, as are the eyes. Food comes via the umbilical cord (e).

Twenty-eight days
All the internal organs have developed. The tiny kitten is about 1in (2.5cm) long.

Thirty-five days
The developing fetus grows rapidly and is now about 2½in (6cm) long.

Sixty-three days
The kitten is ready to emerge. In the last 28 days it has doubled in length.

Giving Birth

THE BIRTH IS seldom very difficult. Any time between 60 and 70 days after mating, the mother's biological clock alters her hormone production and labor begins. She will seek out the site chosen for the birth – a secluded, warm place with a surface she can dig at. Her breathing quickens and she might start to purr rhythmically. As labor continues, she will usually produce a vaginal discharge, and soon after will begin to strain. Once the contractions are occurring about every 30 seconds, a delivery is imminent. A resourceful and healthy mother will usually manage her birth without your help.

Don't fuss. I can manage on my own.

Rear leg held
high out of the way

1 Labor begins
The kitten emerges from the birth canal in a lubricated sac. The mother has good control of her abdominal muscles, and she concentrates on pressing down to get the kitten out. Her leg lifts up out of the way.

2 The birth
The kitten is born and the labor pains ease, allowing the mother to bend to reach the amniotic sac and lick it away. Licking is an instinctive response. The kitten is being born in a "diving" head-and-feet first position; about 70 percent of kittens are born facing this way.

Relaxed leg
indicates easing
of contractions

Tongue peels away
sturdy membrane

Each kitten emerges in
its own amniotic sac

3 Cleaning up

(RIGHT) *The mother tidies the area around the newborn kitten, eating the amniotic sac. The kitten is helpless, and she licks her dry to prevent her from getting cold. At this point she is still attached by the umbilical cord.*

4 The lick of life

(BELOW) *The mother now licks the kitten's face to clear all the mucus from her nostrils and mouth. She is naturally vigorous and quite rough – the licking action must make the kitten gasp. The kitten's lungs will then inflate, and she will start to breathe freely.*

Face is licked to clear mucus and facilitate breathing

5 Hiding the evidence

After the birth of each kitten, the mother prepares herself for the next. She licks all the fetal fluids from her belly, around her genital area and even from the floor. For the time being she disregards those kittens that have been born.

Righting mechanism is a reflex behavior that develops in the womb

Kittens orientate themselves using heat receptors located on the head

After Delivery

1 Two jobs at once
(LEFT) *Lapsing in concentration, the mother licks one kitten while giving birth to another. Soon she will attend to the newborn, licking the membrane away. The more litters a cat has produced, the more competent she will be in the birth process.*

Leg relaxes as attention wanders from the kitten just being born

My babies rely on me for everything.

Newborn kitten still in sac, where he cannot breathe

Umbilical cord is sheared

2 Eating the afterbirth

(RIGHT) The afterbirth, or placenta, is expelled and the mother eats it to hide signs of the birth from predators. It gives her valuable nourishment, as she may not leave the kittens to find food for herself for the next few days.

Mother eats nutrient-rich afterbirth for sustenance

3 Severing the cord

(BELOW) The mother cat chews off the umbilical cord about 1 in (2.5 cm) away from the kitten. With her head at an angle, she uses her side, or carnassial, teeth in a shearing action. An inexperienced mother may need help with this. The mother then cleans up all the bloody discharge.

4 Preparing the meal

(BELOW) Sometimes, even before the last kitten has been delivered, the mother curls into a horseshoe shape, drawing her kittens toward her nipples with her paw. The kittens paddle toward the feeding station and nuzzle in to feed at the exposed nipples.

Licking the kitten's rump stimulates the body functions

Survival

The survival of the litter depends upon the mother's ability to stimulate their breathing and keep them warm. She must also feed all of them and protect them from danger. To hide the signs of the helpless newborn, she licks away all birth fluids and eats the afterbirths.

Caring for the Newborn

THE INTERVAL BETWEEN births can be as little as five minutes or as long as two hours. With very large litters, the mother may deliver only some of the kittens, and settle down, exhausted, to feed them. She will then go into labor once more, up to 24 hours later, to give birth to the remainder of the litter. Newborn kittens are helpless and rely on their mother to provide food, protection and warmth. She is instinctively maternal and will start to lick and feed them as soon as they are born, rarely leaving them during their first 48 hours of life.

The lonesome kitten
(ABOVE) *Huddled against his mother for warmth and security, this single kitten is at a disadvantage because he is denied the social development of growing up in a large litter.*

Location of heat receptors, the kitten's most developed capacity

Kittens snuggle together for warmth

Pink feet indicate that circulation is working well

Sibling rivalry
In a large litter there is competition between the kittens. The rivalry is healthy as it produces a creative environment. However, sometimes a loser, or "runt," emerges.

I'm completely exhausted, but I must look after my kittens.

Undivided attention

The mother cat responds to her kittens' cries by licking them as they burrow in for a meal. The last kittens to be born are still damp, but her licking has stimulated their breathing. Their circulation is now also working well – this can be seen by the pink feet and bellies.

Panting from the exhaustion of labor

Do not disturb

(ABOVE) *The mother will be irritated if you disturb her, and may hiss and spit. Staying close to her kittens, she pants with exhaustion. Soon she will relax and settle down to feed them.*

Legs guide kittens to the nipples

53

Protecting the Kittens

Defenseless at birth
The newborn kitten is unable to see, hear or walk. She uses heat receptors on her face to seek her mother out.

THE MOTHER BONDS quickly with her newborn, and instinctively knows how to care for them. Even a first-time mother responds to her kittens' cries by retrieving them when they wander away from her. She is able to recognize each kitten in her litter by its distinctive smell, secreted from skin glands on the head. Kittens rest only when they are huddled with their mother or with each other. Just when they appear to be accustomed to their new environment, the mother abandons the soiled nest and moves them to a safer site. This behavior stems from living in the wild, where it is necessary to move away from any signs of the birth, which might encourage dangerous predators.

Delicate mouthful
The mother moves from the soiled nest when her kittens are four days old. She carries one at a time, grasping each one in her jaws, while the kitten remains relaxed and passive.

Wide-jawed grasp
carries kitten safely

I don't think we're safe here – let's move on.

Settling in

The mother is happy and relaxed in her new nesting site and seems oblivious to the kittens crawling all over her. The young kittens are drawn to their mother by the warmth of her body.

Powerful, sensitive jaws carry the kitten without harming her

Boldest kitten feeds first

Hind legs flex; tail turns up

Traveling position

The kitten remains passive and assumes a fetal position as she is carried to the nest. Later in life, cats adopt the same tuck position when picked up by the scruff of the neck.

Stepping out

The mother "walks tall" when carrying the kitten in her mouth to reduce the danger of bumps and knocks. If the distance between nests is great, she may move her litter one at a time to a midway rest station, and then on to the new home.

Nursing

Eyes open between four and ten days

Ears will not open until around the tenth day

Eyes open

The kitten, now six days old, has opened his eyes. Although controlled genetically, kittens reared by young mothers or in dark dens open their eyes earlier than normal.

1 Milk station

(BELOW) Nipples toward the rear of the mother have the most abundant milk supply. They are claimed by the more dominant kittens, who usually grow to be strong and secure.

MOTHERS ARE VERY calm when feeding their kittens, an influence of the pregnancy hormone progesterone. This hormone stimulates milk production and gives the mother a voracious appetite. The first milk that she produces, the colostrum, protects the kittens from many diseases. During the first days the kittens' senses develop rapidly. They learn the scent of their favorite nipple and quickly develop a preference for it. Usurpers often give up sucking when an owner claims his preferred nipple.

Come on, there's room for you all.

Total relaxation

The hormone progesterone, which causes the milk to flow, leaves the mother contented. The constricted pupils indicate that her state of arousal is low.

2 Jockeying for position
(RIGHT) *For the first few weeks the kittens are totally dependent on their mother to position herself so that they can suckle. The runt is unwittingly kept from feeding by the mother. She stretches out her paw and the runt is rejected.*

Sleep position assumed for suckling

Less dominant kitten may develop into a runt

Mother pushes kittens towards her nipples

Kittens paddle toward nipples with hindpaws

3 Drinking time
(BELOW) *There is a limit to the amount of time the kittens are allowed to feed. The mother starts to get up, forcing the kittens to release their grasp. The kitten that has not managed to suckle wanders off. Though the mother is watchful, she will show concern only if she hears a distress call.*

Most productive nipples are in abdominal region

Feeding over, the kitten lifts her head and lets go

This kitten has given up and is wandering off

Fostering

I'm not worried that these kittens aren't all mine – they'll all be cared for.

FOSTERING IS NOT a by-product of human intervention in cat breeding. It is a natural feline behavior that evolved to allow some mother cats to leave the den to hunt while others took over the nursing. For several days after birth, the cat's mothering instinct is so powerful that she readily fosters needy orphaned kittens, especially when they are only a few days old. The very young kittens do not discriminate, and willingly take comfort and nourishment from any available female.

Kitten struggles to latch firmly onto a nipple

Two foster kittens suckle the best nipples

The family unit
The kittens are a close-knit group, just like a normal litter, huddling together in the security and warmth of physical contact. Growing up as a foursome will mean more opportunity for play and their mental abilities will mature faster.

The foster mother
This Burmese feeds her own Tonkinese kittens as well as the two Seal point Siamese that were introduced to the family when they were only a few days old. The foster kittens have settled in well, and are competing with the mother's kittens for food.

Plenty for everyone
The Tonkinese kitten has now found a nipple, which she will defend for herself. Her mother continues to feed all the kittens until it is time for weaning. Fostering usually prolongs milk production as the additional suckling stimulates milk flow.

Hand feeding

Even when a kitten is hand-fed from a rubber dropper he will knead with his paws for comfort. He presses on the towel in the same way that he would normally knead the mammary tissue of his mother. This action stimulates milk flow.

Hand rearing

You can hand feed an orphaned kitten on specially prepared milk replacement, using a dropper. The kitten will receive satisfactory nourishment, but unless he is brought up with other cats he will lack vital social contact from other kittens and his nursing mother. This can result in emotional deprivation, and the kitten may not develop a cat's social graces. When an adult he is likely to be a poor breeder.

Kindergarten kittens

Collective upbringing is most common in groups of feral city cats. A contingent of nursing mothers can jointly care for as many as 40 kittens. This form of raising provides intense social activity for the kittens. However, competition for a teat is great, and so smaller kittens are often disadvantaged.

Seal point Siamese have darkened "points" on the ears

THE GROWING KITTEN

Breaking away
This kitten is just starting to investigate life away from mother.

Within a few weeks of birth, your kitten will evolve from total dependence upon mother and siblings to a state of complete independence. At three weeks of age, he will begin to explore and play with the rest of the litter and his mother. The senses of sight, hearing, taste, smell and touch are fully developed by the time he is five weeks old, and by 12 weeks he will have the agility, mobility and all the graces of the adult cat.

Under normal circumstances, play increasingly ends in squabbles within the litter. The more dominant kittens convert play into displays of superiority, and what was previously joyful, uninhibited activity now becomes a more serious show of strength. Play between males and females is less frequent as

Feeling curious
As he develops, a kitten will learn more about his environment.

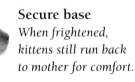

Secure base
When frightened, kittens still run back to mother for comfort.

Making friends
Firm friends at an early age, kitten and squirrel are going to be friends for life.

Becoming agile
The successful hunter must be able to leap and pounce. By 12 weeks the kitten will have developed the full range of adult movements.

the litter becomes more sexually mature. When kittens are raised in our homes, we guarantee them security, warmth, comfort and food. This obviously reduces any need for them to develop into the self-sufficient hunters they need to become to survive in the wild. Self-domesticated by choice, the cat has evolved a pattern of behavior appropriate to the less challenging environment of our homes.

We often interrupt the cat's natural sexual cycle by neutering kittens before they reach puberty. This alters natural odors and reduces many of the tensions inherent in one kitten's relations with another. Therefore, pet cats often have less to fight about, and the kitten's fearless play with siblings can last a lifetime because the struggles over dominance and territory are no longer of paramount importance.

Power games
Ear positions and bite attempts indicate that, in this instance, play has become a serious dispute over issues of dominance.

Developing the Senses

Ears open at ten days, by which time hearing is well developed

Tail remains erect to help with agility

SERIOUS LEARNING begins at three weeks of age when all the kitten's sensory abilities are coming alive. In order to be successful hunters, kittens have to develop a sense of smell and taste; they need to be vocal to express their feelings, and they must be agile and learn to move confidently.

Claws cannot be retracted at this age

One paw raised at a time for stability

Distress call

(LEFT) *With mouth wide open, this anxious kitten cries for her mother. The voice is functional from birth, and the kitten uses her voice box to make the distress cry when hungry, trapped, cold or isolated from her mother or siblings. To us, the sound is similar to that made by a human baby. Mothers soon learn to distinguish the cry of their own kittens from others.*

> *What's going on here? I'm curious – I want to find out more.*

Heads down and sniffing

Curiosity develops early. These kittens are using their sense of smell to explore their surroundings. Smell is the first sense to develop completely and is the most developed at birth.

Tail is large in relation to rest of body to assist with balance

Fluid in the eye is cloudy until five weeks of age

A sense of balance

(ABOVE) *The three-week-old kitten has just mastered walking. Still learning to balance, he is rather clumsy. Tentatively picking up one paw at a time, he makes steps with widely placed feet. Although the touch receptors on the paws are developed, the brain cannot fully understand the stimuli.*

Placement of the paw is still a little haphazard

Relying on Mother

CURIOSITY DEVELOPS in kittens much earlier than fear, and once they can walk they will totter off to investigate any new sight, sound or smell. Although they quickly become gregarious, outgoing and inquisitive, young kittens remain overwhelmingly dependent on their mother for feeding, cleaning and rescuing from danger. It is left to her to observe her kittens' activities and to retrieve them when she thinks they may be at risk. Until about the age of six weeks she is their source of nourishment, providing them with the necessary contact for full physical and emotional development.

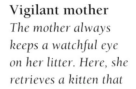

Vigilant mother
The mother always keeps a watchful eye on her litter. Here, she retrieves a kitten that has strayed too far. As the kitten grows, the skin becomes looser and the neck grasp is more difficult.

Rump is presented for mother to lick

Sanitation service
For the first three weeks, the mother stimulates her kittens to urinate and defecate by licking their anogenital regions. She consumes all their bodily discharges. Once they move on to solid food she becomes less inclined to be their sanitation unit.

Barbed tongue combs the fur

First steps
This precocious four-week-old kitten is already venturing out on his own. The mother stands by, observing her kitten's progress.

I know you're always there to get me out of trouble.

Slightly vexed expression suggests irritation

Creature comforts

(ABOVE) *This seven-week-old kitten still thrives on physical contact with her mother. The mother cat's facial expression shows that she is slightly annoyed at being used as a climbing frame, but she offers no resistance.*

Extended leg shows mother is relaxed

Food and security

At six weeks the kittens no longer depend on their mother's milk for nourishment, but they still continue suckling. With their heads close together, the kittens compete with each other for a nipple. They enjoy the security of being with their mother as she relaxes, cleaning the rump of one of them. Weaning kittens earlier than six weeks will restrict their normal emotional development.

Tail is up while kitten burrows in to find a nipple

Limp tail indicates the kitten has settled in to suckle

Stepping Out

KITTENS CAN CRAWL from birth. Heat receptors on the nose tell them where to find their mother. At two weeks the brain is receiving information from the other senses to help develop fluid movement. At seven weeks the kitten moves like an adult, and by ten weeks he will be able to walk along narrow ledges, such as the top of a fence, balancing perfectly.

Let's get going.

Tail held high for balance

Heat receptors on nose leather are extremely sensitive

Tummy drags along the ground

1 Paddling
At ten days the kitten scrambles along with her belly on the ground, paddling with her limbs. Her head is like a battering ram and is used as a probe to locate the warm nest.

2 Flat feet
The kitten can balance at two weeks but cannot yet walk easily. Although able to support her body weight on her limbs, she will topple over if she lifts more than one limb at a time. The feet are kept flat on the ground as she crawls along.

Fluid movement

Messages from each of the senses are sent to the brain. The coordinating center in the brain interprets these messages, then sends further instructions to the appropriate muscles. The messages travel very fast, enabling the cat to operate fluidly. The forelimbs move freely, and because the center of gravity is nearer to the head, most of the activity comes from the front. Hindlegs provide rapid acceleration, and the tail acts as a rudder.

Entire foot on the ground for balance

3 Walking tall
Increased mobility coincides with an intense curiosity. At three weeks, the kitten's hindlegs are in the tiptoe "sprinter's position." She can support her entire body weight and place her feet, but not yet exactly where she wants them.

On tiptoes is the cat's natural position

Tail still raised
for balance

4 Confidence building
*The kitten still has to
concentrate hard on where
to place her feet, but she is
unlikely to topple over
at four weeks of age.
The organ of balance
in the ear is developed
enough for stalking
and chasing siblings
and other objects.*

Homing instinct

Once on the move, cats seem to have
the ability to find their way back home.
Trials have shown that cats use the
earth's magnetic field for navigation:
cats put in a maze emerged in the
direction of home; those fitted with
magnets lost their way. Older cats
fared better than younger ones, and
all performed better when less than
8 miles (12 kilometers) from home.

Paw reaches
out confidently

5 The small adult
*When five weeks old, the kitten
moves fluently. She does
not need to concentrate
so intently and is able
to move naturally,
mimicking her
mother. The
tail drops as it is
no longer needed
as a rudder.*

Tail in a lower
position

6 Complete agility
*The kitten has learned all the
movements necessary for survival
by the time she reaches ten weeks.
She is able to stride confidently
along a branch, with no danger
of falling. Although still small,
she now has all the characteristics
of a fast, agile and silent hunter.*

Paw pads act as
shock absorbers
on uneven surface

Leaps and Bounds

DESIGNED TO BECOME hunters, kittens rapidly develop an enviably fluid and graceful agility. This enables them to alter the position of their bodies and catch unsuspecting prey at a moment's notice. At six weeks their sense of balance is better than a human's will ever be. This is because a large part of the cat's brain is devoted to receiving and interpreting messages from the organ of balance and from the eyes. The skeleton – particularly the backbone and joints – and muscles are well adapted for pouncing, climbing and balancing.

Impromptu jump

Springing spontaneously into the air, the kitten twists at the waist to face the prey, bending her body into a U-shape. One foot is kept on the ground for balance. Extremely strong ligaments around the joints add extra thrust to the powerful thigh muscles.

One paw remains on the ground for stability

Tail drops as forepaws are raised

Ready to pounce

The kitten creeps up on her prey and then, keeping her hindlegs on the ground, springs forward to catch it unawares. The pounce is the hunting maneuver most frequently used by a cat.

Powerful leg muscles allow full height to be reached

Horizontal jumping

With paws ready to grasp the prey, the kitten leaps forward to cover distance, but she may also inadvertently frighten off her victim.

Forepaws free for gripping

Hindpaws land first

Ears alert as kitten lands

Planned leaping

Calculating to reach a particular point, the kitten uses powerful hindleg muscles to make a series of half bounds. She lands, balancing effortlessly, on her front feet.

Tail swings like a pendulum

Flexible shoulders absorb shock

Brain receives information to prepare kitten for landing

Widely spaced frontlegs prepare for crash landing

Tail acts as a counterweight as the center of gravity shifts forward

Crash landing

Not every movement is successful, but the kitten's acute righting reflex ensures that she will land upright. The paws are held far apart to help absorb shock. The lack of bony attachments between the forelimbs and the body makes the landing softer and easier.

Vertical leaping

All four feet lift off the floor as the kitten jumps up and back. Once airborne, the claws unsheathe, ready to grasp on to anything. The leap is used later in life to catch birds and flying insects.

Landing feet first

Cats spend a lot of time on lookout duty. They choose trees, ledges and rooftops for their observation posts. With all this climbing comes the risk of a fall, so in conjunction with their agility cats have evolved a superb sense of balance. If a cat falls, her body rotates in the air, turning her right way up before she reaches the ground.

Claws unsheathed to catch prey

Weaning

SOONER OR LATER kittens become a nuisance to their mother. Exactly when this occurs varies from litter to litter. In general, however, kittens are completely weaned at seven weeks, but some mothers get fed up with the razor-sharp teeth much earlier than this. Others may continue to suckle for several more months, regardless of milk flow.

In both instances the need for independence eventually overcomes all kittens, and they relinquish the security of mother to brave the perils and uncertainties of adulthood.

Separation begins
(ABOVE) This six-week-old kitten does not need her mother's milk, but she will stay close by for several more weeks.

Raised leg lets the kittens suckle

Prominent shoulder blade indicates her energy stores are now exhausted

Cutting the apron strings
(ABOVE AND BELOW) At six weeks, the kittens in this large litter are still voracious feeders. Their mother becomes less willing to spend time with them as they are a physical drain on her. Their milk teeth, which are very sharp, also cause her discomfort.

Breakfast call
Even though these kittens are of weaning age, the mother takes the initiative and licks them gently awake for breakfast. Maternal care varies from mother to mother, but the kitten's personality is certainly influenced by her behavior.

Suckling for comfort
(BELOW) *With only two kittens in her litter, this mother has found feeding much less of a physical drain than would be the case with a large litter. At seven weeks the milk has almost dried up, but suckling is a comfort behavior that sometimes continues beyond seven weeks.*

"*I want to keep on suckling for as long as I can.*"

Head down, the kitten rootles in to suckle

Forming Friendships

BETWEEN THE AGES OF two and seven weeks, it is essential that your kitten is mentally stimulated if he is to mature into a secure, extroverted cat. Initially, the kitten's social activity centers on his mother and gradually transfers to his siblings. At about two weeks kittens start to play with one another, and this social interaction teaches them how to make friends. This playing gently introduces them to the concerns of adulthood.

Let's play grown-ups.

Turning "belly-up" is a relaxed response

Mock aggression

These three-week-old kittens are making mock-aggressive rushes at each other, playing rough-and-tumble games. At four weeks they will be wrestling, and at five weeks they will pounce on each other.

Crouched in the basket, the kitten feels secure

Fleeting friendships

Kittens are happy to play with each other until they are 14 weeks old. In fact, play helps keep them together when their mother is absent, hunting for food. They practice aggressive gestures to establish which displays intimidate their siblings most effectively. Some aspects of play, such as biting the nape of the neck, rehearse sexual behavior; others train the kittens to hunt. The kittens will stalk and pounce as if they were preying on each other.

Flattened-back
ears show play
is more serious

A not-so-
playful pat

Rough and tumble

Aged three-and-a-half weeks, these kittens roll together and tussle. The sparring may look serious, but at this stage it is for fun. A hugging and licking session will usually follow this kind of play fight.

Fighting talk

(LEFT) *This six-week-old kitten backs off from the fight. Games that once ended amicably now often conclude with a glower and a hiss.*

Upright ears reveal
this is just a game

Creative play

(LEFT) *The kittens are relaxed as one turns onto her side to expose her tummy. Her sister plays with her tail, learning that she must react quickly to catch moving objects.*

Paw tries to trap
moving tail

Playful attack

The mother engages in playful advances from one six-week-old kitten while another suckles. As her kittens mature, she will become increasingly intolerant of their antics. Other adult cats seldom respond with aggression, but may swat or growl if pestered repeatedly.

Limp tail
shows kitten
is playing

Making Contact

I've never seen anything quite like that before!

PLAY MIGHT APPEAR purposeless, but nature is seldom frivolous. Each aspect of the kitten's play has significance. Play with toys begins at three weeks, when he paws at movable objects. Soon he will be batting, holding and exploring anything that makes him curious. If introduced to humans at this age, he willingly plays and, when older, he will be happy to be part of the family. Both types of play are a means of preparing the kitten for the adult world.

Playing with humans
When kittens are little, you should play with them for at least 40 minutes every day to ensure that they grow into relaxed and friendly cats. Frequent handling will make the kittens less fearful and more curious.

Learning to play ball
(BELOW) Small balls are favorite toys as they appear to run away. At eight weeks the kitten has full control over the use of his paws and clasps the ball tightly. Like a small child, he is not prepared to share the toy with his sibling.

Claws retract to hold ball tightly

Moving targets

The kittens concentrate on the ball to see if it moves. The ginger kitten touches it inquisitively. The ball rolls away and he watches it intently, just as he will stalk prey in later life. Learning that the ball rolls silently is as important as learning that breaking a twig makes a noise.

Object play

In playing with different objects such as leaves, or toys such as small balls, kittens learn about their environment. If they are to hunt prey successfully, they must be aware of how things move, react or make a noise when touched. The brain and connections between brain cells develop more in young kittens allowed to play than in kittens deprived of object play.

Ears perk
forward
to funnel
in sounds

Kitten stares
at the ball

Hunting skills

The tabby focuses his attention on the ball. Such staying power suggests that he will develop into a good hunter. The ginger kitten's concentration has wandered from the ball, and he now watches something else.

Competing for Position

SOON AFTER THEIR eyes open, kittens begin to tussle competitively with each other. At first the rivalry is playful, but the clumsy paw-blows herald the more serious "ranking" disputes of later life. Eventually, the kitten that is most quick-witted, strongest or most outgoing becomes dominant.

" *I'm the boss.* "

Tail fur on end

Sitting on hind-paws gives superior position

Fixed stare unnerves rival

1 Dominant stare
(LEFT) *All the play moves are identical to those of hunting or fighting. This kitten stares confidently at her sibling, just as she will later stare at prey. She will stay as still as a statue, hiding any intent, until finally one kitten forces the other to make a move.*

2 Play attack
The kitten standing up is still acting dominantly and, judging by the erect fur on her tail, she is more serious about the game than her sibling, who continues to play. With no fear, the kitten on the ground rolls over to expose her tummy. In this instance, "belly-up-ing" is a typical sign of submission.

Stalking circle

(RIGHT) *These kittens circle, trying to sniff each other's anal regions. This is a classic rehearsal of the challenges over territory and rank that occur later in life. Cats that know each other sniff noses.*

Raised tail signifies confidence

Averted eyes indicate submission

Developing a hierarchy

At first it would appear that the litter lives together without friction and with equal rights. When the dinner bell rings, all the kittens gather around their mother with no regard as to who should eat first. Ranking in the litter is not as pronounced as it is in a litter of pups, but a hierarchy does develop. In a game the role of dominant kitten may be freely exchanged, but kittens soon learn that they are able to dominate others, or, conversely, that submission is the most practical response to a sibling who is playing more seriously.

3 Escape route
Suddenly the kitten that was playing realizes that her sibling is serious. The game has evolved into a hierarchy dispute and, with ears pinned back in fear, she retreats. Although the other kitten is lying down, the ear position indicates that she has won the challenge.

Ears perked forward denote play

Ears drawn back in fear

Enter the Hunter

Tail twitches in anticipation

Flexible spine allows unexpected movement

Feet firmly planted

Stalking

(ABOVE) *Stealthily creeping up on her prey, this nine-week-old hunter has mastered the technique of squirming slowly forward. Kittens start stalking each other when they are only three weeks old, and begin to stalk objects a short time later.*

You won't be able to escape me!

Mouse pounce

(RIGHT) *The stiff-legged sideways leap is a favorite maneuver of the nine-week-old kitten, practiced here on a button. She springs down on to her "victim" rather than jumping up. Later in her life she may use the mouse pounce to catch rodents.*

SOME BEHAVIORISTS BELIEVE that play behavior and hunting are manifestations of the same instinct. This does not explain why your cat will hunt for food and still continue to play like a kitten. Hunting behavior is developed by the time a kitten is five weeks old. At that age kittens use three different hunting maneuvers – the "mouse pounce," the "bird swat" and the "fish scoop" – and it is not long before they learn that there is action in the air as well as on the ground. Most kittens become excellent mousers but, due to relatively poor cat camouflage in many gardens, few will mature into expert bird catchers, so their effect on bird populations would appear to be negligible.

Fish scoop

(LEFT) *Practicing on a toy chick, this kitten learns how to make the flipping action that can be used to scoop a fish out of the water. Claws unleashed in readiness, she throws her paw over her shoulder. The kitten does not need her mother to teach her this gesture as it is instinctive.*

Bird swat

This kitten is still too young at six weeks to do a proper bird swat, but with claws out ready to grasp, she extends her paw to reach up at the unexpected movement in the air. When she is older she will be able to leap into the air from a standing position to swipe at moths, flies and birds that catch her attention.

Claws out
in readiness

Claws hook
onto any fast-
moving object

Eyes concentrate
on toy

Balance for hunting

At six weeks this kitten has sufficient balance to free both forepaws to bat airborne objects, but as yet she lacks the muscle coordination to leap successfully. Her tail sticks out straight behind her to help with stability.

Tail used
for balance

Tail up in
excitement

Bringing back the spoils

Once captured, prey must be carried away. This kitten brings her toy chick back to the den just as her mother will bring back mice for her kittens.

Mouth grasps
prey firmly

Breaking Down Boundaries

ROM THE AGE of two weeks a kitten can also start to form relationships with prey (squirrel), predator (dog) or competitor (fox). Provided the kitten is able to play with and head- and flank-rub the stranger without being frightened away, it does not seem to matter where an animal fits in the cat hierarchy. Such friendships can be lifelong, but the period during which these bonds may form is short-lived, lasting for a maximum of five weeks.

Befriending the enemy
(LEFT) *Showing no fear, this kitten clambers up onto the dog to seek out warmth and security. Gentle adult dogs or puppies less than 12 weeks old are ideal for these early social meetings.*

Exploring the differences
(BELOW) *This kitten enjoys a relaxed relationship with the fox cub. Until he is seven weeks old, the kitten looks upon different species simply as other kittens or as cats that either smell or look different.*

Sniffs in curiosity

Critical timing
The permanent fear a cat has of other species, for example a fox or dog, and the instinct to prey on small species such as a mouse or rat, does not develop until after the kitten is seven weeks old. Studies show that when six-week-old kittens are raised with rats they consistently refuse to prey upon that breed of rat later on in life. But if the first meeting is delayed beyond seven weeks, the relationship turns into one of hunter and hunted.

Hindlegs free to kick

Fear of the unknown

Fearful yet inquisitive, this kitten's hackles are partly raised and his back is arched as he investigates the squirrel. There is great curiosity about small species that are the size of prey.

Hello, friend – let's play.

Hierarchy play

(BELOW) The kitten and fox cub play a game of dominance and submission in the same way that kittens play together. Here, the kitten is feigning aggression by rolling over to expose teeth and claws.

Mock attack

(BELOW) The kitten attacks the squirrel playfully, but he will not "bite home." When older it is unlikely that he will kill squirrels. The squirrel is not frightened as it was raised with cats.

Powerful jaws will be used if necessary

Pupils remain constricted as the kitten is not frightened

Ears folded back into angry position

Learning to Survive

Kittens are taught how to catch and kill prey by their mother. This is an essential skill for feral cats, but even your pet cat will teach her kittens how to find and hunt for food, despite the fact that you usually provide regular meals in a food bowl. To begin with, the kittens must learn to identify potential victims, so initially the mother brings prey home dead. Next the kittens must learn how to kill, so she returns with live prey.

At first the kittens may be apprehensive and fearful, but they soon become brave enough to chase and capture chosen prey, throwing it before finally making the kill. Kittens raised by a mother that is a successful hunter are more likely to become successful hunters themselves, as a good teacher passes on special skills. However, kittens can still become adept hunters without training from their mother.

Providing prey
(ABOVE) *This mother cat has just killed a mouse to bring home for her kittens to play with. Her rigid stance and dilated pupils show her excitement. She will warn* *them she is returning with prey. They soon learn to interpret the vowel sounds that tell them if she has a mouse, or, much more dangerous, a rat that may fight tenaciously.*

Touches mouse gingerly

Smells prey to identify

Careful examination
Under the watchful eye of their mother, the kittens examine the dead mouse that she has brought home for them. By mimicking their mother's behavior, the kittens learn to use all their senses to investigate the rodent thoroughly. Its scent will become a lifelong memory.

My mother will teach me everything I need to know.

Preparing to eat
(RIGHT) *While the mother grooms one of her kittens to distract it, the other kitten concentrates on the mouse, holding it in her forepaws and kicking with her hindlegs.*

Paws kick playfully

Ears forward in alert position

Playing with prey
Unfamiliar prey stimulates this kitten to play with her quarry rather than simply kill and consume it. The old story that a hungry cat kills more rats is inaccurate because hunger motivates only the most experienced of hunters.

Eyes look up in curiosity

Making demands
This pet cat stands up on her hind-paws and begs for her food. By watching and listening to her mother, the kitten also learns to beg and make the demand call. Through domestication, the feral cat has evolved from independent hunter into scavenger-beggar.

Paw reaching forward to tap

Mouth open copying begging meow

"Mouse pounce" grab

Hindpaw firmly planted for balance

Becoming Independent

I N THE WILD, where kittens do not experience contact with humans, they mature into lone hunters. There is no incentive to continue the group activity that existed when they were kittens. Independence is often asserted dramatically when the mock aggression of early play determines rank order within the litter. By the time the kittens are 14 weeks old the fights are serious, although the combatants rarely suffer any permanent injuries. The bonds of kittenhood are now broken and the litter disbands. Your kitten continues to accept close contact with you because she regards you as a mother substitute, not a litter-mate.

You're competition. Go away!

Ears perked
and alert

Tail held high
in excitement

Forelimb
stretched out
ready for battle

Claws extended
for attack

1 Play fighting
When fully mobile, at about nine weeks, kittens will start to rehearse aggressive displays. With claws extended, the dominant kitten stands up, ready to pounce. Her sibling is lying down, still thinking that the attack is for fun. But it is for real, and the game may degenerate into a serious fight.

Hindpaw
securely
planted on
the ground

Bite aimed
at the neck

Tail used
for balance

Training ground
The fights of independence are final
training for the duels in which mature
tomcats engage either for territory
or for the right to mate with receptive
females. It is also practice for females
who might later be called upon to
protect their litter or their territory.
At this stage, female kittens begin to
mature sexually, and they are far less
tolerant of physical contact
with male siblings.

Ears perked forward
mean relaxed confidence

2 Neck bite
(ABOVE) *The
submissive kitten suddenly realizes
her opponent is serious. She leaps
up from the prostrate position
and launches a counter-attack,
trying to sink her teeth into
her sibling's neck.*

3 Lull in hostilities
(RIGHT) *At the age of
nine weeks the kittens
may pause and relax during a
fight. The kitten that was mauling
assumes a less aggressive stance,
while her sibling scrutinizes
her, anticipating more activity.*

4 Aggression resumes
(RIGHT) *The kitten that was
initially dominant makes a
flying assault on her
sibling, who starts to
roll over so that she
can defend
herself from
attack with her
claws and teeth.*

Tail-up position
suggests that the
brawl is for fun

Folded-back
ears show
aggression

Ears laid
back for
protection

THE MATURE CAT

Keen eyesight
As the pupils constrict in bright light, the cat is able to look directly into the sun.

WE KNOW THAT cats can see when there is only one-sixth of the amount of light that we need to see, but we are not sure if they see things in exactly the same way as us. We know that their range of hearing is much more extensive than ours, but we do not know what those high-pitched sounds, inaudible to us, really sound like. We know that cats have special taste buds for water, but what do they actually taste?

Varied diet
Many cats enjoy crunchy dry food. Prepared foods are often preferred to natural prey.

Many of the cat's senses are understood by us, although cats use their senses in different ways. Smell, for example, is important for eating, but also for courtship, hunting, territory-marking and even toilet habits. Grooming is important for self-cleaning, but it is also a way of ridding the body of excess heat or reducing tension.

Mutual grooming
The orange cat's gentle grooming of his companion mimics a mother's grooming of her kittens.

Caught cat-napping
This cat might appear to be dozing but he is actually alert to any unusual sights or sounds that may occur around him.

The cat's ability to balance is among the best developed of all mammals. Cats can climb effortlessly, walk tightropes as if they were broad pavements, and, if they do fall, have the ability to right themselves in midflight and land delicately on their feet.

Cats are world-champion sleepers. We know that their sleep patterns are similar to ours, and that like us they probably dream. However, their courtship and mating behavior is completely different, with much caterwauling, shrieking and patient waiting on the part of numerous hopeful males. Old age, however, vividly reflects the same behavior changes that we undergo. Messages simply take longer to get to the brain. Older cats, good companions throughout their lives, have earned and deserve compassionate understanding.

Washing routine
With saliva applied to his paw, this cat grooms his face in a ritualized manner.

Lapping it up
Unlike dogs, cats have almost perfect table manners. These kittens will finish their milk without spilling a drop.

Eating Habits

CATS ARE OPPORTUNIST hunters. In the wild they survive by eating whenever they catch or find a meal. Their feeding habits in our homes, however, are quite different. Typically, a pet cat will choose to eat between 10 and 20 small meals a day, and will continue to feed throughout the day and night. Your pet cat also has a more varied diet than his self-sustaining relatives, and, although hard food is not a natural part of the hunter's diet, many domestic cats actively prefer prepared, crunchy food.

Don't worry, I'll only take as much as I need.

Kittens willingly eat together as they feel no competition

Mother breaks food into manageable pieces

Aid to digestion
(BELOW) *Settling down to eat, this cat adopts a hunched position, with feet drawn back for comfort. The tail is wrapped around the body to prevent it being stepped on, allowing the cat to concentrate on eating.*

Eating in peace
(ABOVE) *To avoid competing with her young kittens, the mother eats separately, removing her food from the bowl. When given a large lump of food, she will slice it into smaller pieces, which she consumes individually.*

Extended neck straightens esophagus to facilitate swallowing

Tongue pushes moist food into the mouth

Dry morsel
Offered dry food for the first time, this cat stands rather apprehensively to investigate the pieces.

Star-shaped morsels are a favorite

Shearing teeth
Using the razor-sharp carnassial, or side, teeth, the cat slices large lumps of food into small pieces before swallowing. The small front incisors are useful for scraping off tiny pieces of meat or fish.

Head tilts to drop unwanted pieces of food

Large canine teeth grasp and tear

Side teeth shear meat

The cat and the cream
Using mobile tongues, the kittens take four or five laps before each swallow. They are fastidious drinkers, never spilling a drop.

Spoon-shaped tongue scoops up milk efficiently

Smelling and Tasting

YOUR CAT HAS twice as many scent receptors in her small nose as you do. She sniffs to pick up information about food, the presence of other cats and potential danger. From smell she can tell whether a tom owns the territory or if a female is in heat. Your cat is drawn to food by smell rather than taste, and will never taste anything without smelling it first. Her taste buds are sensitive, distinguishing between salt, bitter and acid tastes, but she has no taste buds that respond to sweet tastes. Cats that crave chocolate either have been unwittingly trained to do so or are the result of our intervention in breeding.

Cat aphrodisiac

Sniffing the plant catnip stimulates your cat by activating her biochemical pathways. The scent is taken up into the vomeronasal organ. She responds by rolling around on the ground demonstrating her pleasure. This display of excitement is similar to pre- and post-mating behavior. Only about half of all adult cats will sniff, lick or chew catnip.

Eating carefully

Cats are much fussier eaters than dogs. As true carnivores, felines are unwilling to share our diet and they will usually refuse sweet titbits. Cats are attracted to food by its smell, and particularly by the smell of fat in meat. Mouse meat, their natural food, is 40 percent fat.

Once the smell is found to be acceptable, your cat will taste the food. His sensitive palate prefers foods that have high levels of the chemicals nitrogen and sulphur, the constituents of the amino acids that make up meat. Smell memories are stored in the brain and last a lifetime. These memories, together with the sensitive senses of taste and smell, are self-protective, helping to ensure the cat eats healthily.

Grooming tool

Your cat's tongue is long, muscular and flexible. The sandpaper-like hooks are used in grooming. The taste buds, which include receptors sensitive to the taste of water, are located at the tip, sides and back.

Backward-pointing barbs used in grooming and for scraping meat off bones

Sniffing takes air into the vomeronasal organ

Memorizing scents

Sniffing in short bursts, this cat smells a clump of grass. The air is drawn into the vomeronasal organ, a special chamber in the roof of the mouth. Used primarily by males to scent females in heat, this chamber is filled with cells that trap the odor. The smell is converted into electrical signals that are transferred to the brain to create smell memories.

Exploring by smell

Initially attracted to a toad by its movement, this cat explores further by smelling it. Most cats enjoy hunting amphibians, and often present them to their owners as gifts. They will eat them only when absolutely necessary.

If it smells good, it's bound to taste good too.

Reacting dramatically

An unpleasant taste, such as the secretions in the toad's skin, will make a cat salivate profusely in an attempt to dispel the taste as quickly as possible.

Sniffing is a dramatic disruption to regular breathing

Balancing Act

I can't put a paw wrong.

YOUR CAT'S UNCANNY ability to land on his feet, maintaining perfect balance, is directly connected to his acute hearing. Deep in the ear is the vestibular apparatus, which is filled with fluid, tiny floating crystals and millions of sensitive hairs. These instantly orient the cat so that he can turn his body into an upright position. Related to this innate sense of balance is the cat's acute hearing – sharper than either a dog's or a human's. Your cat is able to hear tone so distinctly that he can distinguish between the sound of your car engine and that of an identical size and make of car.

Head rotates first

Loosely attached
back bones allow
180 degree rotation

1 Finding bearings
Falling through the air from a height, this cat begins to orient himself. Sent by the vestibular apparatus, the first messages rotate the head.

Ears can
be rotated
individually

Eyes stare intently
at source of sound

Catching sounds
Natural prey is often hidden in long grass. By moving his ears around, the cat is able to locate the source of the noise precisely and funnel it to the ear drum so that he knows where to pounce. More than 20 muscles in each ear give the cat fine control over its movement.

2 Twisting
Once head and ears have rotated into the correct place, the cat is able to assess his position. Twisting at the waist, he rapidly swings the front of his body around to prepare for landing, despite the fact that his hind-quarters may still be facing skyward.

Hindleg muscles
begin to respond to
instruction to rotate

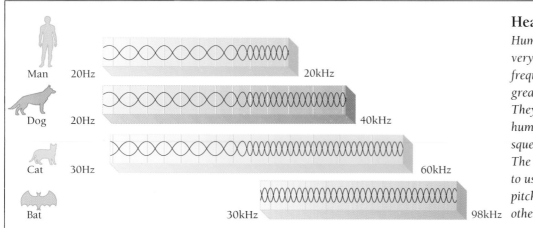

Hearing ranges
Humans, cats and dogs have very similar hearing at low frequencies, but cats have greater sensitivity to high notes. They respond to high-pitched human voices as well as to the squeaks of kittens and mice. The "silent meow," inaudible to us, is really just a high-pitched meow, quite audible to other cats with normal hearing.

Brilliant hearing

Your cat's hearing range covers over ten octaves and can distinguish between two notes that differ from each other by merely one-tenth of a tone. Cats can judge to within 3in (8cm), with 75 percent accuracy, the source of a sound 1yd (1m) away and can hear high-pitched sounds that are inaudible to us.

Turning a deaf ear

This blue-eyed, white cat is suffering from a genetic deafness. She does not turn her head in the direction of a sound or move her ears to locate the position of a noise. White cats with one blue and one yellow eye are often deaf only on the blue side.

Forelimbs stretch out to make ground contact first

3 Absorbing shock
Nearing the ground, the front legs stretch out. With no bone attachments to the rest of the body, the forelimbs absorb shock to prevent injury. The body continues to twist as orientation messages are sent to the hindquarters.

4 Landing feet first
Now ready to land on his forepaws, the cat looks confidently ahead at the landing pad. All his muscles are relaxed because tense muscles are more likely to tear.

Forelimbs act as shock absorbers

Through Your Cat's Eyes

EYES ARE ONE of your cat's most distinctive and mesmerizing features. Appropriate to such opportunist hunters, a cat's eyes are designed to collect the maximum amount of light. The eye's surface, or cornea, is curved, and the lens is very large in comparison to the other dimensions of the eye. In dim light, or when your cat is excited or scared, the pupils dilate; in bright light they can close completely, allowing light to pass through two slits at the top and bottom.

*I've got the eyes
of a hunter.*

Seeing in the dark
(BELOW) *In the restricted light this cat's pupils dilate to become almost spherical, allowing as much light as possible to enter the eye. Contrary to popular belief, cats cannot see any better than us in the pitch dark, but their eyes can function in very dim conditions. This enables the cat to hunt for prey in the dawn light and at dusk.*

Pupils dilate to become spherical

Shading from glare
(ABOVE) *With pupils the size of pin-pricks, this cat can stare into the sun without damaging her retina. Acting like built-in sunglasses, the muscles in the iris allow the pupil to change shape according to the available light. Almost round in the dark, the pupil becomes oval in brighter light. In intense light the slit pupil closes in the middle, leaving two tiny slits at each end.*

Glowing eyes
(BELOW) *A cat's eyes shine green or gold as light is reflected from layers of mirror-like cells behind the retina. The cells improve the cat's night vision by reflecting back light.*

CAT VISION

HUMAN VISION

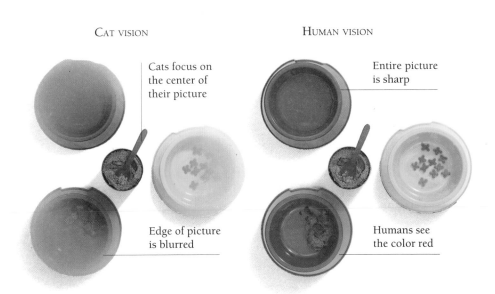

Cats focus on the center of their picture

Entire picture is sharp

Edge of picture is blurred

Humans see the color red

What your cat sees

Cats see green and blue but not red. This is not a significant weakness since smell and taste, rather than color, distinguish prey. Cats focus on the middle of the picture with the periphery remaining slightly cloudy.

The images above demonstrate the differences between what we see (ABOVE RIGHT) and what your cat sees (ABOVE LEFT). He can focus on fast-moving objects clearly because, unlike dogs or humans, his head stays level as he bounds along.

Dilating dramatically

When the "flight-or-fight" response is activated, your cat's pupils dilate. This creates a wider field of vision and actually enables your cat to see more of any potential danger.

Binocular vision

When the two fields of vision overlap, a binocular effect results. Three-dimensional vision is vital to hunting animals, and enables them to judge distances accurately.

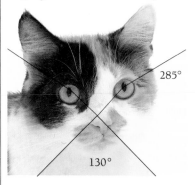

285°

130°

Cat vision

When your cat's eyes face forward, 130 of the total 285 degrees of his field of vision is binocular.

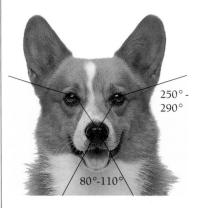

250° - 290°

80°-110°

Dog vision

Eyes are set to the side, with up to 110 degrees of binocular overlap.

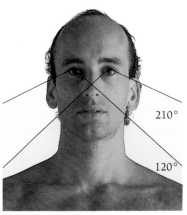

210°

120°

Human vision

Despite a smaller field of vision, our binocular vision is good.

Touching

Aᴌᴌ ᴛʜᴇ ᴛɪᴍᴇ your cat is using her well-developed sense of touch to gather information about her surroundings. The most sophisticated touch receptors are contained in the whiskers which, extending beyond the width of her body, help her to move about confidently. From the information picked up by the whiskers your cat can determine, for example, whether or not she can fit through a narrow gap. Other touch receptors on the body are sensitive to pressure and texture, responding to such things as the sensation of being stroked or the type of surface underfoot. All over your cat's body there are receptors that detect heat and cold. Her preference for the warmth of a fire or radiator may well have come from the ancestors that originated in North Africa.

I know you – so let's rub noses!

Seeking out heat
Cats love heat and are able to withstand much higher temperatures than we can. We start to feel uncomfortable if our skin temperature exceeds 112°F (44°C), but your cat will not feel discomfort until her skin temperature reaches 126°F (52°C).

Touching noses
(ʀɪɢʜᴛ) *This kitten greets another cat she knows by sniffing his nose. The touch receptors on the nose are already developed at birth and help the kitten find his mother.*

Sensing air currents
Every whisker over your cat's eyes, on her elbows and on her muzzle is rooted in a rich supply of nerve endings. As these specialized antennae-like hairs brush past objects, messages are sent to the brain. Even air currents can be felt, and at night she uses her whiskers to help her pick out a clear path. If she loses her whiskers she may bump into objects when moving around in complete darkness, but the problem is short-lived as new whiskers grow in their place.

Importance of touch

Your cat is more sophisticated than almost any other domestic animal when it comes to using touch to investigate surroundings. Touch may even be the most important sense required for social development. But just as touch is important for learning, *being* touched is even more vital for healthy emotional development. Cats deprived of physical contact become fearful and withdrawn, crouching motionless or perhaps compensating by excessive grooming.

Measuring spaces

Using muzzle whiskers, this cat is able to gauge whether or not she can squeeze her lithe body through the narrow gap in the fence. As her head comes through, she will direct her whiskers to feel the surface below.

Whiskers angled down to detect surface

Receptors on the nose pad explore gently

Basking in comfort

(BELOW) *This kitten enjoys the security of the girl's lap. When he is older, he will not remain in this position or let her tickle his tummy because he will feel too exposed.*

Cat assumes relaxed belly-up position

Grooming

Total cleansing process

A born contortionist, this cat sticks her leg straight up in the air and then reaches round to clean herself. As she removes matted or soiled fur, the grooming action stimulates the scent-producing anal and perianal glands.

Grooming is not simply a matter of personal hygiene, it is a reflex behavior. Just as you sometimes scratch your head in thought, your cat may have the urge to groom. Usually your cat will groom herself when she is feeling relaxed, but she may preen if she is frightened. Grooming keeps the fur in pristine condition and, as the saliva evaporates, can also help your cat regulate her temperature.

Abrasive tongue combs fur

Washing routine

(RIGHT) The routine that your cat follows when she washes her face is always the same. Saliva is applied to the inside of the forepaw, which is rubbed from back to front in a circular motion around the side of her face.

Clean from top to tail

With her mobile spine, this cat can reach to groom almost every part of her body with her tongue. Turning her head almost 180 degrees, she nibbles away at grit and flakes of dead skin on her back. The order in which she washes her body is random.

Not just a lick and a promise

Your cat is naturally clean. She will instinctively use a specific site as a toilet, and just as fastidiously groom her fur. The licks stimulate the glands in the skin to produce a film of oil that waterproofs her coat. Her hook-covered tongue removes loose and broken hairs and matts, and she uses her tiny front teeth to gnaw at other debris. Long-haired cats may need extra help with grooming. The fine hairs tangle easily and knots often build up in the coat.

Mutual grooming

This kitten licks her mother behind the ears and provides a practical solution to an anatomical problem. With eyes shut tight the mother feels totally relaxed as her kitten grooms her. Mutual grooming also strengthens the intimate bond between mother and offspring.

Keeping clean makes me feel good.

Finishing touches

Applying saliva for a final rinse, she pulls her paw over her eyes to complete the washing cycle. When your cat grooms herself after you have handled her, she may be tasting your scent or, more likely, she may simply be masking your scent with her own.

Head lowered to reach behind the ears

Paw wipes the eyes

Washing behind the ears

Completing the end of a large washing circle, she brings her paw over her ear. Your cat enjoys being stroked on the head because she cannot reach it with her tongue.

Tail wraps around the body to keep it out of harm's way

Cat Napping

YOUR CAT SPENDS about 16 hours a day sleeping, which is almost twice as long as most other mammals. Exactly why they spend so much time snoozing is not yet understood. They seem to prefer to take their cat naps during the day and are usually active in the early morning and late evening, when hunting is most productive. On waking, they habitually go through a ritual that includes yawning, stretching and grooming.

Nothing's better than 40 winks.

Flexible spine extends fully

Yawning

Awakening gently, this cat gives a wide yawn to stretch his jaw muscles. Although yawning is a sign of nervousness in other species, it does not appear to be the case with cats.

Tongue curls as he yawns

Hind legs stretch backwards

Claws extended in the stretch

Stretching

After arching her back one way, this cat reaches forward to stretch the muscles in her front legs, claws and neck. Circulation to her extremities is revived and her sense of touch is reawakened.

Tail goes up as she arches her back

Flexing the back

Having woken up slowly, she puts her paws close together and straightens her hindlegs. The elegant arch of her back exercises the muscles. She must keep her finely honed body in peak condition so that she is always ready to produce the short bursts of energy that a hunter requires.

Snoozing in comfort

These young kittens snooze together, enjoying each other's warmth and the security of the basket. As they get older and the social bonds between them break down, they will prefer to sleep alone. They will continue to choose warm, secure spots such as cupboards or your bed for their cat naps.

Waking scratch
As the finale of the stretching ritual, the kitten grooms herself, a habit similar to our morning wash.

Sleeping rhythms

Sleeping is not a passive state. When your cat becomes drowsy, she enters a stage of light sleep from which she is easily aroused. Between ten and thirty minutes later, her whole body becomes slack, her position shifts and she enters a period of deep sleep.

During deep sleep your cat may flex her paws and twitch her whiskers. She almost certainly dreams, and, judging from the amount of electrical activity in the brain, her mind is as active as when she is awake. After around seven minutes of deep sleep she returns to a light sleep. The cycle is then repeated.

Relaxing happily
(RIGHT) *This cat shows no fear of humans because she was raised with them. She happily falls asleep in the girl's arms. The cat looks upon the child as a mother substitute, which is why she enjoys the close physical contact.*

Closed eyes show
the cat has no fear

Choosing a Partner

ALTHOUGH ARRANGED MARRIAGES are now the norm for almost all pure-bred cats, when left to nature it is the female prerogative to select her mate. Tomcats might engage in bloody duels for the right to mate with a receptive female, but it is just as likely that she will choose the loser as the father of her litter.

Females normally experience several ten-day cycles of sexual receptiveness each year, which are brought on by increasing daylight in late winter and early spring. Cats housed indoors in artificial light can be sexually active at any time of the year. During her receptive phase, the female undergoes a personality change, becoming affectionate and lascivious.

1 Signalling sexual interest
By rolling provocatively, this female is indicating her availability. She may also tread with her front paws and call out. Even the most withdrawn of females will give these bold signals. Inexperienced cat owners often assume their cat is in distress.

He advances, avoiding eye contact

I'm available.

She keeps her eye on him in case he advances too quickly

2 Tentative approach
While the male advances cautiously, avoiding eye contact and making gentle chirping sounds, the female continues to roll and call repeatedly. He rubs his head against places where she has rolled or rubbed but is careful not to come close to her too quickly. If he does she might turn and swipe at him or run away.

Body is relaxed but not yet receptive to mating

3 Reducing tension
(ABOVE) Now more confident, the male begins to groom the female behind her ears to relax her and make her less likely to respond aggressively to his advances. Although the female appears passive at this stage, the mating initiative comes completely from her, and it is possible that she will withdraw her invitation at any time.

Experienced male
maintains a quiet dignity

Tail to
the side

Hindlegs
push rump up

4 Sexual arousal

(ABOVE) *Seduced by his
grooming, the female turns onto her
front and stretches out. She raises
her rump and swings her tail to the
side to invite mating. In this posture,
the female pads with her forepaws
to maintain her position. If she does
not feel completely at ease with the
male, or if he touches her without
invitation, she may cuff him.*

Relaxed expression
signals that mating
can be attempted

5 Confirming receptivity

*Scenting her rump, the male
sniffs the odors from her vaginal
discharge and her urine into his
vomeronasal organ to confirm that
she is fully receptive. Preparation
for mating is a lengthy business,
but the mating itself will be short.*

Perked forward
ears indicate
apprehension

The Mating Game

CATS DO NOT form pair bonds. When mating ceases, the female has nothing more to do with the male. She is not naturally monogamous, and if several eligible toms are available she might well mate with all of them. Unlike most other domestic animals, cats are induced ovulators, which means that the act of mating stimulates the hormone changes that trigger the release of eggs. Therefore the more frequent the mating, the more likely it is that eggs will be fertilized.

Mouth open in
readiness to grip

6 Getting into position
With her ears back, the female appears fearful as mating begins. The male starts to mount carefully, opening his mouth wide, ready to grasp the back of her neck should she decide to try to attack him.

Forward ear position
signals concentration

7 Penetration
Standing astride the female, the male "pedals" with his hindlegs and then makes just a few pelvic thrusts. Mating is over within a few seconds, but he keeps a firm grasp on the nape of her neck to prevent her from turning on him.

8 Withdrawal
The female shrieks as the male withdraws. Hook-like barbs on the male's penis cause genital irritation, thereby stimulating the chain of nervous and hormonal reactions that culminate in ovulation.

Hindlegs
pull back

Repeated mating

Mating often occurs as frequently as ten times an hour. It ends only when the male is exhausted, and he may well be replaced by another suitor. A succession of males will await their turn patiently. At the beginning of mating the male makes the advances and is often rebuffed. After repeated matings the female beckons another male with a provocative display. Eggs are released from the ovaries 24 hours after successful matings.

9 **Male apprehension**
At the moment of her piercing scream the male instantly disengages and moves away. The female will often lash out at the male as soon as he releases her from the neck grasp.

Ears are pinned back in fear

Facial expression is worried

10 **Relaxing together**
(LEFT) After mating the female allows the male to sit near her. They will groom themselves in preparation for a subsequent mating.

Toms and Queens

THERE ARE SEVERAL subtle behavioral differences between male and female cats. Unneutered males are usually more destructive and more active than females. Females are generally more playful and friendly, more inclined to be affectionate and cleaner than their male counterparts.

Male cats roam over large territories, marking them out frequently with their pungent urine. They fight for possession of the territory and for the right to mate with the females within it. Neutering can help to diminish a male cat's need to roam, spray and fight, although it does not always affect all these behaviors to the same extent. Males that are neutered before they reach puberty do not develop secondary sex characteristics, but if they are neutered after puberty all the physical secondary sex characteristics are retained.

Cheek jowls create illusion of greater size

Protective neck skin

Tomcat
(LEFT) *Secondary sex characteristics – like prominent cheek ruffs and thick neck skin – develop because this tomcat has not been neutered. Likewise, if a lion is neutered before puberty, he will not develop the entire male's mane.*

Entire female
(ABOVE) *This female has a typically delicate face and bone structure. Her slight body is also considerably smaller than a male cat's. In some breeds, females grow to only half the size of their male counterparts.*

Neutered male

(BELOW) *Neutering does not seem to have any significant effect on the excitability or destructiveness of male cats. If males develop unpleasant sex-related behaviors, neutering after the behavior develops is just as effective in correcting it as neutering before the problem arises.*

Neutered female

(ABOVE) *Neutering has a far less dramatic effect on female behavior than on male. Males and females have significantly different behavior repertoires from each other, but once neutered their behaviors tend to be more similar to the unneutered female than the unneutered male. Neutering reduces the need to roam, so all neutered cats are more likely to stay closer to the home territory of your yard.*

Effects of neutering

When a male cat reaches puberty, the male hormone goes into constant production. Secondary sex characteristics then begin to develop. These characteristics include pungent urine odor for territory marking and behaviors such as sex-related aggression. Females, however, display sex-related behavioral changes only when they are in season since this is when high levels of the sex hormone are produced. So while neutering dramatically suppresses male behavior, the neutered female cat simply behaves like a constantly out-of-season female cat.

Getting Older

AS YOUR CAT ages, you may notice that his mood changes. Some cats become grumpy and irritable, while others grow more affectionate, seeking out their owner for comfort. Old age can also bring on a change in your cat's appetite – he may develop preferences for certain foods, or demand to be fed more or less frequently.

Hearing
deteriorates

Matted coat
develops as he
finds grooming
difficult

Reacting slowly

In old age, nerve messages take longer to arrive at and to be sent from the brain. Sometimes the first messages to arrive can temporarily block the entire system. As a result, the brain appears to be working in slow motion, and your cat may not react as quickly as he did when he was younger. This means accidents are more likely. There is also a tendency for your cat to respond in a way that is unfamiliar to you, behaving more like a feral cat. He may even lash out at you when you stroke him. If this happens, it is not because you have provoked him – he has simply forgotten his "learned" behavior and is reverting to natural instincts.

Aging gracefully

The gradual changes of old age are inevitable, but your elderly pet will give you just as much pleasure in his later years as he did when he was a kitten. You may need to change the way you treat your cat when he gets past his prime. For example, try not to disturb him unnecessarily when he is sleeping. Let him decide when he wants to be stroked. Reduce the amount of protein in his diet, since he will need less energy and his kidneys are not as efficient. A well-cared for pet cat should live to be 15 years or older.

Putting on weight

(LEFT) *This Persian has put on a few extra pounds in his old age. His coat has also developed matts because he finds it difficult to groom. It is unusual for a healthy cat to become overweight. Unlike dogs, they are not obsessive about food – although some are accidentally trained by their owners to be so.*

Losing weight

(RIGHT) *In her advancing years this cat has grown to be rather thin. Overactivity of the thyroid gland sometimes causes cats to become hyperactive, which can result in dramatic weight loss.*

I've got to take it easy – I'm not the cat I used to be.

Eyesight begins to fail

Prominent shoulder blade indicates gradual weight loss

Coat becomes patchy in places

TAMING OF THE CAT

THERE ARE FEW differences between the pet cat lying by an open fire and its relative, the North African wild cat. They both have the same fundamental repertoire of cat behavior, but to differing degrees.

It is only in the last 100 years that we have seriously interfered in cat breeding. In previous centuries, by selecting certain cats to accompany them on voyages around the world, our forebears unknowingly helped to create breeds or regional differences. For example, cats with too many toes are common in the northeastern United States because some of the first cats taken there by British settlers had that genetic trait and bred with each other. Through selective breeding, we are now creating breeds not only for their different appearances, but also

Blotched effect
The blotched tabby pattern has become dominant in many parts of the world. The highest concentration is still in Britain.

Rarity value
The Persian's long coat is the result of a genetic accident that has been perpetuated because we admire it.

Temperamental differences
Longhaired cats often tend to be calmer and more retiring than other breeds.

Behavior patterns
Compact, chunky cats like this tom are common in Europe. In North America, similar cats are longer, leaner and more outgoing.

for the resulting variety of cat personalities. Longhaired Persian cats evolved in eastern Turkey, Iraq and Iran but are now selectively bred worldwide. They are quieter and less demonstrative than most shorthaired felines. At the opposite end of the spectrum, the increasingly popular Burmese was restricted to a small area of Southeast Asia until less than 50 years ago. Today, these effusive, gregarious, vocal cats are popular throughout all of Europe, Australasia and the Americas.

Gender differences
This unneutered female is less aggressive, cleaner and friendlier to humans than an unneutered male would be.

New breeds such as the gentle Ragdolls and Burmillas and the more assertive Devon Rexes are also becoming increasingly popular. Your cat's breeding history is a significant factor in determining its personality, so it is wise to bear this in mind when choosing a cat to fit into your home environment.

New breeds
Originally existing in small numbers in Burma and Thailand, the Burmese has achieved worldwide popularity in the last 30 years.

Your Pet's Ancestors

Y OUR PET CAT, a descendant of the North African wild cat, retains instincts and behaviors similar to his wild cousins. The wild cat is highly adaptable, capable of responding to novel situations and shows little fear of humans. In fact, its natural behavioral makeup includes an ability to live in close proximity to man. Thousands of years ago, the wild cat chose of its own accord to become domesticated, willingly relinquishing the life of the lone hunter.

Smooth and oily guard hairs

Woolly undercoat

Instinctive hunter
(*ABOVE*) *Even as the North African wild cat evolved into a domestic animal, it retained the ability to be self-sufficient. The Norwegian forest cat, a descendant of the tamed African wild cat, reverted to the wild where it survived as a superb hunter. Because its ancestors had contact with man it has a more relaxed temperament than wild cats indigenous to northern Africa, which have never been domesticated.*

Living close to man
(*RIGHT*) *Forebear of today's domestic cat, the North African wild cat is drawn to human settlements where it can scavenge for a meal.*

Surviving alone (ABOVE) *Timid and reclusive, the European wild cat does not have the genetic potential to alter its behavior, and has not been able to adapt to living with man. Impossible to tame, this cat has had little part in the evolution of the pet cat.*

Growing a longer coat

The shorthaired coat of the North African wild cat consists of two types of hair – short, fine down hairs and longer, thicker guard hairs. Most longhaired cats evolved as the result of a genetic mutation that allowed the down hair to continue to grow. The long down hairs tangle easily. The longhaired Norwegian forest cat and the Maine Coon have longer guard hairs, which do not get matted, so these cats are able to survive without help from us with grooming.

Maine Coon *A descendant of the hardy American farm cat, the Maine Coon has a luxurious coat to cope with a harsh climate. Thanks to their large size, the cats can catch rabbits, a widely available prey.*

Head small in proportion to large body

Thick coat helps survival in cold weather

Becoming Domesticated

CHOOSING TO LIVE near human settlements, the North African wild cat gradually shifted from hunting for his food in the wild to scavenging. Villages provided a source of food, and the cat's diet was supplemented with the mice and rats that infested grain stores. Inevitably, some of the cats, perhaps the most gentle ones and probably those that begged for food, were adopted as pets. Domestication and selective breeding had begun. Enjoying the considerable benefits of human companionship, the wild cat willingly became tame.

Pupils dilate in fear

Reacting with fear
(LEFT) *This wild kitten reacts viciously toward his handler because he is unused to this kind of contact and has not been socialized by human companionship.*

Silent survivor
Until recently, cats were reviled in the Singapore peninsula. The immigrant cats therefore evolved into small and silent scavengers rather than ardent beggars.

Scavenging successfully
(ABOVE) *Today, the North African wild cat is sometimes seen close to human habitation in parts of the Sudan. The cats show little fear as they scavenge from the waste sites of the communities.*

Nose receptors eagerly
search out new smells

Adapting to circumstance

*There are no obvious physical
differences between wild
and domestic cats, but the
latter has developed a
longer intestinal tract
to cope with a more
varied diet. Domestic
cats can also develop
unusual tastes if
encouraged to do so.*

Mutual benefits

Your pet cat is a beggar and expects
you to provide regular meals. He no
longer needs to be a good hunter to
survive. It is natural for you to enjoy
the fact that your cat depends on you
for the necessities of life. The reliance
behavior is being perpetuated through
intervention in breeding, and,
in time, the ability of cats to hunt
successfully will diminish, and an
exaggerated dependence on humans
will develop.

Mouth open
in begging
meow

Kitten learns
by observing
his mother

Begging effectively

*This kitten learned at an
early age to demand milk
from her mother. This
behavior is perpetuated
in the adult mother cat as
she meows and reaches
up to beg food from her
owner. Mimicking her
mother, the kitten quickly
learns how to survive.*

115

Defining Characteristics

THE DESCENDANTS OF the North African wild cat were first cherished as domestic pets in their native land in about 1000 BC. Merchants then discovered that cats were good traveling companions because they could decimate their ships' rat populations. They were also valuable commodities, fetching high prices in foreign parts. As the merchants sailed the trade routes, so cats spread around the world. Breeding was, of course, restricted to other cats within the same imported group, so the physical and temperamental characteristics that merchants had originally selected were perpetuated.

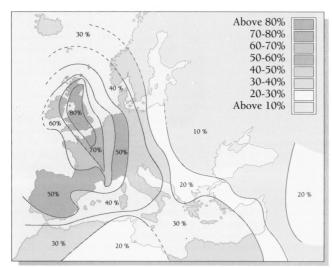

	Above 80%
	70-80%
	60-70%
	50-60%
	40-50%
	30-40%
	20-30%
	Above 10%

Striped tabby

(RIGHT) *The striped tabby is now rare, although it was the original pattern of the northern African domesticated cat. Today, most tabbies have some blotched pattern as well.*

Blotched tabby trail

(ABOVE) *The blotched or classic tabby pattern occurs in less than 20 percent of the cats living in northern Africa. The incidence of this pattern increases as the old trade routes are followed through Europe, reaching up to as much as 80 percent in some areas of Britain, the end of the old trade routes.*

Blotched tabby

(LEFT) *This blotched tabby pattern is uncommon in northern Africa. Traders were attracted to the cats with the most unusual coats to take with them on their ships.*

Tame colors

Merchants often singled out cats with blue, chocolate and other nonagouti coats to take with them on their journeys. (A nonagouti coat is made up of hairs that are uniform in color from root to tip.) Cats possessing these coat colors were possibly less intimidated by humans and also less aggressive. The cats interbred in their new environments, so the resulting cat population tended to have gentler, tamer personalities.

Plain colors

(*ABOVE*) *Cats with uniformly colored coats were originally rare, but through selective breeding they are now abundant. Such coats may be a "self," or solid color, or a mixture, resulting in a "smoke" pattern.*

Following trade routes

The North African wild cat has the genetic potential to produce descendants with a great variety of fur colors, such as this blue and orange coat. The further the distance traveled on the trade routes from northern Africa, the greater the incidence of unusual colors.

Too many toes

All breeds of cats can produce kittens with extra toes on their front paws. These are known as polydactyls. In general, there are fewer than 10 percent polydactyls in any cat population. However, many of the very first cats to arrive in North America in the region from Boston, Massachusetts, to Halifax, Nova Scotia, carried with them the genetic potential for extra toes. A limited availability of breeding partners resulted in a higher than average percentage of polydactyls in the cat population of that region.

Restricted population

A high incidence of polydactyls occurs along the east coast of North America.

Harmless deformity

Instead of the normal five toes, polydactyl cats often have seven toes on their forepaws.

Adapting to Habitats

AS LONG AS 3000 years ago, cats began colonizing the world. The first were taken by merchants from northern Africa to Europe and Asia. Traders also took cats to China via Babylon and India. Cats were initially introduced to Japan around AD 1000, although it was another 500 years before they reached the Americas. The only cats to survive were those able to cope with the demands of a new environment.

Small beginnings
(*BELOW*) *Four thousand years ago, the domestic cat inhabited only a small area of northern Africa.*

Worldwide distribution
(*RIGHT*) *Today cats have colonized almost the entire world, except for the cold Arctic and Antarctic regions.*

Hardy survivor
The large-sized Maine Coon breed developed from the hardy farm cat, originally taken to the United States of America by early British immigrants. Living off a diet of rabbits, the cats flourished. To survive the harsh winters in New England, they evolved thick but trouble-free coats.

Survival of the fittest

The first cats to be introduced to a region could, of course, only mate with other new arrivals. Interbreeding then led to populations with a restricted genetic pool, threatening the health of future generations. Only the fittest survived, and the first breeds began to evolve. Adapting to Thailand's heat, for example, the cat's coat thinned out, while in the mountainous Van district of Turkey, cats developed thicker coats.

Easy-care coat
(*RIGHT*) *Short hair, which is far easier to manage than long hair, is the most common type of coat in domestic cats in Europe. The British Shorthair has sturdy, short legs and a muscular body. There is a wide range of colors and coat patterns.*

Powder-puff tail

(RIGHT) *The result of a genetic mistake, the short, curly, fluffy tail of the Japanese Bobtail survived in the closed breeding population of the Far East. The breed is a firm family favorite in Japan, where it has been established for hundreds of years.*

Keeping cool

(LEFT) *Several breeds of cats developed in what is now Thailand, but the Siamese predominated because it was particularly beloved by Thai royalty. Large ears help the cat to stay cool; the warm climate also favors the light coat.*

Exotic looks

(BELOW) *Longhaired cats originated in Asia Minor. It is thought that the long coat evolved as a result of a genetic change in only a few cats. These cats survived, and so in future interbreeding the long hair was perpetuated. Today, longhaired breeds rely on humans for their survival since they need help with grooming.*

Water-loving cat

The Turkish Van evolved in the isolated region around Lake Van in Turkey. The long, silky coat molts during the hot Turkish summer.

Newcomer

(ABOVE) *The Burmese is a popular new breed and is the result of a cross between a brown female imported from Burma to the United States in the 1930s and a Siamese tom.*

Personality Traits

CAT PERSONALITY AND coat color are probably genetically linked. By developing preferences for cats with certain coat colors and lengths, and specific eye colors, we have created breeds of cats that are distinctive from each other. Although the cats were selected for their appearance, individual breeds also seem to have evolved different personalities. Siamese cats are energetic and vociferous, while long-haired cats tend to be more placid. Oriental shorthairs are extroverts, but intolerant of other cats.

Ornamental Persians
(ABOVE) *Longhaired cats may look cuddly, but they are not as affectionate as some other breeds, although they are friendly toward other household cats.*

Friendly colors
(ABOVE) *Although it has been suggested that nontabby cats are friendlier than tabbies, there is no firm evidence to indicate significant behavior differences between them.*

High-strung types
(BELOW) *Both Siamese and Burmese breeds are excitable. Siamese may also be unfriendly to other felines in your house. Cats are not usually destructive, but these breeds are the most likely to cause mayhem in the home.*

Timid female

Female white cats are often timid, even if their hearing is normal. The combination of white coat and blue eyes usually indicates that an inherited deafness is carried in the genes.

Feline extrovert

(RIGHT) The Siamese is a highly vocal, sociable and gregarious cat, but it can have a nasty side to its character, viciously attacking any cat that intrudes on its territory.

Differences in behavior

As yet there has been very little scientific research into whether individual breeds of cats behave differently. In a recent survey 70 veterinarians were asked about their experiences of cat behavior. The replies that they gave corresponded surprisingly well with the anecdotal advice on behavioral characteristics given in popular descriptive texts on cat behavior.

Attention seekers

(LEFT) Abyssinians are more active, more vocal, more destructive and more demanding than both longhaired Persian cats and most breeds of domestic shorthair cats.

Loving personality

A cross between a Siamese and a Burmese, the Tonkinese has an inquisitive, outgoing personality and is generally very affectionate.

Analyzing Cat Character

CAT OWNERS INTUITIVELY understand that each cat is an individual with its own personality. Defining the individual's uniqueness is difficult. All cats share their behaviors with all other cats, but it is the varying degrees of these behaviors that create temperaments.

Each individual is affected by genetics, hormones, the environment in which the cat finds itself and by learning. This means that some breeds almost certainly have traits that can be described as "breed personality." The Siamese, for example, is more vocal than other breeds. Research with other mammals, such as foxes and rats, has shown that personality is linked to coat color. To date, however, no large surveys have been conducted to find whether personality is associated with breed of cat.

Cat images

Everyone has his or her own perception of cats. Many associate felines with warmth, sensuousness, softness and all things maternal and feminine. Judging from their uses in advertising, this is an increasingly common perception, which is good for cats because it is more likely that we will care for them generously.

Unfortunately, some people – almost one in four – think cats are cunning, spiteful and deceitful, and so they treat them with disdain.

Shy personality
(LEFT) *This long-haired tortoiseshell has a more withdrawn personality and is quieter than the average cat.*

Oriental build
Cats with long, lean bodies are more likely to have gregarious, outgoing personalities than their sturdier cousins. They are also more protective of their home territories and are usually more vocal and demonstrative.

Your cat's personality

Cat owners tend to be good observers. Asking owners about their cat's behavior is one way scientists can research cat personality. You can assess your cat using the questionnaire below. Score each group of questions separately to find out how alert, sociable and equable your cat is.

To analyze your cat's personality, complete this simple questionnaire by checking the appropriate box. If you would like to help in a worldwide study, please photocopy the completed questionnaire and send it to: Bruce Fogle, DVM, Box DK, 86 York Street, London W1H IDP, England.

Assess the behavior of your cat by checking the appropriate box.	Almost always (1)	Usually (2)	Sometimes (3)	Rarely (4)	Almost never (5)
MY CAT:					
Tolerates handling					
Is affectionate					
Demands attention					
Is confident					
Accepts strangers					
MY CAT IS:					
Excitable					
Vocal					
Playful					
Active					
Destructive					
Independent					
MY CAT IS:					
Fearful of familiar cats					
Hostile to strange cats					
Solitary					
Aggressive					
Tense					

Sociable

A low score (12 or less) means your cat is highly sociable and well integrated in human society. Cats that have matured before they meet humans are poorly socialized and likely to have high scores.

Alert

Cats with low scores are the most lively and alert. These felines often have energy to burn and may need organized activity; otherwise they become destructive. A high score (over 15) indicates a reserved or listless pet.

Equable

Cats that enjoy cat company will score high (over 12) and usually include cats raised from kittenhood with other cats. A low score indicates a cat hater, either too territorial to allow another cat on its turf, or too set in its ways to change its attitude.

- How old was your cat when you acquired him/her?_____
- How old is your cat now?_____
- Is your cat male or female?_____ ☐ M ☐ F
- Has your cat been neutered?_____ ☐ Yes ☐ No

- Does your cat have free access to the outdoors?_____ ☐ Yes ☐ No
- In what country do you live?_____
- What is the breed of your cat?_____
- What color is your cat? _____

CAT CARE
MANUAL

A GUIDE TO CARING FOR YOUR CAT

THE ASPCA AND CAT CARE

NO ONE IS sure why cats purr, except that it seems, in part at least, to be one way of showing that they feel very strongly about us. We do not fully understand what constitutes intensity in a cat's mind, or even how, what, and to what degree cats think; but they do think – that much has been determined – and we'd like to believe that they think good things about

us. They certainly purr when they are around us. They apparently like us as much as we like them.

The affection and respect for animals that many people share resulted in the formation of the The American Society for the Prevention of Cruelty to Animals in 1866. It is the Western Hemisphere's oldest humane society, whose purpose, as stated by its founder, Henry Bergh, is "to provide effective means for the prevention of cruelty to animals throughout the United States."

Bergh's initial efforts on behalf of animals struck a resonant cord throughout the country. Within five years, additional SPCAs could be found from coast to coast. Each of these SPCAs was a separate, individual society, formed to meet the needs of its own community. While they were not directly connected with Bergh's ASPCA, they did share his commitment and goals, and still frequently rely on the APSCA for guidance and advice.

Today, more than 125 years later, the ASPCA continues its work by operating shelters and an animal hospital in New York City. Authorized as peace officers, its Humane Law Enforcement agents continue Bergh's work by investigating instances of cruelty to animals. The ASPCA's educational and legislative programs reach millions of people across the country each year.

Many of the problems that all humane societies across the country are forced to deal with are the result of uncaring, irresponsible, or simply poorly informed pet owners. Education plays an integral role in correcting and preventing these problems by providing people with the information they need to care for their companion animals in a humane and responsible fashion.

Cats now outnumber dogs – they are the most popular pets in America, living in over 30 percent of households. Unfortunately, not every cat has the good fortune of living with a caring, knowledgeable owner.

Each year, millions of cats die as a result of neglect, cruelty, for want of good homes, and sometimes simply through ignorance. This book contains valuable information that everyone sharing a home with a cat can use to provide the best care possible for his pet. Such information can only result in good things for your cat, and for you, as you enrich each other's lives.

As you will learn, cats have been domesticated for roughly 4,000 years. Over these many centuries cats have fared quite differently in many cultures. The Egyptians, the first people to live with cats, came to worship them. During the Middle Ages, Europeans blamed them for evil and tied them into witchcraft and other strange beliefs. Thankfully, cats today are valued for themselves and the wonderful companions they make. This no doubt helps to account for their ever-increasing popularity around the world.

Sometimes we can have too much of a good thing. Right now there are many more cats being born every day than there are good homes available. Remember that spaying or neutering your pet will not only help to ensure that all cats have a chance to find a good home, but will help to keep your cat healthier and happier for years to come.

Enjoy those years of companionship, because they will certainly be special for both of you.

Roger Caras
President
American Society for the Prevention
of Cruelty to Animals

INTRODUCTION

It is only during the last few thousand years that the cat has become domesticated, developing from small, wild ancestors that first roamed the Earth about 12 million years ago. Even before then, the larger cats, such as lions tigers, and leopards, were developing from a few prototypes, while other members of the cat family branched in a different direction to become specialist hunters like the cheetah, or small forest-dwelling felines like the ocelot and the margay.

As people moved around the world, the cat went with them. The earlietst signs of domestication were probably seen in the Middle East. The Ancient Egyptians were the first civilization to realize the cat's potential as a vermin hunter, that protected grain supplies on which their lives depended. It is not surprising, then, that this reliance turned to worship. The cat became a deity in Ancient Egypt and was almost as well-loved as it is today. Although it is not regarded as a deity anymore, worship has been replaced with a caring, loving relationship with presentday owners.

Having enjoyed many years of great favor, it was perhaps inevitable that fortune should turn against the cat for a black period in history. In the fifteenth and sixteenth centuries, human ignorance and bigotry were directed at anything that could be blamed for the world's ills, and just as the Ancient Egyptians looked upon the cat as an expression of divinity, religious groups in Europe encouraged a phase of hatred and fear, resulting in the cat being seen as an agent of the devil. This period eventually passed, however, and the elegance, beauty, engaging personality, and inestimable value of the cat as a companion were finally recognized. It is now one of the most popular pets in the world.

Essential Care

Deciding to add a cat to your household should not be taken lightly if you and your pet are to be happy together. Therefore, it is essential that you know exactly how to care for a cat; from choosing a healthy kitten, to reproduction, house training and basic discipline. A major section of this book covers all the varied aspects of day-to-day cat care. Becoming a cat owner is a serious business, and this chapter gives advice on what to look for when adopting or purchasing your pet, basic equipment such as cat collars and baskets, and containers for traveling with your pet.

Nutrition and Health Care

A cat is a carnivore with very specific nutritional needs, and the information in this book makes the basics of its dietary and medicinal requirements as comprehensive and as readable as possible. All cat owners need some guidance on how to recognize health problems with their pets and what action to take when something is not right. The extensive health care section deals with everyday problems such as ear mites, worms, and fleas, as well as first aid in emergencies and treatment of serious illnesses. There is also a diagnosis chart, so you can quickly find the cause of your pet's problem and the appropriate treatment. Owners are also advised how to nurse a sick cat, so that it recovers quickly and without stress. In all cases, owners are urged to consult their local veterinary practice for help and guidance. Reproduction is extensively covered in a special section, with advice on planning a litter, helping your cat give birth, and caring for young kittens. There is even information on how different genes are passed on to give your cat certain characteristics, and first aid for your cat in the event of any problems both during and after giving birth, or if the kittens are sickly.

Showing Off Your Cat

You may want to enter your cat in shows, and this book explains all you need to know about preparing for competition. Even if you do not, grooming is still an essential part of everyday feline care, especially for longhaired cats. The chapter on grooming describes how various types of feline coat should be groomed, and how to bathe your pet and care for its teeth and claws. Special grooming for a cat show is also included, along with information on how a pedigree cat is judged.

Finding Out More

The glossary explains the specialized feline terms used in the book. Finally, there is a short section providing information on the various feline organizations, as well as suggestions for further reading. Once you begin learning about your cat, you might never want to stop!

Chapter 1

INTRODUCING THE CAT

CATS ARE always enigmatic and enchanting; and they have been a source of fascination for mankind throughout history. The cat has been worshiped and persecuted in turn, but it is now in the ascendant again. Cats are perfectly suited to the urban lifestyle of twentieth-century society. Whether pedigree or ordinary housecat, they make attractive, rewarding, and relatively easy-to-care-for pets. Indispensable companions to people of all ages and nationalities, they are chameleon characters; fearless hunters one moment, and purring comforters the next.

THE FIRST DOMESTIC CATS

Even though its ancestors walked the Earth over 12 million years ago, it has only been about 4,000 years since the cat was domesticated. The Ancient Egyptians first used cats to control vermin in their grain stores, but there is evidence of wild cats sharing human caves and villages long before that.

In Egypt, the cat was revered as a hunter, and it became deified as an incarnation of the goddess Bastet. Other ancient civilizations later began to domesticate the cat, and Phoenician traders took tame felines to Italy; from there they spread slowly across Europe. Eventually, they even migrated to the New World with the Pilgrims. Despite a period of persecution in the Middle Ages, when cats were associated with the devil, by the eighteenth century cats had become popular as household pets and had spread all over the world.

ORIGINS OF THE DOMESTIC CAT

Vermin hunter
A 13th century manuscript shows cats in their traditional role as killers of vermin. The first domestic cats had to earn their keep by destroying pests to protect stores of food.

Cat goddess
A bronze statue of the Egyptian cat goddess Bastet, from around 600 BC.

Eastern feline (above)
The domestic cat probably reached India before spreading to China or Japan. This Indian painting dates from around 1810.

Good against evil
An Egyptian wall painting dating from around 1500 BC shows the sun god Ra as a cat, slaying Apep, the serpent of darkness.

ANCESTORS OF THE DOMESTIC CAT

The cats we know today, from lions and tigers to household pets, are descended from early carnivores called the miacids, which evolved from the first carnivorous mammals, the creodonts. While some miacids became lions, tigers, and cheetahs, Martelli's wild cat (*Felis lunensis*) is thought to have been a direct ancestor of all modern small cats. It gave rise to the modern wild cat (*Felis sylvestris*), which developed into three main types: the European wild cat, the African wild cat, and the Asiatic desert cat. The domestic cat (*Felis catus*) is thought to have evolved from the African wild cat.

African wild cat
The African wild cat is the most likely ancestor of the domestic cat. It has tabby markings.

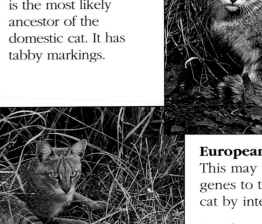

European wild cat
This may have added genes to the domestic cat by interbreeding.

Jungle cat *(left)*
Kept in Ancient Egypt, but probably not related to modern cats.

THE SPREAD OF THE DOMESTIC CAT

1970s *Japanese Bobtail reaches the United States from Japan*

Late 19th century *Longhaired cats reach United States from Great Britain*

Mid-19th century *Longhaired cats reach Great Britain from Turkey*

AD 4 *Shorthaired cats spread across Europe from Italy, reaching Great Britain in AD 900*

16th century *Longhaired cats taken to Italy from Turkey*

Circa 900 BC *Shorthaired cats taken to Italy from Egypt*

17th century *Shorthaired cats taken to United States by first settlers*

1930s *Burmese taken to United States from Burma*

Late 19th century *Abyssinians reach Great Britain from Abyssinia*

Late 19th century *Siamese reaches Great Britain from Thailand*

1950s *Korat reaches United States from Thailand*

16th century *Manx cats taken to Isle of Man from the Far East*

1970s *Singapura taken to United States from Singapore*

Process of domestication

The shorthaired domestic cat spread across the world from Egypt, while longhaired cats came much later from Turkey, Iran, and Afghanistan.

THE FELINE SENSES

The senses of the domestic cat, like those of its wild relatives, are designed for the purpose of stalking and killing prey. Its sense organs are those of a predator, and it can detect the slightest movement and the faintest sound. A cat's hearing, sight, touch, and smell are far more acute than in humans and most other mammals. It can see in the dimmest of lights; it can detect very high-pitched noises; and it can even taste certain smells by using the Jacobson's organ in the roof of its mouth. A cat is highly sensitive to its surroundings and will thrive under the right conditions, but it may not do so well in a home where its needs are not met. Shy cats and children often do not mix; loud noises and sudden movements can be frightening.

THE FIVE SENSES

The mouth and taste

A cat has a discriminating sense of taste. Giving a cat medicine by mixing it with its food can prove difficult, since a cat can usually detect any additions to its food bowl. Unlike dogs, cats do not have a sweet tooth, but some pampered pets do develop a liking for cake and fruit.

The ears and hearing

A cat's hearing is very acute, and it can hear high-frequency sounds up to two octaves higher than a human. A cat can usually be trained to recognize and respond to certain words, such as its name, by the tone of voice used.

The whiskers and touch

The whiskers act as antennae and help a cat avoid objects in dim light. A cat is extremely sensitive to touch, and each individual hair on its body is responsive to the slightest vibration in its environment.

The nose and smell

All cats are territorial and mark their territory with scent to warn off other felines. A cat's sense of smell is enhanced by the Jacobson's organ, which enables a cat to analyze intriguing scents by tasting the molecules on the back of its tongue. This is called "flehming."

The eyes and sight

Although a cat has poor color vision, its eyes are designed to make use of any available light so that it can see in extremely dim conditions. Its sight is that of a hunter, and it possesses a far wider angle of view than a human, which allows it to detect tiny movements of prey animals.

CATS AND CATNIP

The smell of catnip or catmint (*Nepeta cataria*) is irresistible to most, but not all, cats. Many cats react to the plant by sniffing it, rubbing their heads in it, rolling around in a trancelike state on their backs, and purring loudly. The effects of catnip are shortlived, and it is not thought to be addictive or to cause any unpleasant aftereffects. Another plant, valerian, produces similar effects.

Sniffing catnip *(left)*
A cat sniffs the scent of dried catnip for a few seconds before it takes effect. Some cats are not susceptible to the plant and may show no visible signs.

Typical behavior
More than 50 percent of cats respond to catnip by getting very excited and rolling around ecstatically.

MOVEMENT AND BALANCE

The cat is a hunter and predator and needs to be quick on its feet and extremely agile. Its body is specifically designed for maximum speed from minimum effort. Most of the time a cat conserves its energy, but when it needs to, it is capable of sprinting very fast. A cat can travel at a top speed of approximately 30 miles (48 km) per hour over a short distance, enabling it to pounce on its prey before it can escape. Whereas most animals have to spend much of their lives on the ground, a cat has enviable coordination for climbing, jumping, and balancing.

FELINE COORDINATION

Jumping

All cats are superb athletes and can perform an amazing repertoire of vertical, horizontal, and twisting leaps. A cat can jump up to five times its own height in a single bound. Its strong hind-leg muscles and flexible spine enable it to thrust itself into the air and land again safely without injuring itself. A cat will always look before it leaps, carefully assessing the distance before taking off.

The tail maintains perfect balance

The cat's claws are ready to push off from the tree

Balancing

A cat is extremely well coordinated because it possesses a very efficient system for sending messages to the brain from its muscles and joints. It uses its tail as a counterbalance when walking along a narrow branch, in the same way as a tightrope walker holds a long pole for balance.

The eyes are fixed straight ahead

The claws grip the branch

Climbing

From a tree or fence, a cat can patrol its territory and watch its prey without being seen. Using its strong hind-leg muscles and gripping with its front claws, going up is relatively easy, but coming down can be more difficult.

The hind legs are carefully balanced

The eyes survey the ground

The paws are positioned on a narrow branch

THE RIGHTING REFLEX

Turning over

A cat's balance and coordination are unsurpassed, and this has led to the belief that a cat is able to withstand a fall from a great height. This is not always the case, but some cats have survived falls of over 65 ft (20 meters). The cat's righting reflex works automatically and quickly. The cat's eyes and balance organs in the inner ear tell it where it is in space, and it lands on its feet.

137

ASSESSING A CAT'S MOOD

Your cat lets you know when it is pleased, angry, frightened, or unhappy. Eyes, ears, tail, whiskers, and voice are all powerful indicators of your pet's mood. Although sometimes regarded as lone hunters, cats are very sociable animals that have evolved a complex body language and a range of different vocal sounds to communicate with you and with other felines. A cat's face is particularly telling, expressing a variety of different emotions ranging from contentment to fear and aggression.

BODY LANGUAGE

Happy Cat
Your cat may greet you with its tail held high and the tail tip bent slightly forward. An erect tail indicates that a cat is happy and confident. A tail flicked from side to side indicates a state of tension. A cat on the defensive fluffs up its coat and its tail fur in order to appear larger.

The tail is erect and held stiffly

Alert expression with ears pricked forward

First meeting
Cats usually establish their social order without incurring serious injury. Intense staring and emphatic body language may deter more timid cats. The engagement may break up with each cat washing itself in a very deliberate way.

Aggressive cat
A cat lying on its back is not necessarily submitting to a more dominant feline. With its teeth and claws showing, a formidable array of weaponry is displayed.

The ears are flattened against the head

Defensive cat
A cat poised to make a strategic withdrawal may remain still for several minutes. The attention is focused, the gaze intense, and the ears pricked forward to monitor any sound.

Close companions
Cats that are part of the same household will greet each other affectionately by touching noses and rubbing their bodies together. Cats that are best friends will groom each other, sleep huddled together, and play with one another.

Cat calls
The vocal repertoire of a cat is extensive, with more than 16 different sounds. Cat calls include howls of anger, yowls and growls of tomcats fighting, as well as queens in heat looking for mates. According to the intonation, a cat's meow can be used to express many different moods.

Making contact
Rubbing against people is an endearing habit, but your cat is not simply being affectionate. It is marking out territory with the secretions of glands around its face. The tail area and paws also carry the cat's scent.

A cat marks its territory by rubbing against objects

PURRING

The purr is a low-frequency sound that is produced not by the vocal chords but from somewhere deep in a cat's chest. Purring is usually a sign of pleasure or contentment. A mother cat purrs when her kittens are born and when they begin to suckle; tiny kittens purr when they feel secure, warm, and well fed. However, a cat will also purr to comfort itself when it is nervous or in pain.

Purring for pleasure
Purring is a uniquely feline sound that usually means that a cat is relaxed and contented.

THE CAT AS A PET

Cats are becoming ever more popular household pets worldwide. There are at present about 100 million cats in the Western world (*see opposite*) and the numbers are on the increase. There are very many reasons for this immense feline popularity. For example, cats require less time and expense than many other pets and are particularly well suited to living in an urban environment. They are independent, inexpensive to purchase and to maintain, very clean, and keep mice and other vermin out of the home. Cats are also very affectionate and make extremely devoted friends, especially for older people, or for someone who lives alone.

The ideal pet
A cat is extremely adaptable and is equally happy whether living in a small apartment or in a large house.

BUILDING A GOOD RELATIONSHIP

Bonding (*left*)
Unlike a dog, a cat's affection and trust have to be earned, but once you have established a bond, it can last for life. The more you observe your cat's behavior, the better you will understand its basic nature and its likes and dislikes.

Early lessons (*below*)
A cat makes an excellent pet for a child old enough to appreciate how an animal should be picked up and handled (*see page 161*). A child who is brought up in a household with pets will learn to appreciate the responsibilities of caring for another living creature.

Making friends (*above*)
Continue to play games with your cat from kittenhood through to adulthood (*see pages 162-163*). Most cats will pounce on a length of string or chase a bouncy ball, and some can even be taught tricks.

WHY CHOOSE A CAT?

Cats versus dogs (left)
Cats are by nature more independent than dogs and are easier to keep. A dog needs to be taken for a walk on a leash at least twice a day, whereas a cat is quite capable of exercising and amusing itself, although it does enjoy human company.

Dogs are more demanding pets than cats

The appeal of cats (right)
Stroking a cat can help to relieve stress, and the feel of a purring cat on your lap conveys a strong sense of security and comfort. Do not expect your cat to be sociable on demand – it will appreciate some privacy and peace and quiet.

Cats versus other small pets (left)
Cats are much easier to keep clean than other pets, such as birds and rodents, whose cages must be cleaned daily. Other animals make less rewarding pets because they are not as responsive and lead shorter lives.

CAT OWNERSHIP WORLDWIDE
In Great Britain and North America, there are now almost as many cats as dogs. Over 30 percent of households in North America and 24 percent in Europe own a cat.

| Italy 6 million | Spain 1.7 million | Belgium 1.6 million | Sweden 1.1 million | Netherlands 2.2 million | Germany 5 million | France 8.4 m- | U.K. 6.9 million | North America 60 million | Japan 3.5 million | Australia 2.8 million | Denmark 0.6 million |

BASIC CAT TYPES

There are over a hundred recognized breeds of domestic cat. The main feline features that vary are body type, eye color, coat color, and length of coat. Although some pedigree cats are natural breeds, many others are the result of careful breeding. Most cats are of no particular breed and are crosses of different types. These are what we have come to know as "housecats." They can have long or short hair and come in a variety of different colors, the most common of which are tabby, tortoiseshell, ginger, and black.

BODY TYPES

Cobby cat
Pedigree Longhair breeds have stocky, rounded bodies with sturdy, short legs and round faces. Their body type is described as cobby. Other characteristics of this longhaired cat include a broad head and round eyes.

Muscular cat
Most shorthaired cats have muscular builds with sturdy, short legs. This is the most common of the different feline body shapes. Some pedigree cats, such as British and Exotic Shorthairs, have more compact bodies.

Foreign longhaired cat
There are a few breeds of longhaired cat that have slim bodies that differ from the usual cobby type. This group includes Asian breeds such as the Balinese, Angora, and Somali. They have long bodies, with slim legs, wedge-shaped heads, and almond-shaped eyes.

The coat is less woolly and full than that of Pedigree Longhairs

Exotic shorthaired cat

An exotic or oriental cat has an elegant, slim body that is very different from the muscular build of other shorthaired cats. This type of cat has long, slender legs, a wedge-shaped head, large, pointed ears, and slanting eyes. Breeds such as the Siamese, Abyssinian, Tonkinese, and Egyptian Mau all have this slim build.

The coat is very fine and short

TYPES OF EYES

Cats' eyes come in three basic shapes: round, slanted, and almond-shaped. Their colors are basically green, yellow to gold and, most rarely, blue. However, there is a wide range of different shades within these three basic colors. Most non-pedigree cats have green eyes.

British Smoke Shorthair

Non-pedigree Tabby

White Pedigree Longhair

British Tortoiseshell-and-White

Maine Coon

Birman

British Blue Shorthair

Egyptian Mau

Snowshoe

British Tortoiseshell Shorthair

Burmilla

Balinese

Chapter 2
BASIC CARE

WE WANT our cats to live long and happy lives – they contribute so much to our own. A cat is not a demanding pet to keep; all it needs is adequate feeding, regular grooming, and proper veterinary care. A cat thrives best with a sympathetic owner who can devote a lot of attention to it and join in with games. You can keep your cat healthy by ensuring that it is protected from diseases by yearly vaccination and that it is neutered to prevent unwanted kittens. Given time and tender loving care, you will build up trust with your cat. However, it may always regard some aspects of feline care, such as traveling in its carrier and visits to the vet, as tiresome.

BECOMING A CAT OWNER

B ringing a cat into your home will change your life. The benefits of having a feline companion bring with them obligations and, unless you are prepared to make sure that your pet will receive the care and attention that it needs, cat owning is not for you. Having decided that you want to share your home with a cat, you need to decide what type of feline is best for you. Do you want a kitten or an adult cat? A pedigree or a non-pedigree? A longhaired or a shorthaired cat?

THE CAT FOR YOUR LIFESTYLE

Purebred cats
The temperament of a well-bred cat can be fairly reliable. Choose a breed with characteristics that you think fit in with your lifestyle.

Non-pedigree cats *(left)*
A cat may not come with papers, but it can still make a wonderful companion. You can go to your local animal shelter and find one just right for you.

Kittens *(above)*
Kittens demand lots of attention and need to be house trained. They adapt to a new home better than adult cats, so a kitten is a good choice if you already have other pets.

One cat or two? *(right)*
If you are out during the day, consider living with two cats. They will amuse each other and will wreak less havoc in your home.

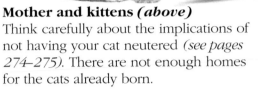

Mother and kittens (above)
Think carefully about the implications of not having your cat neutered *(see pages 274–275)*. There are not enough homes for the cats already born.

Longhaired cats (above)
The Ragdoll is an especially docile cat, set apart by its reputed tendency to relax all its muscles when picked up and cradled. Longhaired cats are generally sweet natured, gentle, and enjoy a quiet life.

Show cats (above)
If you intend to show your cat it will require special attention and grooming. A first-class show cat represents a significant investment in terms of time and money.

Oriental cats (left)
Siamese, Burmese, and other oriental cats are very sociable. They are lively, inquisitive, and love people. They can also be very vocal – if you do not give them enough attention.

WHERE TO OBTAIN A CAT

It is far better to obtain a cat from a friend, neighbor, animal shelter, or recommended cat breeder than from a pet shop. Never take an animal on impulse because you have fallen for its charm. Always examine a cat very carefully before taking it home.

Friends
Friends are a reliable source of kittens since you will probably know the mother.

Animal shelters
Animal shelters often have plenty of kittens and adult cats needing good homes.

Local vets
Your vet may know of cats needing a home. Check the cat's health first.

Breeders
A breeder is a good source of purebred kittens. Specify whether you want a cat for showing.

ESSENTIAL EQUIPMENT

Before you bring a cat into your home, it is essential that you make preparations for the new arrival. A cat is not very expensive to keep, but it must be provided with a litter box, a scratching post, separate food and water bowls, a carrier, and a brush and comb. If you wish, you can also provide it with other useful items, such as a comfortable basket or bed, and a cat flap.

Brush
A brush is essential for longhaired cats. Buy the best quality bristle brush that you can afford.

Comb
A fine-toothed metal comb is useful for grooming a shorthaired cat, but a wide-toothed comb is better for a longhaired variety.

Food bowls
Every cat must have its own bowl and feeding utensils, which should always be kept clean.

Litter box and litter scoop
Even a kitten or adult cat that is allowed outside will need to be provided with a plastic litter box. This needs to be cleaned daily; a plastic scoop allows the used litter to be removed without soiling the hands.

Cat basket (below)
A basket should be comfortable, warm, and easy to clean.

Cat carrier (right)
There is a wide range of different carriers available (see page 168).

Water bowls
Fresh water that is replenished daily should always be available for a cat.

Cat bed (right)
Beds come in many different varieties, including beanbags and hammocks.

CHOOSING A KITTEN

You can share your life with your cat for 14 years or more, so it is crucial that you choose a kitten that will grow up to be a well-adjusted, healthy adult. If you buy a kitten that is weak and sickly just because you feel sorry for it, or to ensure that it gets veterinary treatment, you may be letting yourself in for large medical fees and a lot of heartache. However, if you purchase a kitten and it falls ill or does not improve within a week or two, you may be able to take it back to the breeder, provided that you have both agreed upon such action before buying the kitten.

When choosing a kitten, you should take into consideration how it was reared and its mother's state of health. You should watch the kitten interact with both people and its littermates to determine its personality. Ideally, kittens should not be removed from the litter until they are ten to twelve weeks of age.

Nine-week-old kitten (actual size)
A healthy kitten has a firm, muscular body and feels much heavier than it looks when you pick it up.

The nose is velvety and slightly damp

The eyes are bright and clear

The mouth and gums are pink in color

The fur is soft and smooth to the touch

The limbs show no signs of lameness

The tail has no kink or other deformity

WHAT TO LOOK FOR WHEN CHOOSING A KITTEN

The ears should be clean with no discharge. Constant scratching may be a sign of mites.

The eyes should be clear, bright, and free from discharge. The third eyelid should not be showing.

The nose should be cool and damp, without any nasal discharge or crusting around the nostrils.

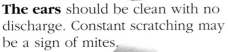

The mouth and gums should be pale pink in color and the breath odor-free.

The abdomen should be slightly rounded but not potbellied, which may be a sign of roundworms.

The coat is a good pointer to how healthy the kitten is; it should be glossy with no signs of fleas.

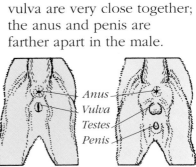

The rear should be clean, with no signs of diarrhea or any discharge from the genitals.

SEXING A KITTEN
The female kitten's anus and vulva are very close together; the anus and penis are farther apart in the male.

Anus
Vulva
Testes
Penis

Female　　　*Male*

FIRST INTRODUCTIONS

If you already have pets, introducing a new cat into your household has to be managed carefully. An adult cat, in particular, will react strongly to the presence of another feline and may defend its territory. The resident pets have to be slowly accustomed to the newcomer, and this will take time and a lot of patience. Feed the animals separately and supervise all meetings for the first few weeks.

A kitten pen
In the security of a pen, two kittens get used to their new home.

ADDING A CAT TO YOUR HOME

INTRODUCING A CAT TO A DOG

Do not let the dog get too close

1 Use a leash to control the dog so that it does not bark or chase and scare the cat. Wait until the dog and cat have become accustomed to each other before allowing the dog off the leash.

2 After a couple of weeks of careful supervision, the cat and dog should have accepted each other's presence and should be able to sit in the same room. Eventually, the cat may become bold enough to actually play with the dog!

INTRODUCING A KITTEN TO AN ADULT CAT

1 Allow the cat to investigate the carrier in which the kitten arrived. If the reaction is neutral, proceed with introducing the kitten. Separate them if the cat attacks the kitten.

The cat will be wary of the kitten at first

2 It may take up to a month for the cats to settle down. It is usually easier to bring a young kitten, rather than an adult cat, into a house that already has another feline.

INTRODUCING A KITTEN TO SMALL PETS

Rabbits
A kitten can frighten a rabbit by clambering all over it. An adult cat should not be left unsupervised with a pet rabbit.

Guinea pigs
A guinea pig will be a source of fascination to a kitten. Never let rodents out of their cages when an adult cat is on the prowl.

Happy pets
Provided all your pets have their own separate living areas, peaceful coexistence between different species can be achieved.

BASIC ROUTINES

You cannot train a cat in the same way as a dog to obey specific commands, but it does need to be house trained in order to live in a human household. Because a cat is by nature a remarkably clean and fastidious animal, it usually learns very quickly how to use a litter box. A cat is a fairly undemanding companion. All it really needs is regular feeding, grooming, clean toilet facilities, health care, and a corner for its bed or basket where it can enjoy a quiet catnap. However, it is important to maintain a daily routine in caring for your cat, since it will be unhappy if it is ignored or if its feeding schedule is erratic. Plan well ahead before introducing a cat into your home. It will be easier for your pet to adjust to its surroundings if essential items *(see pages 148–149)*, such as a litter box, food bowl, and basket, are installed before it arrives in the home.

LITTER TRAINING

House training
Cats are quick to learn how to use a litter box. Keep the box in a place readily accessible to the cat, but with some degree of privacy.

TYPES OF LITTER TRAY

Covered box
A timid cat will appreciate the privacy of an enclosed litter box.

Ordinary box
Place the box in a quiet corner.

TYPES OF LITTER

Reusable Washable, non-absorbent litter.

Fuller's earth Based on natural clay.

Lightweight Very convenient to carry.

Wood-based Good for absorbing liquid waste.

ESTABLISHING ROUTINES

Playtime

Play is vital for a cat's physical and emotional development. Try to spend 10 to 15 minutes twice a day, playing with your cat. Continue the games into your cat's adulthood to maintain a good relationship with your pet *(see pages 162–163).*

Feeding time

Nourishing meals must be provided for your cat. Prepared foods from reliable manufacturers are the safest and most convenient option. They can be supplemented with the occasional fresh food treat.

Bedtime

Every cat should have a quiet spot for its bed. Cats like to sleep for up to 16 hours a day. Do not let your cat stay outside at night, since this is an especially dangerous time.

Regular grooming

Whether your cat is longhaired or shorthaired, it needs to be groomed regularly. Grooming should be started as young as possible *(see page 187).*

TRAINING A CAT

A cat will not do anything that it does not want to, so training has to concentrate on gently enticing your pet to modify its natural behavior. You must keep in mind that a cat is not behaving badly when it scratches a favorite chair – it is keeping its claws trim by stripping away their outer layers, as well as marking its territory with scent. If you want to protect your furniture, provide your cat with a scratching post. The younger your cat is the easier it will be to train it to use a post. If you have an enclosed, protected area, give your cat the freedom to come and go by installing a cat flap.

USING A SCRATCHING POST

Perch from which the cat can survey its surroundings

The rope is impregnated with catnip

Toy balls make the post more interesting

HOME-MADE POSTS

A log complete with bark makes an ideal, natural scratching post. A post can easily be made by attaching a piece of carpet to a wooden plank, pile-side down. Carpet pile does not provide enough "snag."

Training

Whenever your cat looks as if it is going to claw the furniture, caution it and lure it to the scratching post. The post can be made more attractive by rubbing a little catnip on it. Manufactured posts come in a range of designs; this one has a perch for the cat to sit on and balls with which it can play.

USING A CAT FLAP

The clear plastic door allows the cat to see outside

1 The cat flap should be positioned at the right height for the cat to step through, about 6 in (15 cm) from the base of the door. Begin training the cat to use the flap by propping it partly open, and then tempting the cat through with a little food on the other side.

The locking device keeps unwanted visitors out

2 The cat will quickly learn to push open the door itself when it wants to go outside. An electromagnetic cat flap is useful for preventing strange cats from entering the house. This type of door can only be activated by a magnet. The latter should be worn on an elasticized collar.

The magnet worn on the cat's collar opens the flap

6 in (15 cm)

TYPES OF CAT FLAP

Most cat flaps swing in two directions and have a magnetic strip along the sides to keep out drafts. Whatever the type of flap, it should be easy to open, so that the cat can push it with its head without the risk of getting its neck or paws stuck.

Standard cat flap
A standard cat flap like this one is inexpensive and easy to install but does not have a locking device.

Lockable cat flap
A locking device is useful if you want to prevent your cat from going outdoors at night and for keeping other cats out.

COLLARS AND LEADS

A cat does not need much in the way of accessories, but a collar with a nametag is essential, just in case your pet goes outside. A cat should be trained to wear a collar from an early age. Start by putting the collar on for a short period each day until the cat is used to wearing it. A collar with an identification tag giving the cat's name and your address and telephone number is useful in case of accidents and will help prevent your cat from being mistaken for a stray should it wander or get lost. If you take it for a walk outside, you will want to train it to walk in a harness and lead. This will take a lot of gentle coaxing, and even then you may not get your cat to go where you want. Cats that lack confidence should be left at home.

A collar must fit properly

Elasticized collar
A collar must have an elasticized section so that a cat can slip out of it should it get caught.

TYPES OF COLLAR AND LEAD

Flea collars are not suitable for young kittens and must be used as directed

Collars
There is a wide range of different collar designs. Always take the collar off when grooming to check for skin irritations.

There is a collar to suit every budget, ranging from the simple type to diamond-studded ones

A tartan collar is ideal for a fashion-conscious cat that needs a different collar for every day of the week

A harness is essential when trainin because a cat can slip out of a collar

A collar should have an elasticized safety section and felt backing and should be easily adjustable

You can cut down a collar intended for an adult cat to fit a kitten

Select a light leather or cord lead that is suitable for a cat

NAME TAGS AND BELLS

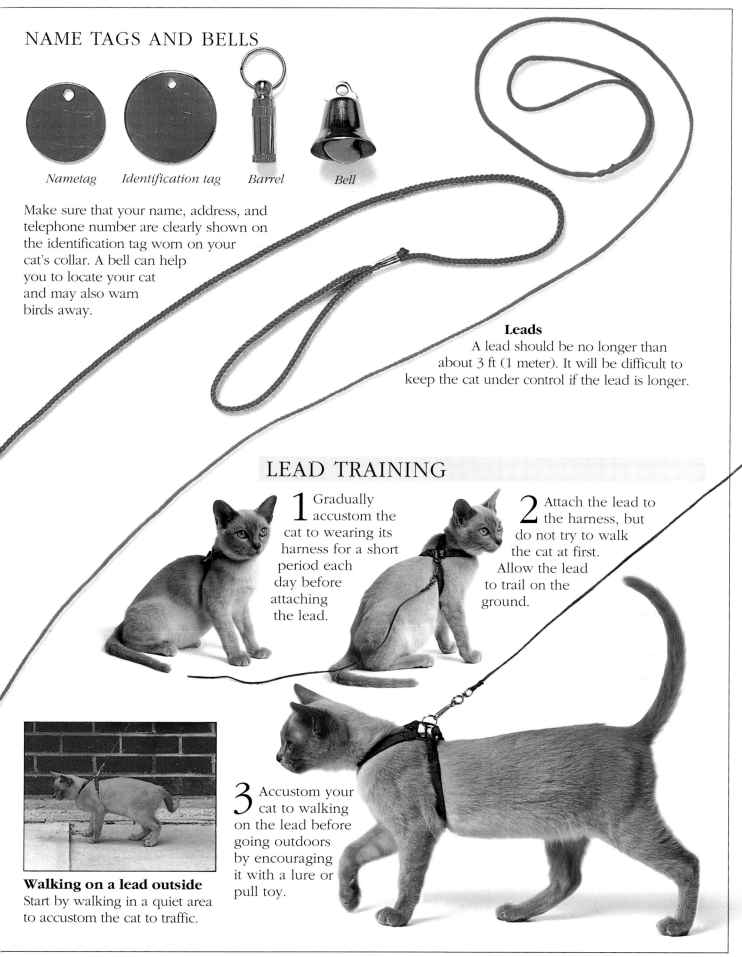

Nametag *Identification tag* *Barrel* *Bell*

Make sure that your name, address, and telephone number are clearly shown on the identification tag worn on your cat's collar. A bell can help you to locate your cat and may also warn birds away.

Leads
A lead should be no longer than about 3 ft (1 meter). It will be difficult to keep the cat under control if the lead is longer.

LEAD TRAINING

1 Gradually accustom the cat to wearing its harness for a short period each day before attaching the lead.

2 Attach the lead to the harness, but do not try to walk the cat at first. Allow the lead to trail on the ground.

3 Accustom your cat to walking on the lead before going outdoors by encouraging it with a lure or pull toy.

Walking on a lead outside
Start by walking in a quiet area to accustom the cat to traffic.

HANDLING A CAT

PICKING UP A CAT

Physical contact is very important for establishing a close relationship with your pet. When holding or carrying a cat, you should allow it to adopt the position in which it feels most comfortable and talk to it in a reassuring way. A cat will soon let you know when it has had enough and wants to be left alone; a determined, protesting cat can be quite a handful. You should also learn where your cat likes to be stroked and which areas of its body are particularly sensitive. When handling a cat, take it in its own time and never use force or sudden movements, which will frighten it.

Support the rear and hind legs

1 First, gain the cat's confidence. Once the cat is relaxed, gently lift it, supporting its hindquarters.

2 Lift the cat in as natural a position as possible. Talk to the cat to reassure it.

3 Use one arm to support the cat's hindquarters, and the other for support and for gentle stroking.

Holding a cat

Cats enjoy being held for brief periods, but they do like to be in control of their own movements and will usually only feel at ease in the arms of a human whom they know and trust. Some individuals can be trained to sit on their owners' shoulders.

CHILDREN AND CATS

Best of friends
Some cats can be frightened by children, who need to be taught how to stroke and play with their pet. This cat has complete confidence in its young companion.

Holding a kitten
Children find kittens irresistible and should be discouraged from picking them up and cuddling them.

First introductions
Introduce a cat to a child very gradually; initial contact should be confined to gentle stroking.

Correct handling
Physical contact should not be forced or prolonged if a cat wants to be put down.

Do not try to hold on to a struggling cat

STROKING ZONES

Chest and ears
Most cats enjoy being stroked or rubbed around the ears and chest.

Neck and back
A relaxed cat appreciates being stroked on its neck and back.

Abdomen
Do not stroke a cat's abdomen and back legs unless you know it well.

PLAYING WITH A CAT

One of the many joys of owning a cat is watching it play. Learning to play is essential for the development of kittens because it teaches them important skills that they will need as adults. After the age of about six months, a cat loses some of its playfulness. It prefers to save its energies for the more serious business of hunting and may need to be encouraged to play games.

You can make any game more appealing for your cat by joining in, but the best way to keep a cat playful is to provide it with a companion. A couple of cats brought up in the same household will continue to play together in adulthood.

Toys
Some favorite toys include catnip mice, sacks filled with dried catnip, bouncy balls, and feathers.

Catnip mice

Small balls

Catnip sack

Fluffy feather

Feather and string

SOLITARY GAMES

Ping-pong ball
A small, bouncy ball is an ideal toy for your cat to pat and push around with its paws. Be prepared to retrieve it from behind doors and underneath armchairs.

Catnip mouse
If your cat likes catnip, this toy will have it purring in ecstasy. Catnip toys do lose their scent after a while and need to be replaced.

Cat's cradle (left)
A ball of yarn makes an irresistible toy. A cat will enjoy trailing it around chairs and table legs. Never allow your cat to play with thread or yarn unsupervised, since it may swallow it.

GAMES FOR SHARING

Hide-and-seek

A cardboard box is ideal for playing games of hide-and-seek. After sniffing every corner of a box, a cat likes to hide itself away, but once inside it will probably be ambushed by its feline companion.

Mouse on a string *(above)*

A cat is fascinated by any object that is dangled or pulled in front of its nose. A piece of string tied to a short pole will keep your cat amused.

A cat tries to paw a feather held just out of its reach.

Fun with feathers

A feather is a good toy for tickling and playing with your cat, but watch out for its claws. If you do not move your hand away very quickly, you are likely to get scratched.

Feline fishing *(above)*

Trail a feather on a piece of string or cord for your cat to chase. Drag the feather slowly in front of the cat's paws and wait for it to pounce, then slowly reel it in.

Pouncing practice

A cat will be fascinated by a cardboard tube and will wait hopefully for something interesting to emerge. Reward its patience by giving it a catnip toy to play with or a tasty cat treat.

THE OUTDOOR CAT

Where it is possible, a cat will enjoy being allowed outside, and will set up its own territory to patrol and defend, even if this consists of only a small yard. A cat marks its home ground with scent by scratching trees and rubbing itself against fence posts. Urine spraying also acts as a warning to other cats to keep away, especially when it is carried out by tomcats. All these feline signals have to be reinforced regularly, since they act as markers to other cats. The more recent the scent, the more other cats take notice. To prevent unwanted pregnancies, never allow an unaltered cat outside.

EXERCISE AND TERRITORY

Climbers
While all cats enjoy climbing for exercise or to survey their territory, kittens can sometimes become frightened by the height and must be helped down. On the whole, however, mature cats have no difficulty in retracing their steps to the ground when they are ready to do so.

Vantage point *(left)*
A roof, fence, or wall makes a good vantage point from which a cat can watch over its territory and make sure that no intruders trespass on its ground. From such a high point, the cat can also see the best hunting and resting places. All cats have favorite areas for sleeping or just watching.

An erect tail signifies alertness to everything that is going on

Cat patrol
A cat will need to patrol its territory regularly to defend it against other cats that might want to muscle in. It will also have to sniff out the scent of its rivals, so that it does not get into trouble by straying into another feline's territory.

The cat's sensitive nose investigates every scent

COMMON DANGERS IN THE YARD

Practically every yard has some hazards in it, since a large number of plants are toxic to animals *(see page 287)*. Even though a cat will not normally eat garden plants, it is wise to keep poisonous ones to a minimum when laying out your garden. A high fence, preferably

with the top sloping inward, may be needed if there is a busy road nearby, both to keep your pet in and to keep out other cats.

All poisonous materials should be kept out of a yard where there are cats or securely locked away. Substances that are toxic to cats

include slug pellets (especially metaldehyde), antifreeze, creosote and other wood preservatives, insecticides, and herbicides. If a cat can get into a garage or garden shed, it may also be at risk from paint, oil, gasoline, sharp tools, and carbon monoxide fumes.

Dangers in the yard
Poisonous plants, garden chemicals, dogs, and rival cats are among the common hazards for a cat in even the most innocent-looking yard. A kitten may fall into a pond or swimming pool and be unable to get out.

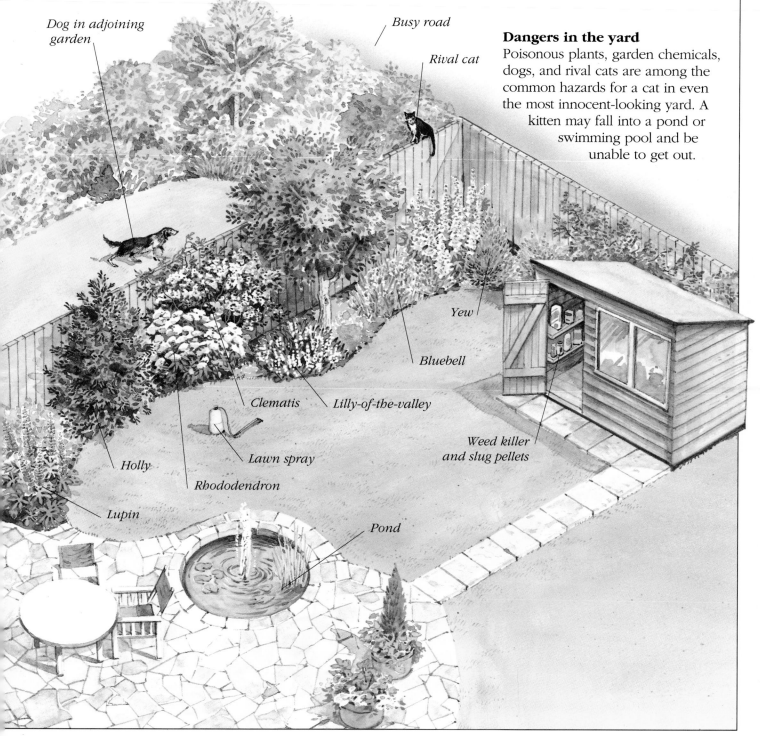

Dog in adjoining garden

Busy road

Rival cat

Yew

Bluebell

Clematis

Lilly-of-the-valley

Holly

Lawn spray

Weed killer and slug pellets

Rhododendron

Lupin

Pond

THE INDOOR CAT

A cat is by its nature a very independent creature that likes to be able to come and go as it pleases. However, some cat owners living in large cities or high-rise apartments may find it impossible to let their pet outside and prefer to keep it safely confined to the home. Most cats can live quite happily indoors, provided that all their needs for amusement, exercise, and safety are provided. It is best to accustom a cat to being inside when it is still a kitten. Its litter box must be cleaned daily, and it should be provided with plenty of toys and games or, better still, a feline companion. You may want to try training your cat to walk on a lead for short trips outside the home *(see page 159).*

Best friends
A feline companion will ensure that an indoor cat never becomes bored when it is left alone.

OUTDOOR RUNS FOR CATS

Outdoor pens
If you wish to allow your cat access to the outside world while still keeping it safe, an outdoor run is the answer. It should be constructed of strong posts and wire netting and provided with a covered shelter in case of bad weather. A cat may also appreciate a tree or post for climbing and scratching.

INDOOR LAWN

Most cats enjoy chewing on grass, as a source of certain extra vitamins. If your cat is kept indoors, you should provide it with a pot of fresh greenery such as lawn grass, catnip, thyme, sage, chickweed or parsley.

Grass in pots
Sow some seeds in a pot for a regular supply of fresh grass.

COMMON DANGERS IN THE HOME

A home can be full of hazards for a cat, especially a kitten or a new arrival. Cats are naturally curious, so washing machines, tumble driers, refrigerators, and ovens should never be left open. Hot irons, tea kettles, and saucepans full of boiling liquids should not be left unattended. Kittens may chew electrical cord, and some cats may chew plants and cut flowers out of boredom. Some houseplants, such as ivies, philodendrons, and poinsettias, can be toxic *(see page 287)*. Fragile ornaments can be knocked off shelves by exploring cats. Open fires should always be protected by a guard, even when unlit. Other dangers include detergents and chemicals, threaded needles, pins, and plastic bags. An open window on an upper floor can lead to a cat falling and injuring itself.

Indoor hazards
Any home can be full of potential dangers for a cat, especially a kitten or a newcomer. They range from open fires and poisonous houseplants to electrical equipment and cooking utensils.

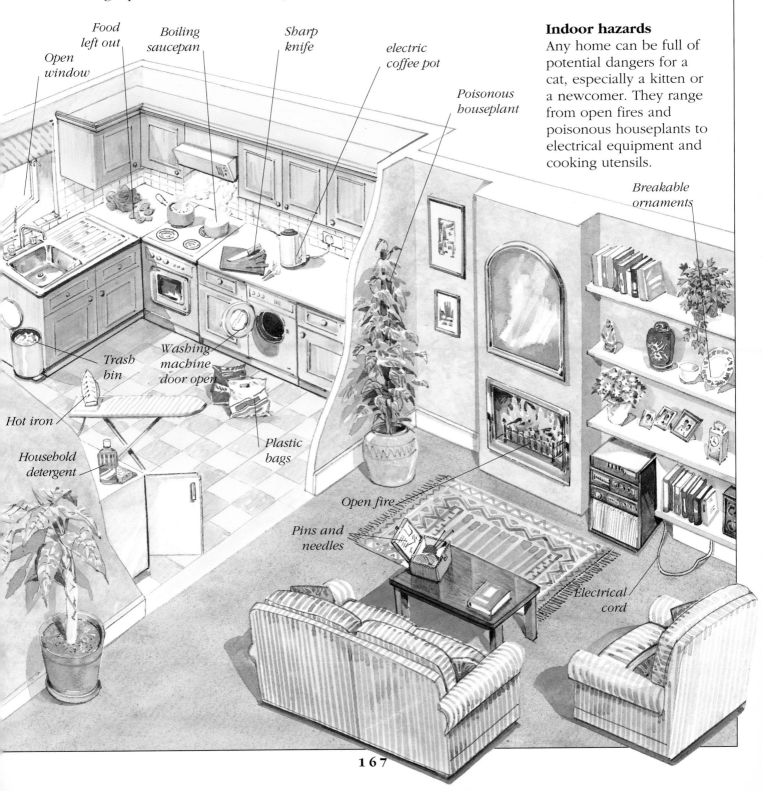

Open window

Food left out

Boiling saucepan

Sharp knife

electric coffee pot

Poisonous houseplant

Breakable ornaments

Trash bin

Washing machine door open

Hot iron

Household detergent

Plastic bags

Open fire

Pins and needles

Electrical cord

TRAVELING AND MOVING HOUSE

Cats do not adjust to travel as readily as dogs and should be confined to carriers for the duration of any trip. Before taking a cat anywhere, you should familiarize it with its carrier. Leave the carrier out and open, and put a treat inside to tempt the cat to investigate. It is essential that your cat sees the carrier in a positive light. A warm blanket will provide good insulation in cold weather, while in very hot weather you may need to cover the carrier with a damp cloth.

Never leave a cat unattended in a car on a hot day, even with a window open, since it may get overheated. Do not allow a cat to travel loose in a car. It may become agitated or get in the driver's way, an accident.

TRANSPORTING A CAT

Wire carrier
Well ventilated, secure, and easily cleaned, a plastic-coated wire carrier is ideal for moving a cat. Line it with a towel or newspapers in case of accidents.

TYPES OF CARRIER

Wicker carrier (left)
Traditional wicker carriers give a cat some privacy, while allowing it to see out. The disadvantages of this type of carrier are that it is difficult to keep clean and may not be entirely "catsafe."

Plastic carrier (right)
Like wire carriers, lightweight plastic carriers are easy to disinfect and clean. Larger carriers will accommodate two cats if they are used to traveling together.

Cardboard carrier
A cardboard carrier is only suitable for emergencies or when taking a calm cat on a short journey.

PUTTING A CAT INTO A CARRIER

1 First close all the doors and windows. Allow the cat to use its litter box before being put into the carrier. Pick up the cat in a firm but gentle way. The cat may start to struggle when it sees the carrier.

CAR SICKNESS

A cat that is a very bad traveler may be tranquilized when being taken on a long journey. Consult your vet about obtaining and administering tranquilizers.

2 Lift the cat into the carrier, supporting its hind legs. The carrier should always be lined with newspapers or a towel, even if you are only going on a short trip.

The carrier should be lined in case of accidents

Make sure the carrier is fastened

3 Keep your grip on the cat until just before you secure the door. Given the chance, a cat will jump out and will become agitated if you have to chase it around the house.

MOVING

Confine your cat to a quiet room of the house while the furniture is being moved, so that it is not scared by all the commotion, or it may try to run away. Do not feed the cat before the journey, since this may make it sick if it does not travel well. When the furniture van has gone, put the cat in its carrier and take it to your new home. Upon arrival, allow the cat time to settle down and become accustomed to its surroundings. Provide it with food, water, and a litter box. Supervise its explorations of your new home for the first few days, watching for situations that may be hazardous for your cat.

Car travel
A cat must be confined for car travel.

TRAVELING ABROAD AND CATTERIES

Vacations and travel abroad require careful planning by the cat owner. For all travel, whether by air, road, rail, or sea, a cat will have to be in a container approved by the carrying company and the U.S. government. For long journeys it will need food, water, and access to a litter box.

Although it is not advisable to sedate a cat for traveling, a vet can prescribe a tranquilizer if you have a nervous animal. A pregnant or nursing queen and young kittens should not be taken on long journeys.

If you cannot take your cat with you, make sure that it will be cared for properly in your absence, whether by friends, neighbors, at a cattery, or by a "cat-sitting" agency.

AIR TRAVEL

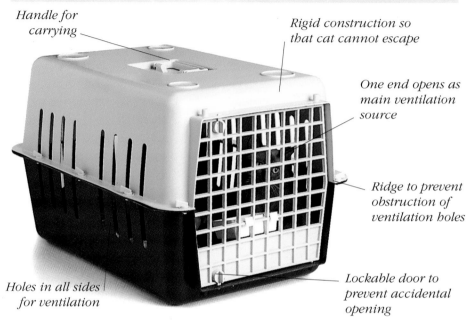

Handle for carrying

Rigid construction so that cat cannot escape

One end opens as main ventilation source

Ridge to prevent obstruction of ventilation holes

Lockable door to prevent accidental opening

Holes in all sides for ventilation

Feline freight
Cats being transported by air must be contained in a carrier like the one above. Such a container must be strong and light, and allow plenty of ventilation, especially for long journeys. Instructions for feeding and watering and the owner's name and address should be clearly marked.

QUARANTINE

In the United States, traveling between states with an animal is forbidden unless you have the required vaccination and health documents. You will need to check with each state you enter regarding the laws on vaccinations.

If you take your cat abroad, you will need to comply with the regulations issued by the transportation company and the country you are visiting. A vet can advise you on regulations and which authorities you need to contact. The penalties for smuggling cats are severe, since they represent a potential health risk to humans.

Confinement
A cat taken abroad may have to spend time in quarantine either upon arrival or on return to its home country to prevent the spread of rabies.

BOARDING YOUR CAT

You should select a cattery well in advance of your vacation. Inspect the premises and make all the arrangements in good time, since many establishments are booked for months ahead. The cattery should be spotlessly clean and tidy, and the cats well cared for. The cats should be able to look out and see each other, but should be kept apart to prevent the spread of infection. All feeding and drinking bowls must be kept clean and sterile, and cat beds should be disposable, or of a material that can be thoroughly disinfected for each new occupant. You should inform the staff if your cat has special dietary needs, and you must ensure that your pet's vaccinations are up-to-date. The cattery should allow you to leave your cat several items to remind it of home, such as a favorite toy. There must be effective security at the cattery, with at least two barriers to the outside world to prevent the escape of boarders or the entrance of strange cats.

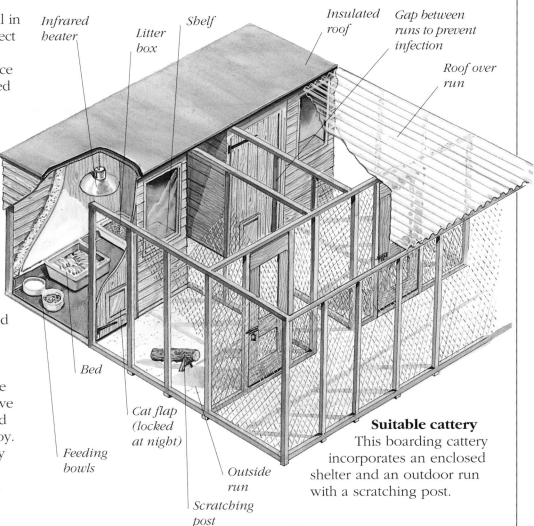

Infrared heater

Litter box

Shelf

Insulated roof

Gap between runs to prevent infection

Roof over run

Bed

Cat flap (locked at night)

Feeding bowls

Outside run

Scratching post

Suitable cattery
This boarding cattery incorporates an enclosed shelter and an outdoor run with a scratching post.

Communal cattery
Some boarding catteries have larger chalets for a nursing queen and her kittens, or for several adult cats from one household. Cats from different households should not share the same accommodation, and, in some areas, this is illegal. Many catteries have longterm facilities for cats that have to be boarded for long periods. Fees vary according to the facilities provided and are usually payable when a cat is picked up.

KEEPING A CAT HEALTHY

One of the responsibilities of caring for your cat involves taking it to the vet for regular checkups, vaccinations, and boosters. This essential part of feline maintenance should start from the first day that you bring your kitten home and continue through to its old age. You should choose a vet in your area who specializes in treating small animals. If the cost of veterinary care is a problem, you may be able to find a low-cost animal clinic in your neighborhood.

CHOOSING A VET

How to find a vet
Ask cat-owning friends to recommend a veterinary practice in your area. Find out what services are available, the fees charged, the consulting hours, and what the arrangements are in the event of an emergency.

USING A VET

You should register your new cat with a vet as soon as you bring it home, and arrange for it to have a complete medical checkup to make sure that it is healthy. If you suspect that your pet is sick, it is advisable to take it to a vet as soon as possible. Never try to treat your cat at home without first obtaining veterinary advice. It will usually be impossible for you to make a correct diagnosis yourself, and your cat's condition is likely to worsen if you delay seeking professional treatment.

HEALTH INSURANCE

You may wish to take out a health insurance policy in case your cat falls ill. In return for paying a yearly premium, the pet insurance will cover most of the vet's fees for any course of treatment. It will not cover routine treatments such as vaccinations or neutering operations. Many pet insurance companies will also pay out a lump sum if a cat is killed in an accident, lost, or stolen.

You and your vet
A vet will advise you on keeping your cat healthy.

BASIC HEALTH CARE

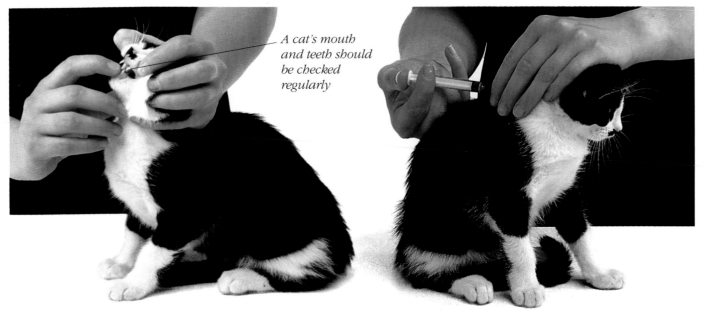

A cat's mouth and teeth should be checked regularly

Regular checkups
Keep a watch on your kitten's health by looking out for unusual behavior and by taking it for regular checkups.

HEALTH CHECKLIST
When you contact your local vet, it is helpful to be able to supply some details of its history. This is a list of questions that you may be asked about your cat:
• Is it alert and active?
• Is it eating and drinking?
• Is it vomiting or retching?
• Is it passing urine and feces normally?
• Is it coughing or sneezing?
• Is it pawing at its eyes or ears?
• Is it showing any signs of pain?

Vaccinations
A kitten should be vaccinated at about eight or nine weeks of age.

Protection from diseases
A kitten must be vaccinated to protect it against infections such as Feline Infectious Enteritis.

TRACING A CAT
If your cat is missing, start by searching your home and yard, since it may simply be locked in a cupboard. Once you have looked in all the obvious places, ask your neighbors for help. Put notices with a description and photograph of your cat in local shop windows, and offer a reward for its return.

You can contact the animal welfare organizations in your area to find out if your pet has been picked up, and local vets in case it has been involved in an accident. Do not give up hope. Cats have a great ability to survive, and there are cases of pets returning home after periods of several months.

A cat that goes outside must wear a collar and an identification disc engraved with your name and telephone number. Alternatively, a tiny identity microchip can be implanted under the skin of the neck. Consult your vet for advice.

Chapter 3
FEEDING

FELINE NUTRITION is an exacting science, since cats are carnivores with very special nutritional requirements. All cats require regular meals of wholesome, high-protein food and a constant supply of fresh water. Cats are by their nature very careful eaters, preferring their food to be fresh and served in a clean bowl. They will turn their noses up at stale food or at any that is served directly from the refrigerator. The nutritional state of a healthy cat is reflected in its appearance; it will have a shiny coat, bright eyes, an alert demeanor, and supple muscle tone. A good-looking, healthy cat is your reward for feeding your pet a well-balanced diet.

CORRECT FEEDING

A cat's unique nutritional needs make it a very demanding animal to feed *(see pages 178–179)*. It is also a very careful eater that quickly rejects its food if it does not have the right smell or if it is served at the wrong temperature. Its keen senses of smell and taste allow it to detect whether food is less than fresh. Try to make sure that your cat is fed at the same time each day and always in the same place.

Sometimes a cat supplements its diet by catching and eating small prey animals, but this does not mean that it is hungry or that you can prevent it from hunting by feeding it more. A cat hunts through instinct, and even a well-fed pet may catch mice given the opportunity.

Protein is essential for the growth and repair of tissues and for the regulation of metabolic processes

Essential fatty acids help give a sheen to a cat's coat

Vitamin A is essential for healthy eyes

Calcium and vitamin D are needed to build healthy bones and teeth

Carbohydrates add fiber to a cat's diet and provide additional energy

Optimum health
A well-fed cat is active and alert; its eyes are bright and its coat is glossy.

FEEDING EQUIPMENT

Even if you have more than one cat, each animal should have its own food and water bowls. You will also need to set aside a can opener, fork, spoon, and knife specially for serving your cat's food. All equipment must be washed after each meal. You can store your pet's utensils in a plastic box so that they do not get mixed up with the household supply. Plastic lids are useful for resealing opened cans. An automatic feeder has a timing device that allows it to open at preset times. It is only suitable if you are leaving your cat for no longer than 24 hours.

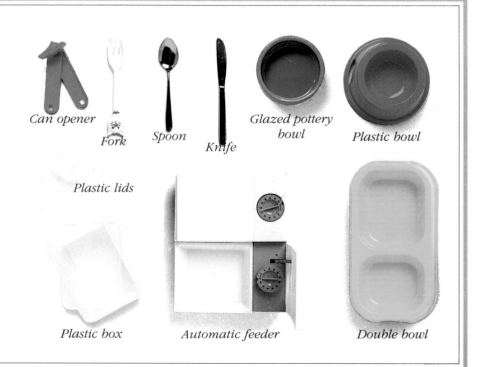

Can opener

Fork

Spoon

Knife

Glazed pottery bowl

Plastic bowl

Plastic lids

Plastic box

Automatic feeder

Double bowl

GUIDELINES FOR FEEDING

Ten basic rules

1 Feed prepared foods only from a reputable manufacturer.
2 Do not feed a cat food intended for a dog or other pets.
3 Always keep food bowls and feeding utensils clean.
4 Do not give a cat any food that is even slightly spoiled.
5 Carefully remove any small bones from fish and chicken.
6 Serve food at room temperature.
7 Dispose of uneaten food once the cat has walked away.
8 Keep a watch on your cat's weight, and do not let it overeat.
9 Do not put reheated food back in the refrigerator.
10 Consult a vet if your cat has refused food for 24 hours.

Do not give a cat too many scraps

Overfeeding
Feed your cat two to three small meals a day, following the manufacturer's recommendations. Do not give many snacks between meals.

Competition for food
A little competition makes for healthy appetites. You will not find a fussy eater in a household where there is more than one cat.

WATER AND MILK

A cat gets most of the moisture that it requires from its food, and many felines seem to drink little. However, you should make sure that fresh water is available at all times. If a cat is fed dry food it will need to increase its water intake because these foods contain very little moisture. Restrict the amount of dry food if your cat is a poor water drinker. Although milk contains a lot of valuable nutrients, it is not essential for a feline diet and may cause diarrhea. As an alternative to cow's milk, try giving one of the lactose-reduced brands available.

Some cats are unable to digest milk

Milk
Milk may cause stomach upset, so give no more than one to two tablespoons in a day.

A Cat's Dietary Needs

Cats require certain dietary components and animal-derived nutrients. They are not vegetarians and, although they can digest some vegetable matter, they are unable to live long on a completely meat-free diet. A cat does not have a strict dietary need for greenery, but you should make sure it has access to grass as a source of certain vitamins, which it cannot obtain in sufficient quantities in its food. A cat may vomit after eating grass, since this helps it to clean out its system and to get rid of unwanted matter, such as hairballs. You should make sure that any chemicals or fertilizer used on your lawn are non-toxic to animals.

Eating grass
Although a cat may sometimes chew grass, it cannot digest much vegetable matter.

YOUR CAT'S WEIGHT

An average adult cat should weigh about 9–11 lb (4–5 kg). Although cats do not vary in size as much as dogs, a cat's weight does vary according to the type of breed. A small cat may weigh only 5½ lb (2.5 kg), and a large cat as much as 12 lb (5.5 kg). The following is a list of average weights:

KITTENS

Age	Weight
One day	2½–5 oz (70–135 g)
One week	4–9 oz (110–250 g)
Three weeks	8–15 oz (215–420 g)
Four weeks	9–18 oz (250–500 g)
Five weeks	10–22 oz (290–620 g)
Six weeks	11–25 oz (315–700 g)
Seven weeks	14–31 oz (400–900 g)

ADULTS

Average	5½–12 lb (2.5–5.5 kg)
Pregnant	8–12 lb (3.5–5.5 kg)
Lactating	8–12 lb (3.5–5.5 kg)

Feline obesity is usually due to a combination of overfeeding and lack of exercise. Neutered and elderly cats are most commonly affected. The occasional cat may have a hormonal problem, but a cat usually becomes fat because it is eating more food than it requires. A very overweight cat will have a large abdomen that hangs down. Its breathing is labored, and it soon becomes less active. Carrying the excess weight puts a strain on the cat's heart and makes it more susceptible to arthritis and other disorders in old age. If your cat is overweight, you should establish how much it is eating. It may be supplementing its diet by hunting, or it may be being fed elsewhere.

REDUCING WEIGHT

Consult a vet to make sure that your cat's excess weight is not due to a medical problem. Cut down the cat's calorie intake by reducing the amount of food given under veterinary guidance. You can obtain a low-calorie diet from your vet or from a store that is especially formulated for feline weight loss.

Obesity
A very overweight cat has a shorter life expectancy than other cats.

THE NUTRITIONAL REQUIREMENTS OF AN ADULT CAT*

Component	Requirement	Source	Comments
Protein	A cat's diet should be made up of 28 percent protein. Kittens require much more.	Complete cat food, meat, fish, eggs, milk, and cheese.	Needs 20 percent more protein than a dog.
Fat	A cat's diet should be not less than 9 percent fat.	Animal and vegetable fats and oils.	Must have certain animal fats only found in meat and fish.
Carbohydrate	Should not be more than 40 percent of the cat's diet.	Cereals, rice, pasta, potatoes, and dry cat food.	A useful source of energy and extra fiber.
Calcium Phosphorus Sodium Potassium Magnesium Iron Copper Manganese Zinc Iodine	1 g per day 0.8 g per day 0.2 g per day 0.4 g per day 0.05 g per day 10 mg per day 0.5 mg per day 1.0 mg per day 4.0 mg per day 0.1 mg per day	All essential minerals are found in a healthy, balanced diet. Two of the most important dietary minerals, calcium and phosphorus, are found in animal products such as milk.	A cat is unlikely to suffer from a mineral deficiency if it is fed a balanced diet. An excess of minerals can be dangerous.
Vitamin A Vitamin B_1 (Thiamin) Vitamin B_2 (Riboflavin) Vitamin B_6 Pantothenic acid Niacin Folic acid Vitamin B_{12} Choline Taurine Vitamin C Vitamin D Vitamin E Vitamin K	550 international units per day 0.5 mg per day 0.5 mg per day 0.4 mg per day 1.0 mg per day 4.5 mg per day 0.1 mg per day 0.02 mg per day 200 mg per day 100 mg per day No dietary requirement 100 international units per day 8.0 mg per day No dietary requirement	All essential vitamins are found in a healthy, balanced diet. Vitamin A is found in liver, egg yolk, and butter. Vitamin B_1 is found in eggs, liver, cereals, and milk. Vitamin C is not needed in a cat's diet, since it can be manufactured in the body. Fish liver oils and animal fats are good sources of vitamin D.	Vitamins are essential for regulating all bodily processes. Any deficiency or excess may cause disease. Vitamin A poisoning is usually caused by ingestion of too much liver. A diet based on oily fish, such as tuna, can cause a deficiency of vitamin E.
Water	50–70 ml per kg of the cat's body weight.	Water is supplied in a balanced diet.	Water must always be available.

* Source: NRC National Academy of Sciences (1986), Washington, DC.

VITAMIN AND MINERAL SUPPLEMENTS

A variety of vitamins and minerals is essential to your cat's health and to the maintenance of its bodily functions. If you feed your cat a well-balanced, varied diet, extra vitamins should not be necessary since it will get all the nutrients it requires from its food. Giving vitamin and mineral supplements can be potentially harmful. An excess of vitamins A, D, or E, or of calcium and phosphorus, can cause serious health disorders, while an excess of cod liver oil can cause bone disease. Always seek the advice of a vet before giving supplements – they may be helpful if a cat has some metabolic problem, or for a pregnant queen or young kittens that require extra vitamins for growth.

Yeast tablets are a source of B vitamins.

Vitamin powder for adding to food.

Cat sweets containing added vitamins.

PREPARED CAT FOODS

Cats are nutritionally very demanding animals, requiring a high level of protein and fat. It is unwise to feed a cat on fresh foods alone and far safer to rely on a reputable manufacturer to supply a balanced diet. Most canned cat foods are complete: in other words, they contain all the necessary dietary constituents in the right proportion (see page 179). Note the feeding recommendations given, and spend a little time reading the labels to check the nutritional content of the ingredients. Do not overfeed your cat, since it may become overweight and lazy.

TYPES OF CAT FOOD

Canned whitefish, flaked and with the bones removed

Canned foods
These contain meat, fish, gelling agents, fat, water, vitamins, and cereals.

Canned tuna chunks

Canned chicken and turkey with herbs

Canned, medium-textured lamb chunks

Salmon-flavored dry food

Chicken-flavored dry food

Dry foods
Usually fed as part of the diet. Fresh water must also always be available.

Beef-flavored dry food

Seafood-flavored dry food

Chicken-and-fish-flavored dry food

DAILY FEEDING REQUIREMENTS

Life stage	Type of complete food	Energy	Amount	Number of meals
Weaning to 8 weeks	*See page 153*	–	–	–
2–4 months	Canned kitten food	250–425 calories	10.50–18 oz (300–500 g)	3–4
4–5 months	Canned kitten food	425–500 calories	18–25 oz (500–700 g)	3–4
5–6 months	Canned kitten food	500–600 calories	25–28 oz (700–800 g)	2–3
6–12 months	Canned kitten food	600–700 calories	25–28 oz (700–800 g)	1–2
Adulthood*	Canned food	300–550 calories	13–28 oz (400–800 g)	1–2
	Semi-moist food	300–550 calories	13–26 oz (400–750 g)	1–2
	Dry snack food	Feed only as an occasional meal or mixed with a canned cat food.		–
Late pregnancy (last third)	Canned food	Feed at least a third more than normal, especially in the late stages of pregnancy *(see page 146)*.		2–4
Lactation	Canned food	Feed at least three times more than normal to satisfy the mother's and kittens' increased requirements.		2–4
Old age**	Canned food	Feed more where absorption is poor but less if the cat is inactive *(see page 139)*. Take veterinary advice.		1–2

*Cats vary in activity and may need less or more food overall. ** Cats with special dietary needs should be fed under veterinary supervision.

Semi-moist foods
Semi-moist foods can be alternated with canned or fresh foods.

Chicken-and-liver-flavored dry food

Beef-flavored semi-moist food

Liver-flavored semi-moist food

Chicken-flavored semi-moist food

Tuna-flavored dry food

Liver-flavored dry food

Cat chews
Cat chews provide exercise for a cat's teeth and gums.

Cat treats
Milk-flavored drops can be fed as a treat.

FRESH FOODS

The easiest way to ensure that your cat enjoys a balanced diet is to feed it a canned cat food produced by a reliable pet food manufacturer. However, you can feed your cat a meal of fresh food once or twice a week, to add variety and interest to its diet.

PREPARING FRESH FOODS

Fresh food treat
Your cat will like the taste and texture of fresh food and, if it is fed mainly on canned cat food, it will enjoy the change from its usual diet.

Cooked meat
Give your cat an occasional treat by cooking it some fresh beef, lamb, pork, or fish. Meat can be baked, grilled, or boiled and should be cooled and chopped into small chunks before serving.

Cooked meat with vegetables
Cooked carrots, peas, or greens can be added to meat for extra vitamins.

Cooked meat with pasta
Add a little cooked rice, pasta, or potato to your cat's food bowl to make the meat or fish go further. Vegetables and carbohydrates should only make up a very small proportion of your cat's diet.

Minced meat
Your cat will enjoy the occasional meal of cooked minced beef.

Cooked fish

White fish such as scrod, cod, or haddock is good for tempting a cat that is sick or that has a poor appetite. Fish should never be served raw; gently poach or steam it and remove bones.

Cooked poultry

Feed your cat all the leftover parts of a chicken, including the skin and giblets. Chop the chicken into small pieces, taking care to remove bones.

Canned sardines

Sardines, mackerel, or herring make a very nutritious treat.

Canned tuna

Canned tuna or salmon make a quick occasional meal. Bones should be removed before serving.

Scrambled egg

A lightly scrambled egg makes an excellent light meal. Never feed a cat raw egg whites.

Oatmeal

Oatmeal or baby cereal made with warm milk is appreciated by growing kittens. Do not add any sugar.

A satisfied cat

When a cat has finished eating a tasty meal, it will sit and wash its face with its paw.

Chapter 4

GROOMING

CATS ARE meticulous about keeping themselves clean and tidy. It is rare to see a healthy cat looking bedraggled. Cats only fail to groom themselves when they are sick or when they become elderly and frail. However, owners of longhaired cats do need to give their pets daily help with grooming. Fortunately, Pedigree Longhairs are generally placid  and good-natured and tend to enjoy the prolonged attention. If you accustom your cat to a grooming routine when it is young, it will be much easier when it gets older. A well-groomed cat, fed on a balanced diet, is a happy and active individual.

FIRST STEPS IN GROOMING

Grooming needs to be regular and frequent, but it does not have to take up much of your time unless you are preparing a cat for showing. If you accustom your pet to being groomed from a young age, it will be much easier to handle when it is an adult. Do not encourage a kitten to play with combs or brushes; if it continues to do this in later life, it is likely to scratch you and make grooming difficult.

Cats should have their claws trimmed regularly. If your cat is difficult, try doing just one or two claws a day. Declawing (the surgical removal of a cat's claws) deprives a cat of its natural means of defense, and may cause stress, resulting in behavioral problems. This practice is actively discouraged in most countries.

TRIMMING THE CLAWS

1 Light pressure on the cat's foot will expose the claws. A badly overgrown claw can grow into the paw pad and become infected, requiring veterinary treatment.

2 Using sharp clippers, cut off the white tip. Take care not to cut the sensitive quick.

GROOMING EQUIPMENT

Clippers   Comb   Brush   Toothbrush

You will need sharp nail or guillotine clippers for trimming your cat's claws, a bristle brush and comb for removing tangles in the coat, and a small, soft toothbrush for cleaning the teeth. All items should be used on only one cat.

WHERE TO TRIM THE CLAWS

It is safer to err on the cautious side and cut less claw rather than more. Cutting into the pink quick is painful and will result in bleeding. If you are unsure, ask a vet to show you how to trim your cat's claws correctly.

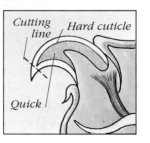

Cutting line   *Hard cuticle*

Quick

GROOMING A KITTEN

Use a comb to remove tangles

Hold the kitten still while gently stroking it

1 To calm the kitten and get it used to being groomed, stroke it gently before starting to use the brush and comb.

2 Comb through the kitten's coat from head to tail, looking for signs of fleas or other parasites at the same time *(see page 223)*.

3 Brush the fur to remove any dead hair. Pay particular attention to the legs and to the area between the toes, which can become soiled.

Contented kitten
Grooming from kittenhood will strengthen the bond between you and your cat, and ensure that it develops into a pet that loves attention.

4 Gently brush the teeth and gums to accustom the kitten to a routine of dental hygiene from an early age *(see page 189)*.

GROOMING A CAT'S FACE

Before grooming your cat, you should examine its eyes, ears, and teeth for signs of health problems and clean them if necessary. In most cases, the eyes and ears will only require a quick wipe with a cotton wad. Discoloration of the fur around the eyes may occur in Pedigree Longhair breeds as the result of blockage of the tear ducts and should be cleaned off. Consult a vet if the problem is recurrent. Your cat's teeth should ideally be brushed once a week.

The corners of the cat's eyes should be free from discharge

The ear flaps should be kept clean with no signs of dirt or dark wax

The teeth should be brushed weekly

Facial grooming
A cat's eyes, ears, and teeth need regular attention. Examine your cat once a week before grooming.

CLEANING THE EYES

1 A healthy cat's eyes rarely need much attention. Consult a vet if there is any sign of a discharge. Dampen a piece of cotton with water.

2 Wipe gently around each eye with a separate a cotton ball. Be careful not to touch the eyeball itself.

Remove staining from the corners of the eyes

3 Dry the fur around the eyes with a cotton ball or tissue. Owners of longhaired cats may need to remove any staining in the corners of the cat's eyes.

GROOMING EQUIPMENT

Cotton ball *Baby oil* *Small bowl*

Use a cotton ball dampened with warm water or baby oil.

CLEANING THE EARS

1 Inspect the cat's ears for signs of inflammation. Dark-colored wax may be caused by ear mites and requires veterinary attention (*see page 227*).

2 Moisten a cotton ball with a little baby oil and wipe away any dirt on the insides of the cat's ears.

3 Use a circular motion to gently clean the cat's ears but do not probe inside. Never poke cotton swabs in a cat's ears.

FELINE EARS

A cat's ear is a very delicate structure and should be treated with caution. Do not poke anything into the ear.

CLEANING THE TEETH

DENTAL EQUIPMENT

Toothbrush

Toothpaste   *Cotton swabs*

You need cotton swabs, a small toothbrush, and a tube of toothpaste.

Examine the gums and teeth

1 Gently open the cat's mouth to check that its gums and teeth are healthy. The gums should be firm and pink, and there should be no broken teeth.

2 Accustom the cat to having its teeth brushed by lightly touching its gums with a cotton swab. Put a little pet toothpaste on the cat's lips so that it can get used to the taste.

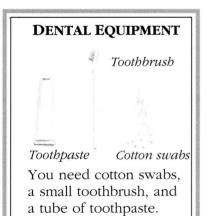

3 After a couple of weeks, try brushing the cat's teeth using a small, soft toothbrush. Use either a pet toothpaste or salt and water.

COAT TYPES

Types of feline coat can be divided into the following basic categories: longhaired, shorthaired, curly, wirehaired, and hairless. A cat's coat has a topcoat of "guard" hairs that are thick and weatherproof. The undercoat consists of soft "down" hairs and bristly "awn" hairs. Different cat breeds have different grooming requirements.

Sphynx
The virtually hairless Sphynx has fine fur on its face, ears, paws, and tail. The skin should be regularly washed with a sponge.

COAT COLORS AND MARKINGS

The basic domestic cat has a tabby coat; all other coat markings are the result of selective breeding. There is an enormous variety of coat colors, including black, white, chocolate, blue, lilac, red, cream, and tortoiseshell. Coat patterns and shades also vary.

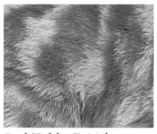

Red Tabby British Tabby Shorthair

Silver Spotted British Spotted Shorthair

Tortoiseshell British Tortoiseshell Shorthair

Gray British Blue Shorthair

Gray and white British Bicolor Shorthair

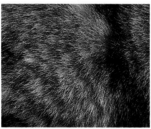

Tortoiseshell British Tortoiseshell Shorthair

White Pedigree Longhair

Classic tabby Non-pedigree Shorthair

Chocolate tortoiseshell Cornish Rex

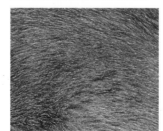

Pale gray Exotic Lilac Shorthair

Black British Black Shorthair

Brown Abyssinian

GROOMING DIFFERENT COAT TYPES

Shorthaired coat
A shorthaired cat requires little help with its appearance. However, grooming once a week will keep your cat's coat looking glossy and smooth.

Longhaired coat
Longhaired cats need the most attention and require daily grooming. Check for knotted fur on the abdomen and legs.

Angora *(right)*
An Angora's fur is fine and silky, with a tendency to wave. Grooming is particularly important in the spring, when this type of cat sheds its thick winter coat.

Rex *(right)*
A Rex's curly coat is very easy to groom. The fur is short, very silky to the touch, and particularly curly on the back and tail. Use a leather chamois to polish the coat.

Exotic Shorthair
An Exotic Shorthair's coat is very dense and slightly longer than that of other shorthaired cats. This cat should be combed or brushed daily.

Maine Coon
The fur of a Maine Coon is thick, but the undercoat is slight, which makes grooming easy. Gentle brushing every few days is all that is needed.

GROOMING A SHORTHAIRED CAT

Grooming your cat is a task that requires some patience, but your efforts will be rewarded if you make time for regular sessions. Cats are fastidious animals that wash themselves daily with immense care, but most appreciate and enjoy a little human help.

Start grooming your cat from as early an age as possible *(see page 187)*. An older cat that is set in its ways will not be so willing to submit itself to being brushed and handled. Establish a routine by setting aside a time for grooming, preferably when the cat is relaxed, perhaps after feeding. One or two sessions a week should be sufficient for most shorthaired cats.

As cats approach old age, or if they are ill, they become less competent and not so inclined to groom themselves properly, and may need more help in keeping neat and tidy.

GROOMING METHOD

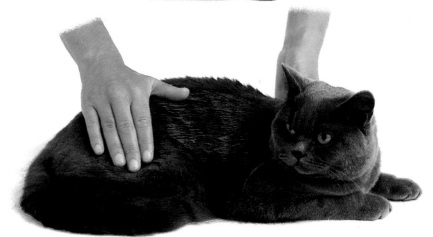

1 With a metal comb, work through the cat's fur from head to tail to remove any dirt. Look for signs of fleas at the same time *(see page 223)*.

4 Every few weeks, apply a few drops of coat conditioner to help remove grease from the coat.

5 Using a leather chamois or cloth, rub the conditioner into the coat to bring out the natural gleam.

GROOMING EQUIPMENT

Metal comb *Bristle brush* *Rubber brush* *Leather chamois*

You will need a metal comb, bristle and rubber brushes, and a leather chamois. Keep all equipment as clean as possible.

2 Using a bristle brush, work along the lie of the coat. Brush all over the cat's body, including the chest and abdomen.

3 A rubber brush is excellent for removing dead hair and is particularly good for oriental-type cats with fine, short fur.

FLEAS AND PARASITES

While grooming your cat, examine its coat. You are unlikely to see many fleas, but you may be able to see flea droppings as black specks.

6 Stroking is enjoyable for your cat and will also help remove dead hair and keep the coat smooth.

British Blue
If your pet is fed a balanced diet and given plenty of daily care and attention, this will show in its glossy, healthy coat.

GROOMING A LONGHAIRED CAT

In the wild, a longhaired cat would only molt in the spring but, because domestic cats are kept in artificially lit and heated surroundings, they tend to molt throughout the year. Longhaired pedigree cats, in particular, need daily grooming sessions to keep their fur free from tangles. As well as keeping the coat clean, neat, and glossy, grooming serves to remove loose hairs and dead skin, and tones up the circulation and muscles.

It is important to accustom a longhaired kitten to being groomed from an early age (*see page 187*). Neglect by an owner can have serious consequences, leading to a deterioration of the cat's coat, painful, matted hair, and even swallowed fur forming balls in the stomach.

If your cat dislikes being groomed, brush it very gently, a little at a time, until it becomes used to the process.

GROOMING EQUIPMENT

Wide-toothed comb   *Talcum powder*   *Bristle brush*

You will need a wide-toothed comb, talcum powder, and a natural bristle brush.

GROOMING METHOD

1 Start by combing the fur on the abdomen and legs to untangle knots.

2 Gently comb the fur upward toward the cat's head one section at a time to pull out all the dead hairs.

5 Comb the fur around the neck in an upward direction so that it forms a ruff.

6 Vigorously brush the fur the "wrong way", working from head to tail. Remove all talcum powder from the cat's coat before showing.

3 To help remove grease and dirt, sprinkle a little talcum powder on to the coat once a week.

4 To remove tangles, first sprinkle with talcum powder and then gently tease the knots out by hand.

MATTED FUR

Knots must be teased out by hand or with a mat-splitter, available at many pet supply stores. You may have to consult a vet for advice.

Do not forget to brush the cat's tail

7 Finally, make a parting down the middle of the tail and gently brush the fur out on either side.

Smoke Longhair
A longhaired cat's fur should be luxuriant and silky to the touch.

BATHING A CAT

BATHING METHOD

Some people may be surprised at the idea of bathing a cat, but there may be times when this is essential, for instance if your cat's coat becomes contaminated with oil or grease. Show cats are bathed regularly, usually a few days before a show *(see page 302)*. Make sure you get everything ready beforehand, with the shampoo, towels, comb, brush, and pitcher for rinsing all within easy reach. You may need to enlist the aid of an assistant who can help you keep the cat calm and reassure it while it is being bathed.

Use a safe cat shampoo or a tearless shampoo, and be careful not to get any soap into the cat's eyes or ears. If you have a shorthaired cat, you may prefer to give it a dry shampoo. Rub warm bran into the coat, then vigorously brush it out.

1 Fill a bath or large bowl with about 4 in (10 cm) of warm water. Test the temperature of the water and lift the cat firmly into the bath.

4 Rinse the cat, using plenty of warm water, until all traces of soap have been removed.

BATHING EQUIPMENT

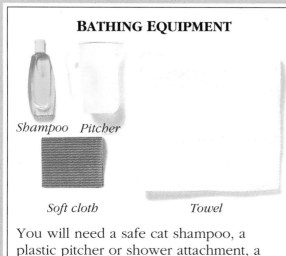

Shampoo *Pitcher*

Soft cloth *Towel*

You will need a safe cat shampoo, a plastic pitcher or shower attachment, a soft cloth, and a large towel for drying the cat off so that it does not catch a chill.

5 Lift the cat out of the bath and wrap it in a large, warm towel. Dry it off.

2 Wet the cat with a little shampoo mixed with warm water from the neck downward, using a pitcher or shower attachment.

3 Gently massage the shampoo well into the cat's coat. Take care not to get any soap into the cat's eyes or ears.

Do not put undiluted shampoo on a cat's coat

HANDLING DURING BATHING

Handle the cat firmly but gently. A cat does not like getting its fur wet and may try to scratch or bite. Talk to the cat to reassure it.

7 If the cat is not frightened, dry it thoroughly with a hairdryer. Hold the dryer at a safe distance, gently brushing the fur at the same time.

6 Carefully wipe around the cat's eyes, ears, and nose, using a soft, damp cloth *(see page 188)*.

Chapter 5

THE PROBLEM CAT

BADLY BEHAVED cats are a nuisance. Some normal feline behavior may be difficult for a human owner to understand and even more difficult to curb. Unacceptable feline behavior, such as soiling and spraying inside the house, and aggression, may relate to stress and can often be tackled if the cause of the upset can be identified. Alternatively, you may find that your cat is extrovert or introvert by nature. Understanding and patience are essential if you are living with a problem cat.

RECOGNIZING SIGNS OF STRESS

Even though a life in the wild would be more stressful for a cat than living with humans, a pet may suffer from stress if it is exposed to certain stimuli, or if its needs are not properly met. Anxiety can cause a cat to react in bizarre ways, such as soiling and spraying indoors, chewing wool, biting and scratching, and nervous grooming. There are different causes of stress, usually involving illness, pain, fear, or a change in the routine of the household due to the arrival of a new baby or pet. A cat may also suffer from stress following the loss of an owner or a change in living quarters.

ANXIOUS FELINE BEHAVIOR

The anxious cat
An anxious cat may appear nervous, crouching low, on the ground. Other feline responses to stress include panting and shedding fur.

The body is tense

The pupils are dilated

Aggression (left)
A normally placid, affectionate cat may suddenly start to behave in an aggressive way, biting and scratching its owner. There is usually a good reason for this type of behavior. It may be a sign that the cat is sick and should be taken to a vet. A cat may also become aggressive or destructive through boredom or unresolved stress (see page 206).

The tail is held upright as the cat sprays the chair leg

Territory marking indoors (right)
A cat may spray inside the house if it is suffering from stress due to a change in its routine, or if another cat has been introduced into the home. The area must be washed with an odor neutralizer to remove the odor and discourage the cat from repeating the behavior.

House soiling

A cat that soils floors or furniture may be suffering from a urinary problem that requires veterinary treatment. If the cat is otherwise healthy, it may be a sign of stress. Do not scold or strike the cat. Provide it with a clean litter box until the problem is resolved. Deter the cat from soiling in the same place again by covering the spot with tin foil or plastic sheeting.

An anxious cat may lick and chew its fur

Nervous grooming (above)

There are cases of cats responding to stressful situations by over-grooming. The cat may continually lick and chew one particular area of its body for no apparent reason. This can lead to skin conditions such as dermatitis, eczema, and even baldness. A vet may treat the cat by prescribing tranquilizers to help while the stress is being resolved.

IDENTIFYING PROBLEMS

If there is no obvious reason for your cat's problem, consult a vet who may refer your pet to an animal behaviorist for treatment.

Chewing wool

Certain breeds of oriental cat, especially Siamese and Burmese, may sometimes obsessively chew wool and other types of fabric. Such cats may be reverting to infant behavior as a result of stress.

DEALING WITH UNWANTED BEHAVIOR

UNWANTED FELINE BEHAVIOR

We need to recognize the the difference between normal but unwanted feline behavior and more serious problems, such as phobias. Some aspects of normal cat behavior can put a strain on your relationship with your pet, but you must remember that your cat is just following its natural instincts when it chooses a favorite plant for its toilet or scratches your best armchair. If you teach your pet boundaries and give it direction from the time it is a kitten, it will be less likely to behave in an undesirable way as an adult cat.

Never shout at or strike a cat; a firm "No" will usually stop it in its tracks. As a last resort, a quick squirt of water from a water pistol may stop a cat persisting with bad behavior.

Digging up plants
A cat's habit of digging up the soil around plants (both indoors and out) when selecting a site for its toilet is a nuisance to many gardeners. If your cat selects a nearby garden for its toilet, you and your pet will soon become very unpopular with neighbors.

The cat dislikes the feel of the gravel

Remedy (right)
Garden plants can be surrounded with wire mesh or netting to discourage a cat from using a particular spot. Various odors, such as buried moth balls, may also act as deterrents. Probably the most effective way to stop a cat's gardening activities is to place sharp gravel around precious plants.

Fighting with other cats
An unneutered tomcat is likely to fight with other rival cats. An intact male cat's natural instinct is to defend its territory against other males and to seek out females to mate with. If you own such a cat and allow it to roam free outdoors, you can expect it to often come home battle-scarred from brawling.

Remedy (above)
Neutering a male cat makes it less aggressive toward other cats. It is likely to have a smaller territory to protect, stray less, and make a more affectionate pet (see page 274).

DEALING WITH UNWANTED BEHAVIOR

Eating houseplants

Cats often like to nibble at the leaves of houseplants. A cat that is confined indoors may eat plants as a substitute for grass, which all cats like to chew on. Do not keep any plants that are toxic to cats in your home *(see page 287).*

A cat may eat houseplants if it has no access to grass

CAT SANCTUARY

Simple touches can enrich your cat's life and improve its behavior. Every feline needs a quiet place where it can sleep undisturbed.

Remedy *(right)*

Houseplants can be protected by putting an anti-chew agent on the leaves. If this does not work, try spraying the cat with a plant spray or water pistol (using only clean water) every time it misbehaves.

Scratching furnishings

A cat scratches furnishings not merely as a way of manicuring its claws, but also to mark the extent of its territory as a signal to other felines. The more confined or threatened a cat feels, the more likely it is to mark its home.

Remedy *(right)*

Think carefully when choosing curtains, carpets, and chairs. Some textured fabrics or rough wallpaper will be irresistible to a cat. Train your cat to use a scratching post *(see page 156).*

A post is good for sharpening claws

CARING FOR AN INTROVERT CAT

Cats are well known for their independent natures, but some individuals may be rather timid and withdrawn. The root of the problem usually lies in the way a cat was raised. A kitten should be brought up in a stimulating environment, in which it feels secure. It should be encouraged to investigate new objects and to interact with other cats. A kitten that is not used to being handled and that is deprived of human attention will grow up into a cat that is timid and wary of humans.

THE TIMID CAT

Wary of humans
A timid or nervous cat may have been mistreated or undersocialized when it was young. A sudden noise or the appearance of a stranger in the house is enough to to make it hide away in a corner.

The eyes are wary

The tail is held between the legs

Gentle reassurance *(below)*
Never reach for a timid cat; let it come to you in its own time. A cat often perceives any unwanted advance as aggression. Reassure the cat by speaking to it softly and, if it will allow it, gently stroking it at the same time. The cat may feel safer if it is on a table or raised surface above floor level – lure it there. Avoid making sudden movements or loud noises. Keep visitors away until the cat has gained confidence.

A secure refuge *(above)*
A timid cat needs a quiet refuge where it can retreat in times of stress. An enclosed cat bed may help it to overcome its nervousness.

THE DEPENDENT CAT

The ears are forward and alert

The mouth is open; this cat is very vocal

Demanding attention

Another type of introvert cat is completely reliant on its human owner and will probably follow you around looking for reassurance. A dependent cat will seek constant love and attention. It will probably cry when it wants to be picked up or when it wants to be fed, or sometimes simply because it wants attention.

The body is held upright, demanding attention

Making friends *(right)*

A dependent cat is likely to suffer from loneliness whenever it is separated from its owner. Provide it with a feline companion, and encourage it to be more independent by allowing it to explore and experience new situations.

Companionship *(above)*

A kitten may help encourage a dependent cat to be more outgoing and less reliant on its owners for amusement. The kitten will make an ideal companion for the older cat to play with if it is to be left alone for long periods, and will prevent it from getting bored or lonely. The younger the kitten, the more likely it is to be accepted by the adult cat *(see page 153).*

CARING FOR AN EXTROVERT CAT

A boisterous or extrovert cat can be quite a handful. It will require constant attention to keep it out of mischief. Most felines grow out of kittenish behavior, but an extrovert cat will stay lively and playful into adulthood. It is neither possible nor practical to train a cat in the same way as a dog. However, a kitten or young cat should be taught some basic discipline to prevent it from developing bad habits in later life.

THE AGGRESSIVE CAT

Biting and scratching
A cat may bite or scratch during play, or when stroked. There is usually a reason for aggressive behavior. The cat may be sick, in pain, or overstimulated.

The ears are held back

The claws are out

The back legs are used to kick

Tap the cat's nose gently with two fingers

Discipline (left)
Never hit or strike out at a cat. This will only make it nervous and cause it to run off and hide. However, you should scold a cat every time it misbehaves, using a firm, sharp tone of voice. A gentle tap on the cat's nose with two fingers may also be effective.

An extrovert cat needs toys for stimulation

Attention seeking
Most cats get all the stimulation they need by exploring their environment. A cat that is not given enough attention may become aggressive and destructive. Cats needs plenty of human contact and stimulation in the form of games and toys *(see pages 166–167)* to keep them amused. A feline companion may help, especially if the cat is left alone for long periods.

THE STRAYING CAT

Leaving home

An unneutered cat or one that is not getting the care and attention that it needs (for example, if it is left alone or fed at irregular times) may stray or desert the home altogether. A cat can survive very well without humans or, if it wants, find a new home. However, it may be picked up as a stray or become wary of humans and revert to a semi-feral state.

The eyes and ears are alert

The tail is held high

The stride is confident and purposeful

Keeping a cat confined

A cat that has a tendency to stray may need to be confined indoors for a short period. To prevent your cat from wandering too far from home, train it to come when you call it at feeding times. A cat should not be allowed to stay outdoors all night since this is a dangerous time.

A cat relies on its owner to provide it with food

Feeding times *(right)*

If a cat is fed at regular times in the morning and evening, this will ensure that it is not far from home at feeding times. Your relationship with your cat is based on the principle that you provide it with food. If this supply is withdrawn, a cat is likely to go off in search of a new home.

Chapter 6

YOUR CAT'S HEALTH

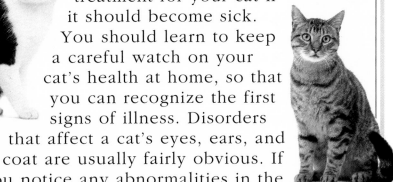

WHEN YOU take a cat into your home, its health becomes your responsibility. Your vet will provide vaccinations against infectious diseases, as well as regular checkups and treatment for your cat if it should become sick. You should learn to keep a careful watch on your cat's health at home, so that you can recognize the first signs of illness. Disorders that affect a cat's eyes, ears, and coat are usually fairly obvious. If you notice any abnormalities in the appearance of your cat or any changes in its behavior, contact a vet immediately.

THE HEALTHY CAT

A healthy cat is a glorious sight. It is confident, alert, and interested in and aware of everything that is going on around it, even when it appears to be taking a quiet catnap. Assessing your cat's state of health by regularly examining it *(see pages 216–217)* and carefully observing its behavior is not difficult, but does need to be done in a routine way so as not to miss any vital sign. A sick cat often does not show any symptoms, and you may not notice that there is anything wrong until it is too late for minor medical treatment.

It is best to look over your cat when it is fairly relaxed and, if possible, without it realizing what you are doing. If you know what to look for, a quick survey of your cat when you are grooming it or when it is sitting on your lap should tell you much about its condition.

A cat's behavior is usually the best indicator of whether it is healthy. If you notice any small changes, such as a loss of appetite, a marked decrease in levels of activity, or listlessness, do not hesitate to consult a vet immediately. If you are worried about any aspect of your cat's health or notice any type of unusual behavior, you can telephone the clinic first and ask the advice of the trained staff before you make an appointment for a consultation.

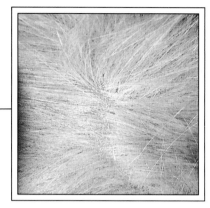

Skin and coat
A cat's coat should look sleek and glossy, and be springy to the touch. The skin should be free of scratches or fight wounds, and there should be no signs of fleas or baldness.

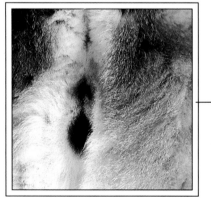

Rear
A cat will keep the area under its tail very clean. There should be no evidence of soreness or diarrhea.

Feline fitness
A healthy cat should have a good appetite and, when it wants, can be very active, moving with grace and agility. It should groom itself regularly and enjoy being petted and handled.

Ears

The outer part of a cat's ears tend to become dirty and should be gently cleaned once a week *(see page 189)*. The ears should be a healthy pink color inside, and there should be no signs of discharge or accumulation of dark-colored wax. Never poke anything into the ear canal.

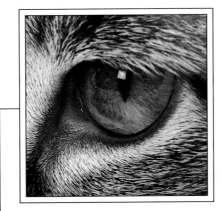

Eyes

A cat's eyes should be clear and bright and free of any discharge. If the third eyelid is showing, this is a sign that a cat is sick.

Nose

A cat's nose should feel soft and velvety and damp to the touch. The nostrils should be free of discharge and have no crusting on the surface. Consult a vet if a cat is sneezing continually, since this may be a sign of a respiratory virus.

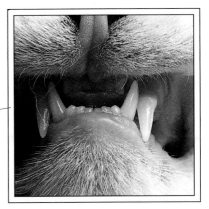

Mouth and teeth

Regular brushing will keep a cat's teeth clean and its breath free of smell. There should be no broken teeth, and the gums should be pale pink and free of inflammation.

SIGNS OF ILL HEALTH

The signs described below and opposite may be accompanied by changes in your cat's general behavior; these can often be the first indication that something is wrong. Your cat may spend more time sleeping, drink more than normal, be reluctant to play, or lose its appetite. It is difficult to tell whether your cat is in pain and which part of its body is affected; it may be restless, cry out, or just want to hide itself away. If you can say when your cat first showed signs of ill health, this will help the vet make a diagnosis.

EYE DISORDERS
(see page 225)
- Discharge from the eye
- Inflammation of the eyelid
- Change in the eye color
- Abnormal sensitivity to light
- Visible third eyelid
- Problems with vision

EAR DISORDERS
(see page 227)
- Discharge from the ear
- Dark brown wax in the ear
- Persistent scratching or rubbing of the ears
- Head shaking or holding head to one side
- Swelling of the ear flap
- Hearing problems

RESPIRATORY DISORDERS
(see page 229)
- Labored breathing
- Persistent sneezing
- Persistent coughing
- Discharge from the eyes and nose
- High temperature

MOUTH AND TOOTH DISORDERS
(see page 235)
- Drooling and pawing at the mouth
- Inflamed gums
- Missing, loose, or broken teeth
- Bad breath
- Difficulty in eating
- Loss of appetite

When to call a vet
Contact a vet immediately if your cat appears to be in pain or if it is obviously injured. Keep the telephone number of the clinic in a prominent place, so that you can find it easily in case of an emergency.

SKIN PARASITES
(see page 223)
- Persistent scratching
- Loss of hair
- Excessive grooming
- Biting at the skin and coat
- Signs of parasites in the coat

DIGESTIVE DISORDERS
(see page 231)
- Repeated vomiting
- Persistent diarrhea
- Loss of appetite
- Blood in the feces or vomit
- Persistent constipation

NERVOUS DISORDERS
(see page 241)
- Convulsions and fits
- Muscle spasms and tremors
- Partial or complete paralysis
- Staggering gait
- Acute skin irritation

SKIN AND COAT DISORDERS
(see page 221)
- Persistent scratching
- Excessive licking and grooming
- Biting at the skin and coat
- Swelling under the skin
- Bald patches in the coat
- Increased shedding of the hair

BLOOD AND HEART DISORDERS
(see page 243)
- Collapse or fainting
- Bluish discoloration of the gums
- Breathing difficulties
- Unwillingness to exercise
- Coughing while exercising

REPRODUCTIVE DISORDERS
(see page 237)
- Failure to breed
- Bleeding from the genitals
- Abnormal discharge from the vulva
- Swelling of the mammary glands
- Swelling of the testes

INTERNAL PARASITES
(see page 233)
- Worms passed in the feces
- Persistent diarrhea
- White "grains" visible on the rear
- Licking and rubbing of the behind
- Potbellied appearance
- Loss of weight

URINARY DISORDERS
(see page 239)
- Straining to pass urine
- Abnormal urination or incontinence
- Blood or excessive cloudiness in the urine
- Excessive thirst
- Persistent licking of the genitals

BONE, MUSCLE, AND JOINT DISORDERS
(see page 219)
- Lameness and limping
- Swelling around the affected area
- Tenderness when area is touched
- Reluctance to walk or jump
- Abnormal gait

DIAGNOSIS CHART

T his flow chart is intended to be a rough guide for you to find out what is wrong with your cat. If your pet is showing any of these clinical symptoms, it may be the first sign of a health problem. Always contact a vet if you are in the slightest doubt about your cat's health.

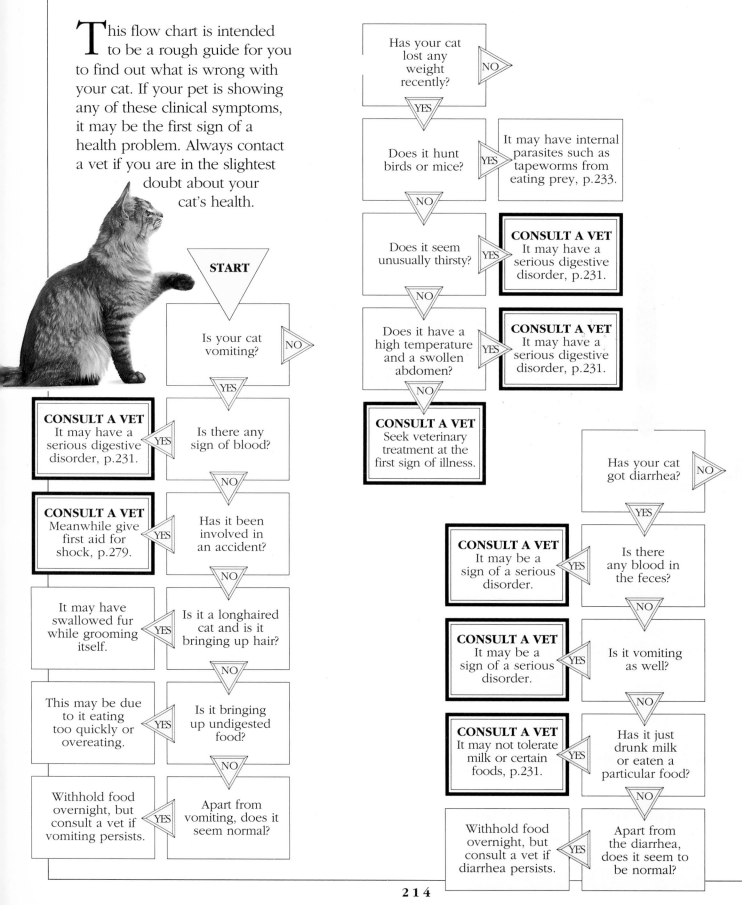

START

Is your cat vomiting? — NO

YES

Is there any sign of blood? — YES → **CONSULT A VET** It may have a serious digestive disorder, p.231.

NO

Has it been involved in an accident? — YES → **CONSULT A VET** Meanwhile give first aid for shock, p.279.

NO

Is it a longhaired cat and is it bringing up hair? — YES → It may have swallowed fur while grooming itself.

NO

Is it bringing up undigested food? — YES → This may be due to it eating too quickly or overeating.

NO

Apart from vomiting, does it seem normal? — YES → Withhold food overnight, but consult a vet if vomiting persists.

Has your cat lost any weight recently? — NO

YES

Does it hunt birds or mice? — YES → It may have internal parasites such as tapeworms from eating prey, p.233.

NO

Does it seem unusually thirsty? — YES → **CONSULT A VET** It may have a serious digestive disorder, p.231.

NO

Does it have a high temperature and a swollen abdomen? — YES → **CONSULT A VET** It may have a serious digestive disorder, p.231.

NO

CONSULT A VET Seek veterinary treatment at the first sign of illness.

Has your cat got diarrhea? — NO

YES

Is there any blood in the feces? — YES → **CONSULT A VET** It may be a sign of a serious disorder.

NO

Is it vomiting as well? — YES → **CONSULT A VET** It may be a sign of a serious disorder.

NO

Has it just drunk milk or eaten a particular food? — YES → **CONSULT A VET** It may not tolerate milk or certain foods, p.231.

NO

Apart from the diarrhea, does it seem to be normal? — YES → Withhold food overnight, but consult a vet if diarrhea persists.

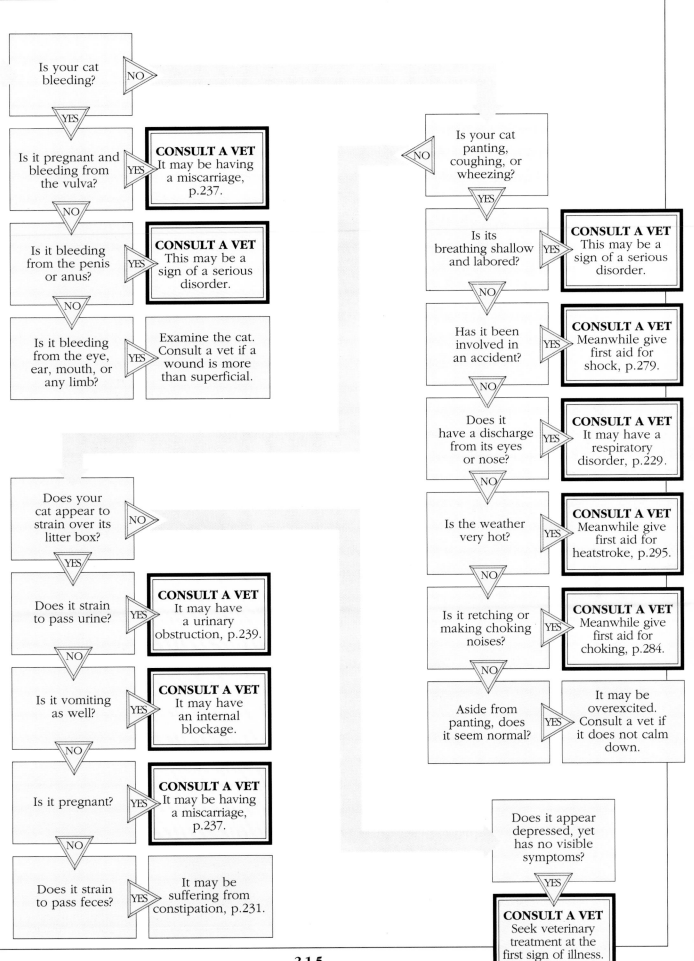

Is your cat bleeding? — NO

Is your cat bleeding? — YES

Is it pregnant and bleeding from the vulva? — YES — **CONSULT A VET** It may be having a miscarriage, p.237.

Is it pregnant and bleeding from the vulva? — NO

Is it bleeding from the penis or anus? — YES — **CONSULT A VET** This may be a sign of a serious disorder.

Is it bleeding from the penis or anus? — NO

Is it bleeding from the eye, ear, mouth, or any limb? — YES — Examine the cat. Consult a vet if a wound is more than superficial.

Does your cat appear to strain over its litter box? — NO

Does your cat appear to strain over its litter box? — YES

Does it strain to pass urine? — YES — **CONSULT A VET** It may have a urinary obstruction, p.239.

Does it strain to pass urine? — NO

Is it vomiting as well? — YES — **CONSULT A VET** It may have an internal blockage.

Is it vomiting as well? — NO

Is it pregnant? — YES — **CONSULT A VET** It may be having a miscarriage, p.237.

Is it pregnant? — NO

Does it strain to pass feces? — YES — It may be suffering from constipation, p.231.

Is your cat panting, coughing, or wheezing? — NO

Is your cat panting, coughing, or wheezing? — YES

Is its breathing shallow and labored? — YES — **CONSULT A VET** This may be a sign of a serious disorder.

Is its breathing shallow and labored? — NO

Has it been involved in an accident? — YES — **CONSULT A VET** Meanwhile give first aid for shock, p.279.

Has it been involved in an accident? — NO

Does it have a discharge from its eyes or nose? — YES — **CONSULT A VET** It may have a respiratory disorder, p.229.

Does it have a discharge from its eyes or nose? — NO

Is the weather very hot? — YES — **CONSULT A VET** Meanwhile give first aid for heatstroke, p.295.

Is the weather very hot? — NO

Is it retching or making choking noises? — YES — **CONSULT A VET** Meanwhile give first aid for choking, p.284.

Is it retching or making choking noises? — NO

Aside from panting, does it seem normal? — YES — It may be overexcited. Consult a vet if it does not calm down.

Does it appear depressed, yet has no visible symptoms? — YES — **CONSULT A VET** Seek veterinary treatment at the first sign of illness.

EXAMINING A CAT

If you suspect that your cat is sick, a basic check on its bodily functions will be useful in assessing its condition. You can make such health checks a routine, beginning when the cat is very young. Regular examination has a number of benefits. It allows you to detect early changes in your cat's health, and makes it possible for you to give the vet a full report on any unusual signs that you have observed. Most important of all, it helps to reinforce the bond between you and your cat.

When subjecting your cat to examination, always be firm but gentle, and talk to it in a reassuring way. None of the techniques shown on these pages is difficult. They just require a little understanding of feline behavior and practice.

TAKING THE PULSE

1 Place the cat on a table or other raised surface. Make sure that the cat is as calm and relaxed as possible by talking to it in a soothing way.

2 The cat's pulse is best felt high up on the inside of the hind leg. You should always count the pulse beats for at least two separate minutes.

TAKING THE TEMPERATURE

1 First, shake the thermometer and lubricate it with petroleum jelly. Lift the cat's tail and insert the thermometer.

2 Carefully hold the thermometer in the cat's rectum for at least one minute. Remove and wipe it before reading.

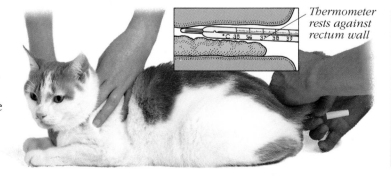

Thermometer rests against rectum wall

READING A THERMOMETER

100-102° F

A healthy cat's temperature is between 100 and 102°F (38 and 39°C).

VITAL SIGNS

Normal pulse, temperature, and respiration rates are: pulse: 160–240 beats per minute; temperature: 100–102°F/38–39°C; respiration: 20–30 breaths per minute.

CHECKING BODY FUNCTIONS

Breathing
Listen to either the breaths out or the breaths in. Here the cat's breathing is being checked by a vet, with a stethoscope.

Abdomen
With the cat at ease, gently palpate the abdomen for any signs of swelling or tenderness. Use a gentle touch, since the cat may react if it is in pain.

Ears
Look into the ears but do not put things in them. Note any scratches to the outer ear, inflammation, or dark-colored wax, which may be a sign of ear mites.

Eyes
Look for discharges, inflammation, or signs of injury. Do not put any drops in a cat's eyes without consulting a vet, and never touch the eyeball itself.

Mouth
Open the cat's mouth and look for broken teeth, inflamed gums, or a buildup of dental deposits that may require scaling by a vet.

Claws
Gentle pressure on the cat's foot will unsheathe the claws. Note any broken or missing claws and any injuries to the soft web of skin between the cat's paw pads.

BONE, MUSCLE, AND JOINT DISORDERS

A cat's agility and elegance are made possible by its highly refined skeleton and the joints and muscles that make it work. Cats are seldom victims of muscle or joint disorders, although an elderly feline may suffer from inflammation of the joints and lameness, which require treatment by a vet. The most serious problems are bone fractures, joint sprains, and injuries from fighting. Always consult a vet for treatment of any serious injury, since the cat is likely to be suffering from severe shock.

Fractures
Although a cat's skeleton is very strong, fractures do occur as a result of accidents.

THE FELINE SKELETON

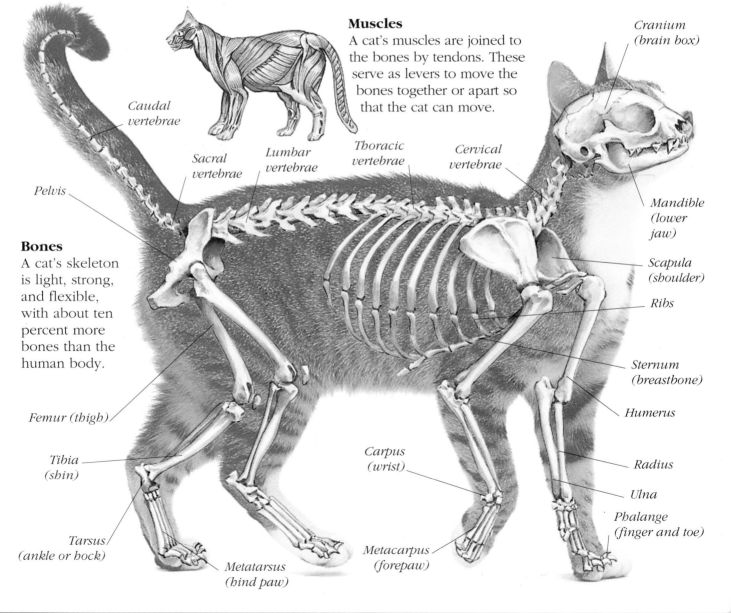

Muscles
A cat's muscles are joined to the bones by tendons. These serve as levers to move the bones together or apart so that the cat can move.

Bones
A cat's skeleton is light, strong, and flexible, with about ten percent more bones than the human body.

Caudal vertebrae

Sacral vertebrae

Lumbar vertebrae

Thoracic vertebrae

Cervical vertebrae

Cranium (brain box)

Mandible (lower jaw)

Scapula (shoulder)

Ribs

Sternum (breastbone)

Humerus

Radius

Ulna

Phalange (finger and toe)

Metacarpus (forepaw)

Carpus (wrist)

Metatarsus (hind paw)

Tarsus (ankle or hock)

Tibia (shin)

Femur (thigh)

Pelvis

BONE, MUSCLE, AND JOINT DISORDERS

Disorder	Description and signs	Action
Bone fractures	Most fractures are caused by traffic accidents or awkward falls. Broken bones are classified according to their severity. A simple fracture does not break through the skin, whereas in a compound fracture the bone is exposed. Fractures are associated with shock, blood loss, and internal injuries.	Consult a vet immediately for setting of the broken limb. Do not attempt to treat a fracture yourself by splinting the limb (see page 281).
Dislocation	A dislocated joint can be the result of a fall or other accident. The hip is the joint most commonly affected. Signs are a sudden pain with an inability to put weight on the limb.	Urgent veterinary treatment is needed. The vet will replace the joint in its socket under an anesthetic.
Bone infection	A deep fight wound may worsen and the infection spread to the bone. Signs of a bone infection include lameness, fever, swelling, and perhaps a discharge.	All serious bite wounds must be treated by a vet. Antibiotics may be prescribed to prevent infection.
Mineral deficiency	Kittens fed a diet of all muscle meat do not get enough minerals. This leads to poor bone development and stunted growth. The condition can also affect adult cats.	A vet can advise on the necessary corrections to the diet. Treatment may involve giving a mineral supplement.
Vitamin excess	Feeding a cat an excessive amount of foods high in vitamin A or D, or overdosing with a vitamin supplement can result in deformities of the spine.	The diet must be corrected at once. Do not give vitamin supplements unless recommended by a vet.
Cleft palate	A birth defect caused by a failure of the bones of the hard palate to develop fully (see page 235).	Surgery to correct the defect may sometimes be possible.
Arthritis	This condition sometimes occurs following a joint infection, dislocation, or trauma. It is most often due to a degeneration of the cartilage in joints as a result of old age. Signs include painful, stiff joints and lameness.	Consult a vet immediately if your cat shows any signs of lameness. Anti-inflammatory drugs may be prescribed to relieve the condition.
Sprains	Although muscle problems are rare, a sprain may sometimes occur when a tendon or ligament is stretched beyond its limits. The signs are swelling and a temporary lameness.	If there is any swelling of the limb, consult a vet immediately. Treat with cold compresses.

BONE FRACTURES

When bones break as the result of an accident, the surrounding tissues are likely to be damaged as well. The cat will probably be in severe shock, and the fractured limb will be swollen and painful due to internal bleeding and bruising. The bones must be immobilized for as long as it takes for them to heal properly. Cats make good subjects for treatment, since they take to cage rest and can cope with splints and pins. Even if a limb has to be amputated, a three-legged cat quickly learns to get around without difficulty.

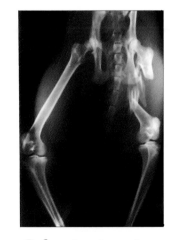

Before treatment
A radiograph shows the extent of injuries to a thigh bone. Although the femur is shattered into several pieces, it is not beyond repair.

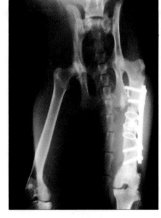

After treatment
Following surgery, the broken bone fragments have been realigned and immobilized. Healing usually takes several weeks.

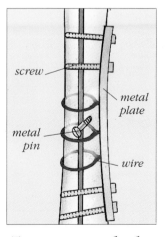

Treatment method
The bone fragments are carefully pieced together. They are immobilized using a combination of encircling wires, a steel plate, and some screws.

screw

metal plate

metal pin

wire

SKIN AND COAT DISORDERS

There are two types of skin disorder: parasitic and nonparasitic. External parasites such as fleas, lice, and ticks are very common in cats *(see pages 222–223)*. Other nonparasitic conditions that can affect the skin and coat are dermatitis, ringworm, stud tail, feline acne, tumors, and abscesses due to fight wounds. Most problems are not contagious and respond well to treatment. Ringworm, however, can be transmitted to other cats, and even to humans.

The main signs of skin disorders are irritation, inflammation and changes in the surrounding skin, and hair loss. They are not specific to any one ailment. Changes in the skin and coat can sometimes be an indication of a serious illness, and if a cat stops grooming itself this may be an early sign that it is sick.

Self-grooming
Meticulous grooming keeps skin and coat problems to a minimum.

ANATOMY OF THE SKIN

Layered protection

The skin helps to control a cat's temperature and to minimize water loss. The coat is made up of heavy guard hairs and finer secondary hairs, all joined to a system of muscle fibers that allow the hair to come erect and bristle, especially along the back and over the tail.

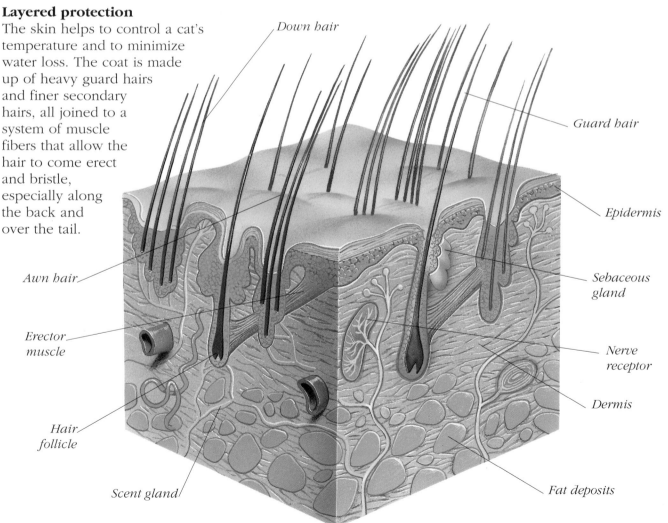

Down hair

Guard hair

Epidermis

Awn hair

Sebaceous gland

Erector muscle

Nerve receptor

Dermis

Hair follicle

Scent gland

Fat deposits

SKIN AND COAT DISORDERS

Disorder	Description and signs	Action
Abscess	This is a painful swelling that becomes infected and filled with pus. It is usually caused as a result of a fight wound (see page 289). The most common sites of abscesses are on the face and around the base of the tail.	Consult a vet if your cat has been bitten. The wound may become septic and require veterinary attention.
Dermatitis	Dermatitis is a term for several skin problems (commonly called eczema) that can cause inflammation and dry, scaly skin. Allergic dermatitis is caused by an allergy to certain foods (such as fish) or to flea dirt and may result in hair loss. Flea collar dermatitis is the result of a reaction to the insecticide in the collar and causes itching and redness. Solar dermatitis may affect the skin on the ears of white cats in sunny areas (see page 227).	Consult a vet. Treatment for dermatitis may involve giving the cat antibiotics and using anti-inflammatory or hormonal agents. Solar dermatitis may be controlled by applying protective suntan cream to the cat's ears. Flea collars should be removed at the first sign of irritation.
Ringworm	A skin infection caused by a parasitic fungus, not a worm. Signs of infection can be difficult to spot and vary from a few broken hairs on the face and ears to small, round patches of scaly skin on the cat's head, ears, paws, and back. A cat may carry the disease without showing any symptoms.	Ringworm can be treated with a variety of antiseptic creams and, in severe cases, antifungal drugs. Disinfection of all bedding is important because it is transmissible to humans (see page 245).
Tumor	A skin tumor is a swelling on or beneath the cat's skin and can be either benign or malignant – the latter means that it is cancerous. Cancerous growths usually grow very rapidly and cause bleeding and ulceration.	Examine any lump or growth that appears on your cat's skin. Consult a vet immediately if you are concerned.
Nervous grooming	Nervous licking or grooming of the coat may result in partial hair loss and sometimes dermatitis. This behavior may be caused by boredom or anxiety (see page 201).	Treatment involves identifying the reason for the stress. Tranquilizers or sedatives may be prescribed.
Feline acne	Acne on a cat's chin and lower lip is caused by blocked ducts leading to blackheads, pimples, and small abscesses forming on the skin.	Consult a vet if you notice any skin abnormality. Antibiotic treatment is sometimes needed.
Stud tail	This is an excessive secretion of oil from the sebaceous glands at the base of the tail. It commonly affects unneutered male cats and may cause staining on pale-colored cats.	Wash the coat with a safe shampoo, but consult a vet if it becomes infected or if there is irritation.
Hair loss	A neutered cat may suffer from hair loss on its hindquarters and abdomen. This may be due to a hormonal imbalance.	Consult a vet to identify the reason for the baldness.

RINGWORM

This skin infection is caused by a parasitic fungus, not a worm. It lives on the surface layers of the skin, causing inflammation and scratching. Signs of ringworm infection are usually seen as bald patches of scaly skin on the head, ears, paws, and back.

Some cats show no symptoms of the disease other than a few broken hairs. Diagnosis can be made using an ultraviolet lamp and by examining affected hairs under a microscope. Ringworm is highly contagious among cats living in a household and can be transmitted to other animals, even humans. Disinfection of baskets, bedding, and bowls during an outbreak is essential.

Treating ringworm (above)
The fur around the affected area may be clipped before treatment.

DERMATITIS

This is an inflammation of the skin and can be associated with many different factors. It is commonly caused by an allergic response, such as a reaction to flea dirt or certain foods. This results in an inflamed, itchy rash developing on the cat's skin. The condition can be aggravated by self-mutilation and infection. All skin conditions require careful investigation by a vet so that a proper diagnosis can be made. Procedures include various skin tests in which small samples of skin are removed and examined under a microscope.

SKIN PARASITES

A variety of parasites can inhabit a cat's coat. Fleas are the most common cause of feline skin problems. Specks of "flea dirt" are easily seen in the coat, looking like large soot particles. Irritation can result from the fleas themselves or from sensitivity to their saliva or droppings. Fleas are involved in the life cycle of tapeworms and can lead to anemia.

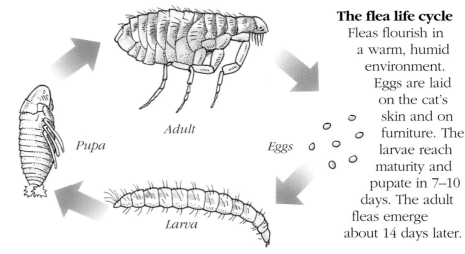

Pupa   *Adult*   *Eggs*

Larva

The flea life cycle
Fleas flourish in a warm, humid environment. Eggs are laid on the cat's skin and on furniture. The larvae reach maturity and pupate in 7–10 days. The adult fleas emerge about 14 days later.

COMMON FELINE PARASITES

Flea Visible as pinhead-size, red-brown insects. Found around the neck and at the base of the tail.

Signs of infestation
Continuous or persistent scratching may be the first sign of infestation by parasites. Check the irritated area, then take appropriate action.

Ear mite The most common feline health problem, producing reddish-brown wax.

Fur mite Highly contagious. Visible as dry scales (dandruff) on the cat's back.

Tick Round, blood-sucking parasite. Must be removed carefully from skin.

Harvest mite Visible as tiny red dots on the cat's feet in autumn. Can be very irritating. Also known as "chiggers."

HUMAN INFECTION

Most parasites prefer not to live on humans. When they do get into clothing or onto skin, they are fairly easy to remove with sensible hygiene.

Louse Pinhead-size insect that feeds on the skin. Its white eggs (nits) may be visible on the cat's fur.

SKIN PARASITES

Parasite	Description and signs	Action
Fleas	The most common skin parasite. Fleas can carry tapeworm larvae *(see page 232)*. The presence of fleas is shown by persistent scratching and small black specks ("flea dirt") in the cat's coat. Some cats are allergic to flea bites due to a sensitivity to the flea's saliva.	Ask your vet to recommend a suitable insecticide spray or powder. Do not use a flea collar on a kitten or sick cat. Always follow the manufacturer's instructions very carefully.
Ticks	Sheep ticks are sometimes found on cats in country areas. They resemble small, blue-gray swellings and suck the cat's blood. A heavy infestation can sometimes cause anemia. There are some ticks in Australia that secrete a toxin that can result in paralysis (tick poisoning).	Dab the tick with alcohol and then remove it with tweezers. If the mouthparts remain in the skin, this can cause an abscess. Ask your vet to advise you on a suitable insecticide.
Lice	Lice are uncommon in healthy cats. They are found on the head and along the back and can be seen as white eggs (nits) attached to the cat's fur.	Consult a vet. In severe cases, the fur may need to be clipped, and the cat bathed in a suitable insecticide.
Mange mites	These minute skin parasites burrow into the cat's skin and cause a range of skin conditions, including inflammation and hair loss. The head mange mite affects the cat's head and neck. Other mites that can cause skin irritations are fur mites (also known as "walking dandruff"), harvest mites, and ear mites *(see page 227)*.	If you suspect that your cat has mites, consult a vet for identification and treatment of the skin parasites with a safe insecticide.
Fly strike	This condition especially affects longhaired cats with neglected or matted fur. Blowflies lay their eggs in the cat's fur, and the larvae burrow under the skin, causing skin damage and bacterial infections.	Consult a vet. The matted hair and damaged skin need to be cleaned with a safe antiseptic and treated with a suitable insecticide.
Bot flies	This type of fly is found mainly in parts of the United States. The bot fly grubs penetrate the cat's skin and may be seen as swellings on its neck, back, sides, and abdomen.	Veterinary treatment is needed if a cat has multiple swellings.

FLEA COLLARS

Collars are a useful aid to flea control, supplying continuous anti-flea medication. They should complement, rather than replace, normal household hygiene. Over-exposure to the medication in flea collars can sometimes cause skin irritation.

Safety *(right)*
Regularly remove flea collars to check for irritation.

TREATING PARASITES

The first rule in controlling fleas and other parasites is to maintain a high standard of hygiene in the cat's environment. No amount of dressings, powders, or sprays will be completely effective if this rule is not followed, since many parasites live or lay their eggs away from the cat and thrive in well-heated, modern homes. As well as treating the cat, you should also disinfect its bedding and all surrounding furnishings with a house spray to prevent parasites recurring. Cats are highly sensitive to a variety of insecticides, so you should ensure that preparations are always used as directed. A flea collar *(see page 158)* should have an elasticized section and should be replaced every few months to ensure its effectiveness. Do not put a flea collar on a cat unnecessarily, if you have already managed to eliminate fleas from the house.

Sprays *(left)*
Keep any sprays away from the eyes. A cat may be frightened of the noise.

EYE DISORDERS

Changes in the appearance of a cat's eyes, whether due to infection or injury, are usually very noticeable. The most common eye conditions affect the cat's outer eye and the conjunctiva (the membrane covering the eyeball). The third eyelid is an extra protection that is not normally visible in a healthy animal, but which may come across the eye if a cat is sick. Signs of problems to watch out for are discharge or watering, closure of the eye, and any cloudiness or change in color. Consult a vet if you notice any abnormality – if left untreated, many eye conditions can lead to impaired sight or even blindness. Most common eye disorders can be treated with antibiotic drops or ointments prescribed by a vet *(see page 252)*.

Inspecting the eyes
A vet can examine the deeper parts of a cat's eyes using an ophthalmoscope.

HOW THE EYE WORKS

Pupil dilation
The cat's vertical pupil protects the retina from bright light and can adjust to different light levels.

Pupil in darkness

Pupil in bright light

The structure of the eye
Light passes through the cornea and the lens to the light-sensitive cells of the retina, where impulses are sent to the brain via the optic nerve. A cat's eyes are specially designed to collect the maximum amount of light.

Optic nerve

Vitreous humor

Retina

Lens

Upper eyelid

Aqueous humor

Cornea

Pupil

Lower eyelid

Iris

Conjunctiva

Suspensory ligaments

EYE DISORDERS

Disorder	Description and signs	Action
Conjunctivitis	This common disorder is an inflammation of the outer layer of the eye (conjunctiva). The eyes will look red and swollen, and there will be a discharge. One or both eyes may be affected. Conjunctivitis can be a symptom of a viral infection such as Feline respiratory disease *(see page 229)*.	Consult the vet for an examination of the cat's eyes. Treatment will usually be in the form of antibiotic drops or ointment. Never use medicines intended for humans.
Corneal damage and ulceration	Injuries to the eyes and eyelids during fights are common and normally heal quickly. If the wound becomes infected, there may be ulceration and even penetration of the cornea.	Consult a vet immediately. Urgent treatment of corneal ulcers is essential to avoid complications.
Protrusion of the third eyelids	The inner eyelid in the corner of the eye is not normally visible, but it may come across to protect an injured eye. If both eyes are affected, this is a sign that the cat may be out of condition or suffering from a viral infection.	Urgent treatment is needed where there is any injury to a cat's eyes. A cat should always be examined by a vet if it is out of condition.
Keratitis	An inflammation of the cornea results in the eye becoming cloudy. Signs include watering and sensitivity.	Urgent treatment is needed to prevent the condition from deteriorating.
Cataracts	An opacity of the lens of the eye is sometimes a congenital condition, but it is more often associated with elderly or diabetic cats.	Careful veterinary assessment is needed. Surgery may be possible to restore vision if both eyes are affected.
Glaucoma	This serious condition occurs when there is an increase in pressure within the eyeball. As a result, the cornea becomes cloudy and the eyeball enlarges.	Any apparent enlargement or change in the eyes should receive prompt veterinary treatment.
Bulging eye	Severe bulging or even dislocation of the eyeball may occur following an accident or as the result of an eye tumor.	Emergency veterinary treatment is needed as soon as possible.
Retinal diseases	Degeneration of the light-sensitive cells at the back of the eye (retina) may be inherited or due to a dietary deficiency. This eye disorder results in sight loss and may eventually lead to blindness.	Urgent veterinary treatment is required for diagnosis and to prevent the condition from deteriorating.
Watery eyes	An overproduction of tears or blocked tear ducts may cause facial staining.	Usually an inherited defect, associated with Pedigree Longhairs *(see page 253)*.

THE THIRD EYELIDS

Gentle pressure on a cat's eyeball will expose the tiny shutter at the corner. If these eyelids are visible, this can be a sign that a cat is out of condition or is suffering from diarrhea or worms. Exposure of the third eyelid on one side only may be due to an injury, fight wound, or object in the eye.

Third eyelid

Eyelids *(left)*
Consult a vet if the third eyelid is visible.

BLINDNESS

Severe eye conditions such as retinal diseases or cataracts can result in a loss of sight. Cats cope surprisingly well with failing sight brought on by old age, or even with the loss of an eye following an accident or trauma. In familiar surroundings, they soon learn to adjust their behavior by using their other senses to compensate.

You should consult a vet immediately if your cat appears to have a sudden loss of vision. This may not be apparent if you look at the cat's eyes, but you may notice it misjudging heights or bumping into furniture.

Eye test *(left)*
To test sight, cover one eye and move your finger toward the other one, making the cat blink. Or shine a flashlight in the eye to see the pulpil reflex.

EAR DISORDERS

A cat's ears not only control its hearing, but its sense of balance, as well. Infections of the middle and inner ear can therefore cause problems with a cat's mobility, as well as with its hearing. The most common causes of infection are certain microorganisms, foreign bodies, and ear mites. The signs of ear disorders to watch for include persistent scratching, shaking of the head, twitching of the ears, discharge, and the presence of dark wax. Deafness can occur following an infection, but it is more often a congenital defect associated with cats with white coats. Old age usually results in some loss of hearing.

Examining the ears
A vet can inspect the lower part of the ear canal using an otoscope. Do not poke anything into a cat's ears.

HOW THE EAR WORKS

Ear flap

The outer ear
Sound waves are gathered by the sensitive outer ear and channeled to the ear drum.

Semicircular canals

The inner ear
The ear drum vibrates, moving the ossicles in the middle ear, which pass on the movement to the inner ear. The sound waves are translated into electrical impulses and conveyed to the brain.

Auditory nerve

Ossicles (hammer, anvil, and stirrup)

Cochlea

Outer ear

Oval window

Eustachian tube

Ear drum

Middle ear

EAR DISORDERS

Disorder	Description and signs	Action
Ear mites	Mite infestation is very common in cats (especially in kittens). Tiny mites live in the ear canal and can cause irritation if they are present in large numbers. Signs of ear mites include persistent scratching and the accumulation of dark brown, pungent wax in the ears.	An examination of the cat's ears with an otoscope can confirm the presence of ear mites. All cats and dogs in the household will need to be treated with ear drops *(see page 253)*.
Ear infection	An inflammation of the ear canal can be caused by the presence of a foreign body, fungus, or bacteria in the ear. The cat will scratch the inflamed ear, leading to infection and sometimes a discharge.	Consult a vet for examination of the cat's ears. Treatment will usually involve administering ear drops *(see page 253)*.
Middle and inner ear infections	If an infection spreads to the middle or inner ear, it can result in damage to a cat's hearing. Signs of this disorder include loss of hearing and sense of balance. An affected cat may tilt its head to one side.	Prompt veterinary treatment with a course of antibiotics is usually needed. Delay may result in permanent damage to the cat's hearing.
Blood blister (hematoma)	Fighting or constant scratching may rupture blood vessels in the ear flap, producing a large blood blister. This is not painful, but it will cause irritation and the cat may continue to scratch and paw at it.	Consult a vet, who will drain the fluid from the ear. If the blood blister is left untreated, this may lead to scarring and a "cauliflower ear."
Sunburn	Pale-colored cats living in sunny areas, such as Florida, are prone to sunburn on their ear tips because of the lack of protective pigment in the skin *(see page 293)*. In time, skin damage may lead to cancerous growth and to the cat's ear becoming thickened and inflamed.	The cat should be kept indoors during the sunniest part of the day. A sunblock cream may provide some protection. Amputation of the ear tips is the only treatment for cancer.
Deafness	Loss of hearing may be the result of old age, middle ear infections, head injuries, or the ear canal becoming blocked with wax. Some cats are deaf from birth, especially some white cats with blue eyes *(see page 253)*.	A thorough veterinary examination is required where deafness is suspected.
Foreign bodies	Foreign bodies, such as grass seeds, can sometimes get caught in a cat's ears and may cause irritation and eventually lead to infection *(see above)*.	Consult a vet if the foreign body is not visible and cannot be easily removed *(see page 285)*.

EAR MITES

Most cats harbor some ear mites, but they usually only cause health problems if they are present in large numbers. The tiny mites feed on the delicate lining of the ear canal, causing irritation and the production of brown wax. This makes the cat scratch or shake its ears, thereby causing inflammation. Early veterinary attention is vital to make sure that any ear infection does not spread to the inner ear and affect the cat's centers of hearing and balance. It is important to keep your cat's ears clean and check regularly for signs of irritation or infection.

Ear mites are very contagious, so always treat both ears and treat all animals in the household.

Signs of mites (above)
Persistent scratching and head shaking are signs of mites.

EAR INJURIES

Because of their exposed position, a cat's ears are very prone to being bitten, torn, or scratched during fights. Such injuries can become infected if the wound is deep and may require veterinary treatment. Violent or persistent scratching may sometimes rupture blood vessels on the ear flap, producing a blood blister. Although this is not painful, it will irritate the cat, which will continue to scratch it. A vet can drain the fluid from the ear and support it, so it can heal in its correct shape. The ears of white cats are prone to damage from both frostbite *(see page 293)* and sunburn – the latter can lead to cancerous growth.

RESPIRATORY DISORDERS

Most respiratory illnesses that affect cats are due to infections by bacteria or viruses, and the upper respiratory tract is usually affected. Although the majority of conditions are mild and respond to careful nursing, they can become serious if neglected. Like human beings, cats can sometimes suffer from colds and occasional sneezing, coughing, and wheezing. Signs of respiratory disorders include breathing difficulties and discharge from the eyes and nose. A sick cat's breathing may be deep and labored or rapid and shallow. Coughs may be fluid and chesty or dry and harsh. It is important to get prompt veterinary help if your cat is showing any sign of illness, in order to prevent the condition from becoming chronic or life-threatening.

Listening to breathing
A vet can listen to a cat's breathing with a stethoscope. Radiographs may also help with the diagnosis.

THE RESPIRATORY SYSTEM

Breathing
Air is drawn into the cat's lungs through the nasal passage, which filters and warms it. The air passes down the trachea into the bronchi and the lungs, where the oxygen is absorbed by the blood and taken around the body.

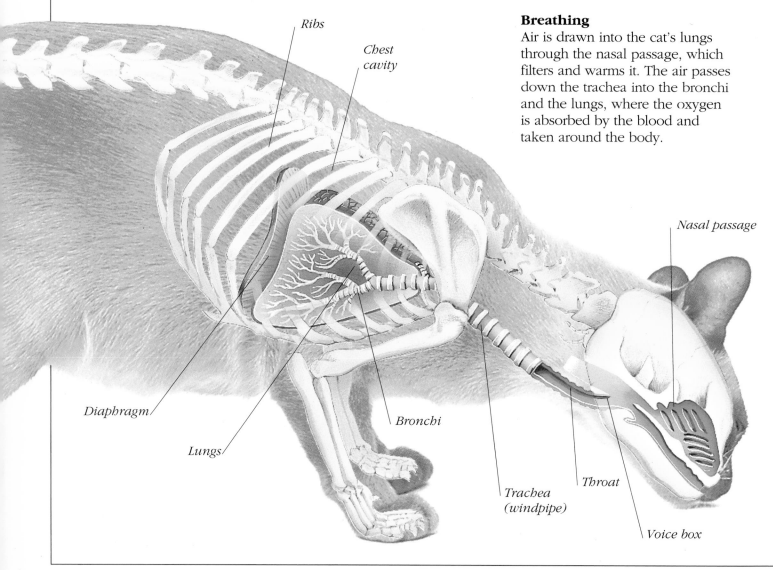

Ribs

Chest cavity

Nasal passage

Diaphragm

Lungs

Bronchi

Trachea (windpipe)

Throat

Voice box

RESPIRATORY DISORDERS

Disorder	Description and signs	Action
Feline respiratory disease ("cat flu")	The two most common respiratory viruses are Feline Viral Rhinotracheitis (FVR) and Feline Calici Virus (FCV). FVR is usually the more serious disease. The main sign of FVR is a watery discharge from the eyes and nose which becomes thicker as the disease progresses. A cat with FCV may also have a runny nose and eyes, and it will typically have ulcers on its tongue and mouth.	Prevention of FVR and FCV by vaccination is essential. Antibiotics may reduce the severity of the disease's effects, but much depends on the cat's immune system being able to fight off the virus. Recovery is often due to careful home nursing.
Pneumonia	A lung infection may follow severe respiratory diseases. Fever, difficulty in breathing, nasal discharge, and a cough are often associated with pneumonia.	Urgent veterinary treatment is needed. Careful nursing and cage rest are both an important part of the treatment.
Bronchitis	This condition usually accompanies other respiratory diseases. It is caused by an inflammation of the air tubes (bronchi) that link the windpipe to the lungs. Persistent coughing is the main symptom.	Urgent veterinary treatment is needed. Careful nursing and cage rest are both an important part of the treatment.
Pleurisy	A bacterial infection may lead to an inflammation of the layer covering the lungs (pleura). This causes a buildup of fluid in the chest cavity that makes breathing difficult.	Urgent veterinary treatment is needed. The fluid in the chest cavity may need to be drained.
Asthma	An allergic sensitivity can sometimes bring on an asthma attack. It is characterized by a sudden difficulty in breathing and wheezing and coughing.	Urgent veterinary treatment is needed to ease breathing and prevent repeated asthma attacks.
Chlamydial disease	This is caused by bacteria that produce signs similar to Feline respiratory disease (see above).	A vaccine may give some protection against the disease.
Nasal discharge	A watery discharge from the nose and eyes is a sign of several infections. If the discharge is accompanied by sneezing and sniffling, the irritation may be due to an infection of the nasal cavities.	Consult a vet for examination and diagnosis of the infection.
Lungworm	This tiny parasite may be found in the lungs of cats in rural areas. Severely affected animals may have a dry cough.	A vet can prescribe drugs to treat the lungworm parasite.

LUNGWORM

The most common lung parasite that can infect cats is the lungworm. The signs of infection are usually mild, and most cats show no symptoms at all. A few, however, may develop a persistent dry cough. The lungworm life cycle is complicated, since it involves a snail or slug, as well as a rodent or bird, before it matures into an adult in a cat. An infected cat can often cough up parasites and get rid of them, but drugs are also available. In parts of North America tiny lung flukes can also infest cats.

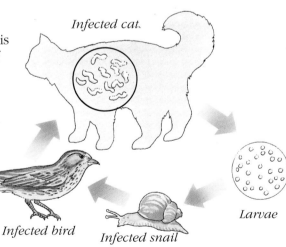

Infected cat.

Larvae

Infected bird *Infected snail*

Lungworm life cycle (above)
Larvae are eaten by a snail or slug, which, in turn, is swallowed by a bird or rodent. When this host is eaten by a cat the cycle is completed.

CAT FLU

The term "cat flu" is misleading, since there are several different viruses known by this name. Cats should be vaccinated against the main two feline respiratory viruses, Feline Calici Virus and Feline Viral Rhinotracheitis. However, other viruses exist for which there is no vaccine. The signs of all these infections are similar. An infected cat will have a runny nose and eyes, and may be sneezing or coughing. Cat flu can be serious, so it is best to consult a vet if your cat is showing any signs of illness. Telephone the clinic first, so that any necessary precautions can be taken to prevent the infection from spreading to other cats.

DIGESTIVE DISORDERS

Nutrients are broken down and used in a variety of ways to make a cat function properly. The digestive system is the center of this mechanism, converting food eaten by a cat to energy. The most common problems affecting the digestive system are vomiting, diarrhea, constipation, and appetite and weight loss. A cat may stop eating because it feels ill or has difficulty swallowing. Or it may eat too much, for a variety of reasons. Food may be vomited immediately after eating or only partly digested. A cat may show signs of excessive thirst or of constipation or diarrhea. Watch the symptoms carefully, since such health problems may require immediate medical attention.

Careful feeding
This is a cat's best protection against major diseases.

THE DIGESTIVE SYSTEM

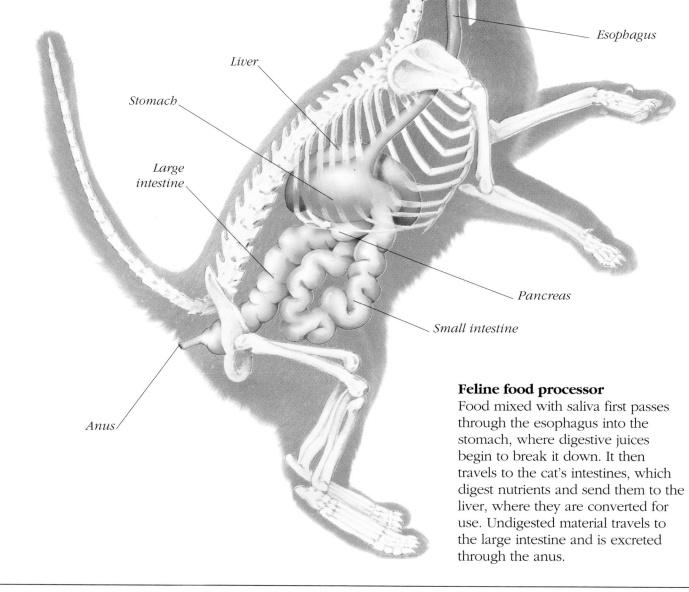

Liver

Stomach

Large intestine

Anus

Mouth

Esophagus

Pancreas

Small intestine

Feline food processor
Food mixed with saliva first passes through the esophagus into the stomach, where digestive juices begin to break it down. It then travels to the cat's intestines, which digest nutrients and send them to the liver, where they are converted for use. Undigested material travels to the large intestine and is excreted through the anus.

DIGESTIVE DISORDERS

Disorder	Description and signs	Action
Feline Infectious Enteritis (FIE), also known as Feline Panleukopenia	This widespread viral disease is highly contagious. It is spread by direct or indirect contact with an infected cat. FIE develops rapidly, so that in severe cases young kittens may die before a diagnosis can be made. The virus attacks the gut and the white blood cells. The main signs are depression, loss of appetite, and persistent vomiting, and diarrhea.	Vaccination is effective in protecting a cat against FIE infection (see page 173). Early diagnosis and isolation of an infected cat is important to stop the disease from spreading. Careful nursing is essential to prevent dehydration.
Feline Infectious Peritonitis (FIP)	This virus primarily causes an infection of the abdominal cavity, but it also affects the liver, kidneys, nervous system, and brain. FIP mainly attacks cats under three years of age; older cats are more resistant. The main signs are loss of appetite, fever, weight loss, and a swollen abdomen.	Consult your vet on the availability of a vaccine. An infected cat must be isolated to prevent the disease from spreading to other cats. Treatment is not usually effective.
Vomiting	It is normal for a healthy cat to vomit occasionally, for example after eating grass or when getting rid of hairballs. Severe vomiting, abdominal pain, and excessive thirst indicate a serious digestive disorder that may be caused by a cat ingesting an irritant or contaminated food.	Vomiting or regurgitation of food may be due to several reasons. Consult a vet if the vomiting is severe or if it persists for more than 24 hours.
Diarrhea	Mild diarrhea may be caused by stress or a change in diet, but if the symptoms persist it may suggest a bacterial or viral infection. Diarrhea accompanied by vomiting or blood in the feces is a sign of a serious disorder.	Consult a vet if the diarrhea persists for longer than 24 hours or if there is any blood in the feces. Do not allow the cat to become dehydrated.
Liver disease	The liver may be damaged as a result of a viral disease or ingesting a poison. Signs of liver malfunction may include vomiting, diarrhea, excessive thirst, and abdominal pain.	Consult a vet immediately. Diagnosis can be aided by analysis of blood, urine, and fecal samples.
Diabetes	This condition is due to the inadequate production of insulin by the pancreas. Early signs are frequent urination, excessive thirst, increased appetite, and unexplained weight loss.	Treatment involves careful dietary control and, in some cases, daily injections of insulin.
Dietary sensitivity	Some oriental cats are unable to digest the sugar in milk, and this may cause diarrhea and vomiting. Other foods that may cause allergic reactions include fish and eggs.	A full veterinary examination is required to determine the cause of the sensitivity when it is not known.
Constipation	A cat should have a bowel movement at least once a day. Elderly cats, particularly longhaired types, are the most likely to suffer from a blockage in the bowel due to constipation.	Treat the cat with liquid paraffin by mouth. If there is no movement after two days, seek veterinary treatment.

DIARRHEA AND VOMITING

Cats vomit fairly readily as a means of protecting themselves against harmful substances. Anything more than occasional vomiting should be investigated by a vet, since it may indicate a serious problem. Diarrhea can be very debilitating and requires prompt veterinary attention, especially if the cat is vomiting or if blood is present. If not treated, severe diarrhea and vomiting can lead to collapse and even death through rapid dehydration. Such symptoms may be due to poisoning or Feline Infectious Enteritis, both of which need immediate veterinary treatment.

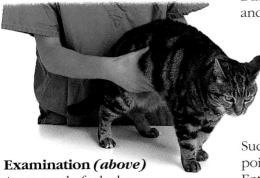

Examination (above)
A vet gently feels the abdomen for signs of swelling.

REFUSING TO EAT

Tempting a sick cat to eat is a delicate task. Try warming small amounts of a favorite food to body temperature and feeding several times daily.

Appetite loss (above)
Always consult a vet if a cat refuses food for more than 24 hours.

INTERNAL PARASITES

Parasites do not cause a cat much discomfort except when they are present in large numbers, but your cat is better off without them. The most common feline parasites are the worms that infest the intestinal tract, but there are also flukes, lungworms, heartworms, and protozoan organisms such as *Toxoplasma (see page 245)*.

Many parasites spend their immature stages in another host, such as a rodent, flea, or bird, which must be eaten by a cat in order for the parasite to complete its life cycle.

Young cats are most at risk from parasitic infections, so it is essential to worm kittens from as early as four weeks old.

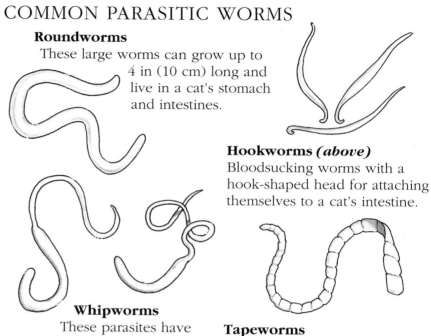

COMMON PARASITIC WORMS

Roundworms
These large worms can grow up to 4 in (10 cm) long and live in a cat's stomach and intestines.

Hookworms (*above*)
Bloodsucking worms with a hook-shaped head for attaching themselves to a cat's intestine.

Whipworms
These parasites have the appearance of a whip and live in the large intestine.

Tapeworms
Flat, segmented worms that attach themselves to a cat's intestine.

LIFE CYCLES OF COMMON PARASITES

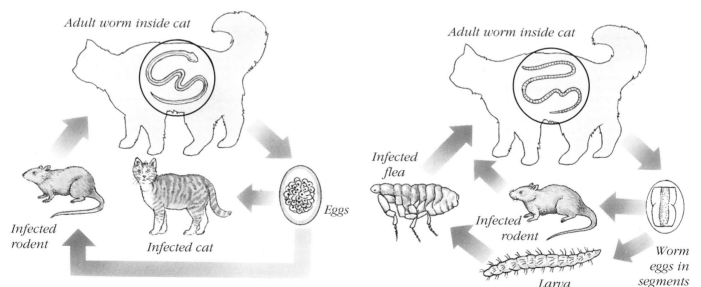

Adult worm inside cat

Infected rodent

Infected cat

Eggs

Adult worm inside cat

Infected flea

Infected rodent

Larva

Worm eggs in segments

The roundworm life cycle
The adult worm lives in the cat's intestinal tract. It lays eggs that pass in the cat's feces, and the eggs may then be eaten by a rodent. Cats are infected by direct contact with the eggs, perhaps while grooming, or by eating a secondary host.

The tapeworm life cycle
The adult tapeworm sheds segments full of eggs, which pass in the feces. The eggs may then be eaten by a rodent or bird, and develop into larvae. The life cycle is completed when this host is eaten by a cat. Larvae can also be transmitted by fleas.

INTERNAL PARASITES

Parasite	Description and signs	Action
Roundworms	Roundworms live in the stomach and intestines and feed on digested food in a cat's gut. An adult cat may show no signs of having worms, but occasionally mature worms may be passed, or eggs may be detectable in the feces. Kittens can be infected via their mother's milk and become seriously weakened. Symptoms of a severe roundworm infestation include diarrhea, constipation, anemia, a potbellied appearance, and a loss of weight and condition.	Consult a vet, who can advise you on a suitable roundworm treatment. It is important that kittens and pregnant queens should be treated with worming tablets. Cats that hunt should be treated routinely two or three times a year.
Tapeworms	Tapeworms are most often found in adult cats. The worm has a long, segmented body and attaches itself to the intestine wall. The segments containing eggs are passed with the cat's feces, sometimes becoming stuck to the fur under the tail and drying out to resemble grains of rice. The shedding of segments may cause irritation, and the cat will lick its behind.	A vet can prescribe an appropriate tapeworm treatment. Flea control is also essential to prevent reinfection, since fleas can be intermediate hosts for certain species of tapeworm.
Hookworms	Bloodsucking hookworms are found in parts of North America. They live in the small intestine and can be passed to unborn kittens. Signs are diarrhea and weight loss.	A vet can prescribe an appropriate hookworm treatment. Strict hygiene measures are also recommended.
Threadworms and whipworms	Tiny threadworms and whipworms live in the gut and can infect cats in parts of North America and Australia. Signs may include diarrhea, but these worms rarely cause illness.	A vet can prescribe an appropriate worming treatment.
Flukes	Flukes are rarely found in cats, but these flatworms can sometimes infest the small intestine and liver in North America. They are caused by a cat eating infected raw fish. Signs include digestive upsets, and sometimes anemia.	A diagnosis by a vet is required to confirm a fluke infestation. Treatment is not always effective, and preventive measures are very important.
Lungworms	These tiny parasites sometimes infest a cat's lungs and can cause respiratory disease *(see page 229)*.	Consult a vet for treatment with a safe deworming drug.
Heartworms	Cats in some countries are infected by worms that live in the heart *(see page 243)*.	Consult a vet for treatment with a safe deworming drug.

PREVENTING INFESTATION

Discuss a worming program with a vet as soon as you get your cat. Maintaining hygiene standards around the home and keeping your cat free of external parasites, such as fleas, will also reduce the numbers of internal ones. Kittens should be treated from about four weeks old, and if worms and eggs are found in the feces, a course of treatment should be prescribed. Adult cats, particularly those that hunt prey and are allowed to roam freely, should be checked for worms at least twice a year.

Even though it may not be possible to prevent your cat from eating prey, you can reduce the risks of infestation by keeping its indoor environment unhospitable to parasite carriers such as mice and fleas. When you spray or dust your cat with insecticide, treat its bedding as well. Do not use any rodent poisons in the house, since they can be extremely toxic to cats *(see page 287)*.

Worming *(left)*
Try concealing a worming tablet in a small piece of food.

TREATMENT

There are many different worming preparations. It is important to obtain the correct remedy for the type of parasite infesting your cat. Worming medicine may be given in the form of a paste, which can be added to food or given directly by mouth. When giving pills, make sure that your pet swallows them and does not spit them out. Some pills may be only for roundworms, while others may kill a variety of parasites.

Pills for roundworm.   **Pills** for tapeworm.

MOUTH AND TOOTH DISORDERS

The cat's mouth and teeth are adapted to their role of hunting and catching prey, while the tongue is equipped with hooked, abrasive papillae used for grooming. Damage or inflammation to a cat's mouth, teeth, gums, palate, or tongue can make it difficult for it to eat, and it may be unable to groom itself. Eventually, the animal's life is endangered if action is not taken in good time.

Cats do not often get cavities in their teeth, but bacteria and debris may sometimes build up on the tooth surface to form plaque, and when mixed with minerals in the saliva, this hardens into tartar or "calculus". If not treated, gingivitis may result, followed by recession of the gums and the loss of teeth. There are a number of microorganisms, especially those associated with Feline respiratory disease or "cat flu" *(see page 229)*, that cause mouth ulcers. Occasionally, objects such as fish bones can become lodged in the mouth and need to be removed *(see page 284)*.

Carnivore
Although a cat's teeth are not very prone to decay, they benefit from regular cleaning. This is especially the case with older cats.

THE CAT'S TEETH

Feline fangs
Adult cats have 30 teeth, shaped for cutting and tearing meat, rather than for grinding or chewing. The carnassial teeth are adapted for slicing through flesh. A kitten gets its milk teeth at about 14 days old, and loses these to adult teeth at four to six months old.

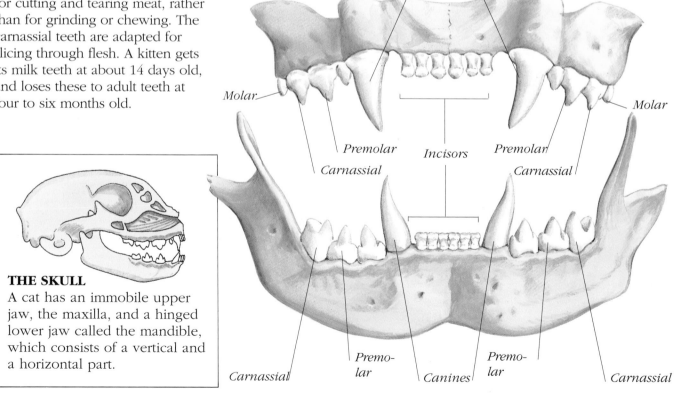

Canines

Molar

Premolar

Carnassial

Incisors

Premolar

Carnassial

Molar

THE SKULL
A cat has an immobile upper jaw, the maxilla, and a hinged lower jaw called the mandible, which consists of a vertical and a horizontal part.

Carnassial

Premolar

Canines

Premolar

Carnassial

MOUTH AND TOOTH DISORDERS

Disorder	Description and signs	Action
Cleft palate	Kittens are sometimes born with the two sides of the hard palate at the roof of the mouth not properly joined. Affected kittens will not be able to suckle milk properly.	Surgery to repair the hard palate may sometimes be possible.
Dental problems	Dental problems are common in older cats. The deposition of plaque on the tooth surface leads to brownish-yellow tartar ("calculus") forming on the teeth. This results in food being trapped, which causes inflammation of the gums (gingivitis). If the infection invades the tooth socket (periodontitis), the tooth will become loose or an abscess may form. A cat with dental problems may have bad breath and it may experience difficulty in eating and paw at its mouth.	Regular brushing of your cat's teeth with a toothbrush helps prevent the build-up of plaque. If there is extensive tartar or a cat is very uncooperative, a vet can descale the teeth using an ultrasonic scaler under an anaesthetic.
Gingivitis	An inflammation of a cat's gums is the first sign of dental problems and is usually associated with a buildup of tartar on the teeth. Gingivitis may start as a dark red line bordering the teeth, but if it is left untreated the gums will become sore and ulceration may occur. A cat with gum disease may have bad breath, drool, and experience difficulty in chewing food.	Consult a vet if you notice any redness around a cat's mouth and gums. Regular brushing of a cat's teeth will help to keep the gums healthy.
Mouth infection	Stomatitis is an inflammation of the mouth lining. It may result from a foreign body in the mouth, a viral disease, or dental problems. An affected cat will have difficulty in eating and the inside of the mouth will appear reddened.	Treatment depends on the cause of the infection. A vet will be able to identify the underlying cause.
"Rodent ulcer"	A "rodent ulcer" is a slowly enlarging sore or swelling on a cat's upper lip.	Consult a vet for treatment. "Rodent ulcers" tend to recur if the treatment is stopped too soon.
Salivary cyst	If the salivary glands or ducts that carry the saliva to the mouth become blocked, this can result in the formation of a salivary cyst (ranula) under the tongue.	Prompt veterinary treatment to drain the cyst is required since the cat will be unable to eat.
Mouth ulcers	Ulcers on a cat's tongue and gums are sometimes caused by Feline respiratory disease *(see page 229)* or kidney disease.	Consult a vet for an examination to determine the underlying cause.

GUM DISEASE

An inflammation of the gums is known as gingivitis. This is most commonly associated with an accumulation of tartar or "calculus" on the teeth, but can also indicate an internal disease if it is very severe. Health problems such as kidney disease *(see page 239)* and Feline Immuno Deficiency Virus *(see page 243)* and are often associated with inflammation of the gums. When an infection becomes established, the gums will recede and in time the teeth

Gingivitis (above)
A dark red line along the gums is a sign of infection.

will become loose in their sockets. Occasionally, a cat may have bad breath without any visible changes in its mouth. All clinical signs must be investigated by a vet, since they can lead to your cat losing its teeth or being unable to eat. Gum disease may be prevented by feeding your cat a sensible diet. A cat fed on soft food alone is especially prone to dental problems. Meat chunks or dry food in the diet will provide a cat with something to chew on and help remove debris.

CLEANING TEETH

Tartar buildup can be retarded by cleaning a cat's teeth regularly. You may need someone to hold the cat steady while you brush its teeth using a special toothpaste or a weak saline solution *(see page 189)*.

Brushing (above)
While the upper lip is held back, the back teeth can be brushed.

REPRODUCTIVE DISORDERS

Since a large number of male and female cats are neutered *(see pages 274–275)*, problems with the reproductive system are fairly uncommon. Most intact cats are very fertile and experience no difficulty in producing offspring, but there are disorders that can prevent queens from conceiving, or males from producing sperm.

There is no equivalent of the human menopause in cats. Reproductive activity does slow down as they grow older, but they can still reproduce and give birth at an advanced age.

Tumors of the testes are rare, but mammary tumors are fairly common. They usually occur after the cat is ten years old and need urgent attention. There is no evidence that having a litter of kittens before being neutered is good for a queen. Neutering will prevent the development of tumors if carried out before one year of age. Males with one or both testicles undescended are best castrated, since the condition is inherited.

Ultrasound scans
Ultrasound scans can be used to help monitor pregnancy in cats, just as in humans.

THE REPRODUCTIVE ORGANS

The male
The testes produce sperm that travel down the spermatic cord to the urethra. The penis is equipped with spines that trigger ovulation.

The female (below)
The female cat comes into heat, or "estrus", when the brain signals the pituitary gland to release a hormone that causes the ovaries to produce eggs. Another hormone causes behavioral changes, such as "calling" *(see page 264)*.

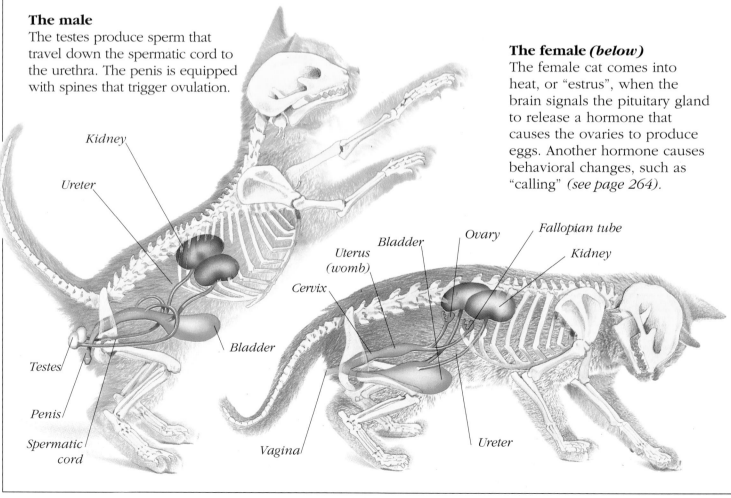

Kidney

Ureter

Testes

Penis

Spermatic cord

Bladder

Uterus (womb)

Cervix

Bladder

Ovary

Fallopian tube

Kidney

Vagina

Ureter

REPRODUCTIVE DISORDERS

Disorder	Description and signs	Action
Female infertility	If a female cat fails to conceive after mating, this may be due to a number of factors. The queen may be suffering from a nutritional deficiency (such as lack of vitamin A) or she may have been mated at the wrong time.	A proper diagnosis of the cause of infertility can only be made after a thorough veterinary examination.
Male infertility	Infertility is very rare in male cats, but it may be due to an infection of the male reproductive organs or an inherited problem. Although a male cat with one undescended testicle (monorchid) can still be fertile, a cat with both testicles undescended (cryptorchid) will probably be sterile.	A proper diagnosis of the cause of infertility can only be made after a thorough veterinary examination. Do not breed from a monorchid cat, since the condition is inherited.
Ovarian cysts	A queen that is not mated may develop ovarian cysts. These cysts produce large quantities of the female sex hormone, which causes frequent or continuous heat periods.	Consult a vet if a queen has abnormal heat cycles.
Abortion and resorption	Miscarriage may be brought on by stress, trauma, an infection, or a fetal abnormality. Signs of miscarriage include bleeding and discharge from the vulva, and the onset of premature labor. Developing kittens less than seven weeks old may sometimes be absorbed from the uterus.	If you notice any unusual signs that may indicate a premature birth, you should contact a vet immediately.
Queening problems	Most cats have no difficulty in giving birth, but occasionally a queen may require assistance (see pages 294-295).	Consult a vet immediately if a cat appears distressed during queening.
Metritis	The uterus can become infected following a difficult birth, particularly if a queen is elderly. Signs may include abdominal pain and a bloody discharge from the vulva.	Consult a vet immediately if there are any abnormal signs following queening.
Pyometra	An accumulation of fluid in the uterus is most common in aging queens. Signs include loss of appetite, high fever, depression, and a vulval discharge.	Consult a vet immediately. An affected cat will need to be spayed.
Mastitis	Mastitis is an inflammation of the mammary glands. The glands appear reddened and swollen, and the kittens are unable to suckle and may show signs of hunger or weakness.	Consult a vet immediately. In severe cases, the kittens may need to be reared by a foster mother or by hand.

FEMALE REPRODUCTIVE PROBLEMS

While a spayed cat will not be affected, an unneutered female cat may suffer from several disorders of the reproductive tract. Pyometra is due to a degeneration of the uterus, occurring as the queen gets older. Cysts develop in the uterus, causing inflammation and the womb to fill up with fluid. The condition can result in toxemia and death if not treated. Immediately after giving birth, a queen may suffer a prolapse of the uterus, when the womb is pushed outside the body. If this happens, contact a vet immediately, since the condition can lead to severe shock and death. Other health problems associated with the female reproductive system include ovarian cysts, infertility, miscarriage, and problems with queening (see pages 294-295).

Birth problems (left)
Seeking veterinary help sooner rather than later is the rule for kittening.

NURSING PROBLEMS

Several disorders can prevent a queen from producing milk. Mastitis causes a swelling of the mammary glands. Lactational tetany ("milk fever") results from a fall in the calcium in the blood.

Perfect mother (above)
Most queens are excellent mothers and will suckle orphan kittens.

URINARY DISORDERS

Problems that affect a cat's urinary system warrant urgent veterinary investigation, since such disorders can be serious and life-threatening. If your cat strains when passing urine, or cannot pass any at all, you should contact a vet at once. A cat's urine is fairly clear or pale yellow, and if it becomes cloudy or colored, this may indicate a bladder infection or even the start of kidney disease. Excessive thirst and frequent urination can sometimes be a sign of diabetes or liver disease, while incontinence may often be associated with a hormonal imbalance, or a spinal injury. To prevent urinary problems, make sure water is always available, and do not feed a cat only on dry food, since too little fluid can lead to a urinary obstruction.

Drinking too much
If your cat is drinking to excess or passing more urine than usual it must be examined by a vet without delay, since this may be a sign of kidney disease.

THE URINARY SYSTEM

Urination
The urinary system is responsible for keeping optimum levels of useful chemicals in the blood and eliminating toxic ones. Waste material is filtered through the kidneys and released as urine down the ureters to the bladder. The urine then passes through the urethra and out of the body.

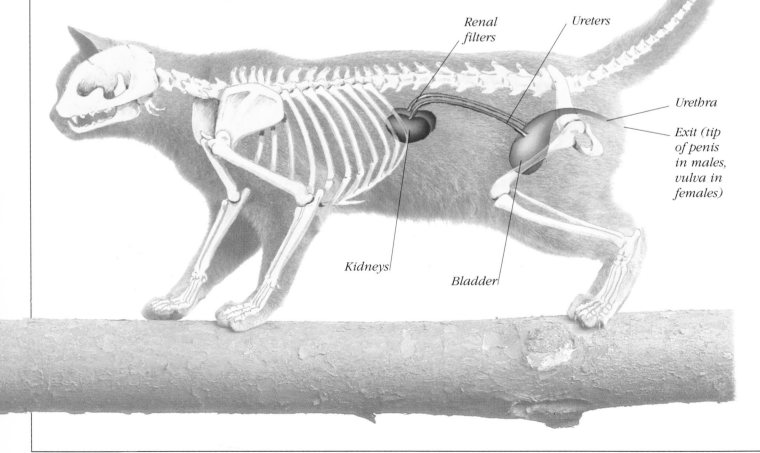

Renal filters

Ureters

Urethra

Exit (tip of penis in males, vulva in females)

Kidneys

Bladder

URINARY DISORDERS

Disorder	Description and signs	Action
Chronic kidney disease	This is the most common disorder that affects elderly cats. The gradual deterioration of the functioning of the kidneys makes it difficult for a cat to eliminate waste products from its body. An affected cat may start to urinate more frequently and will have an increased thirst. Other common signs of kidney disease are weight loss, bad breath, and mouth ulcers.	Consult a vet, who will be able to make a proper diagnosis after taking a sample of blood. Careful dietary management is essential in order to compensate for kidney damage.
Acute kidney disease	Acute kidney disease is not as common as the chronic form and usually affects younger cats. It may be caused by bacterial or viral infection, or as the result of a cat swallowing a toxic substance. The signs are vomiting and loss of appetite, severe depression, and dehydration.	Consult a vet immediately, who will try to combat the toxin if the disease is caused by poisoning. Fluids need to be given to combat dehydration.
Urinary obstruction or Feline Urological Syndrome (FUS)	Minute crystals or a sandy sludge can sometimes cause a blockage of the bladder if they build up to plug the urethra. This particularly affects neutered male cats because the urethra of the female cat is relatively wide. A cat with urinary problems will strain to pass a little bloodstained urine and, in severe cases, it may not be able to pass any water at all. The bladder may be distended and the abdomen tense and painful to the touch. This condition causes an affected cat a great deal of pain and distress.	Urgent veterinary treatment is required to relieve a bladder obstruction. Left untreated, a cat may die in two days. Careful dietary control is needed to ensure that a cat has a high water intake. A cat should not ingest excessive amounts of magnesium, since this produces an acid urine.
Cystitis	An inflammation of the bladder is most commonly caused by a bacterial infection or may be associated with FUS (see above). In Australia, cystitis can be caused by a bladder worm. Signs include frequent urination accompanied by straining and an increased thirst. The urine may be blood-stained and the cat may persistently lick its rear end.	Consult a vet immediately in order to ensure that the condition does not worsen – if this happens, the bladder may become blocked.
Incontinence	Frequent or constant urination due to a loss of voluntary control may be due to old age, injury, or an infection of the bladder. This is not the same as urine marking or spraying, which is territorial behavior.	If there are any other signs, such as straining, consult a vet immediately. Do not limit the cat's water intake.

URINARY INFECTIONS

An inflammation of the bladder, known as cystitis, may be due to a bacterial infection and can be treated successfully if it is detected early. The symptoms of infection are frequent urination with some discomfort, straining, and constant licking under the tail. Cystitis can affect both sexes, but it is mainly toms and young neutered males that suffer from the more serious Feline Urological Syndrome. If a cat does not drink enough water, or is fed only dry food, the urine may become too concentrated and the salts in it form a sandy deposit or stones, which block the urethra, the narrow passage to the outside.

The cat then experiences difficulty and pain when urinating. FUS is not usually found in females. It is a condition that requires emergency veterinary treatment.

Straining *(below)*
A cat should show no signs of discomfort when passing urine.

KIDNEY PROBLEMS

The kidneys are often the first organs to show signs of aging, deteriorating gradually *(see page 258)*. Without treatment the cat's condition may worsen, until the kidneys produce little urine, resulting in a build-up of toxic material inside the cat, which can be fatal. Urgent medical treatment is needed before the condition becomes irreversible. However, if the symptoms are recognized early enough, the cat may be treated successfully and go on to enjoy a long and normal life. Apart from deterioration through old age, kidney failure can also occur as the result of an injury, or following a serious disease, such as Feline Infectious Peritonitis *(see page 231)*.

NERVOUS DISORDERS

The grace, coordination, and agility of cats require a highly sophisticated system of nervous control. The intricate network of nerves runs without mishap for most of the time, but if a problem does occur, it tends to be of a serious nature. Although relatively rare, cats are occasionally subject to fits and seizures. These may be due to several causes, including brain tumor, poisoning, or an inherited epileptic condition. However, the most common cause of nervous problems is physical damage as a result of road traffic accidents. An inflammation of the brain or spinal cord can be associated with some infectious diseases. Paralysis of a limb can result if the spinal cord or the nerves supplying that part of the body are damaged in an accident. If the nerves do not heal, the paralysis may be permanent.

Poisoning
If a feline eats a rat or mouse killed with poison, it may become very ill, since the substance often attacks the nervous system.

THE CENTRAL NERVOUS SYSTEM

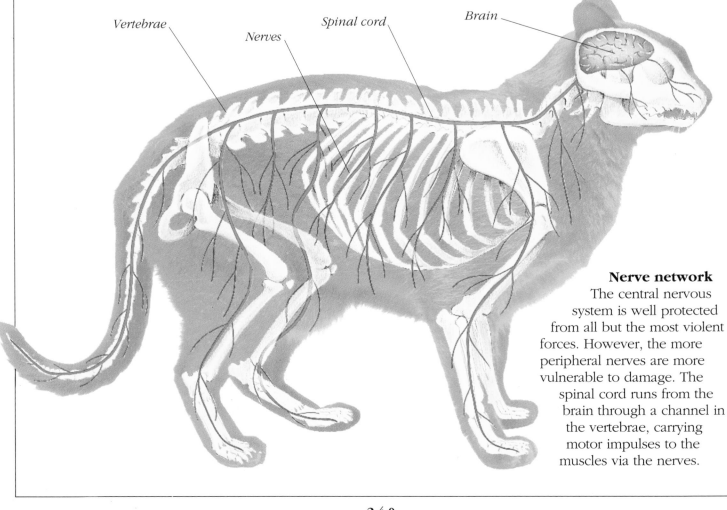

Vertebrae

Nerves

Spinal cord

Brain

Nerve network
The central nervous system is well protected from all but the most violent forces. However, the more peripheral nerves are more vulnerable to damage. The spinal cord runs from the brain through a channel in the vertebrae, carrying motor impulses to the muscles via the nerves.

NERVOUS DISORDERS

Disorder	Description and signs	Action
Brain damage	Severe trauma to the brain is most often due to a road traffic accident or fall and is usually fatal. Strokes are very rare in cats. They are due to a blood clot forming in a vessel to the brain and often result in a loss of functioning of one part of the body. Brain damage can also be caused by a tumor or a congenital defect, or by the spread of a bacterial infection from another part of the body.	Urgent veterinary treament is essential following an accident or fall, especially where head injuries are suspected. Most cats recover from a minor stroke, but they may need treatment for residual problems, such as loss of sight or recurring seizures.
Meningitis	This uncommon nervous disease affects the membrane covering the brain and the spinal cord. It results in fever, dilated pupils, loss of appetite, and convulsions.	Urgent veterinary treatment is required. The vet may take a specimen of the spinal fluid for examination.
Encephalitis	Encephalitis is an inflammation of the brain itself and may be caused by some viruses such as rabies, or bacterial infection. Signs can be variable and include fever, dilated pupils, seizures, and paralysis.	Urgent veterinary treatment is required. The vet will need to establish the cause of the infection.
Seizures	Seizures are relatively rare in cats. They may be connected with brain damage, poisoning, or a vitamin deficiency or may even be inherited. Epileptic episodes may begin when a kitten is about six months old or they may suddenly start following an accident or blow to the head.	Consult a vet immediately. Do not move a convulsing cat. Seizures can sometimes be controlled by anticonvulsant drugs.
Paralysis	The spinal cord and nerves supplying a part of the body may be damaged following an accident, resulting in paralysis of the affected area. This usually happens to a cat's tail or limb. The cat will be unable to bear any weight on the affected limb and may drag it along the ground.	If the nerve is severely damaged and the limb is fractured in an accident, amputation may be necessary. Most cats are able to cope surprisingly well with only three legs.
Feline Dysautonomia (Key-Gaskell Syndrome)	The cause of this rare condition, which affects a cat's nervous system, is unknown. Signs include rapid weight loss, appetite loss, vomiting, regurgitation of food, and pupil dilation.	Urgent veterinary attention is essential if there are to be any prospects of the cat recovering.
Poisoning	There are a number of household substances that are extremely poisonous to a cat should it ingest them. Poisoning may cause signs such as convulsions or muscle tremors.	Seek veterinary attention immediately if you suspect that your cat has been poisoned (see pages 286–287).
Loss of balance	Unsteadiness and lack of coordination when walking may be the result of faulty development, injury, vitamin deficiency, or a disorder of the inner ear (see page 227).	Seek veterinary attention immediately for a thorough examination of the cat.

TESTING REFLEXES

While half the nervous system is concerned with feeling, using the sensory nerves, the other half controls the cat's movement with the motor nerves. Examining a cat's reflexes is the first step in investigating any nervous disorder. A cat's reflexes (see page 279) give an indication of which part of the nervous system is not working normally. A vet may also test the ability of the cat's pupil to contract when a bright light is shone into the eye. A semiconscious cat may be unable to react to stimulus if it is suffering from shock. X-ray examinations and samples of blood or fluid from the spinal cord may also be required if a cat is suffering from any suspected nervous disorder.

If there is no feeling in a limb, or an absence of reflexes, and the cat is unable to control its urine or fecal movements, the prospects for recovery are not very good. However, a cat can recover from some neurological injuries, and an assessment must be carried out by a vet in every case.

Feline Dysautonomia (below)
Permanently dilated pupils are a sign of this rare disease.

BLOOD AND HEART DISORDERS

Disorders of the blood are more prevalent in cats than problems with the heart. Even though the heart is fairly small, it is well adapted to the feline lifestyle, capable of rapidly accelerating from a resting heart rate to one that provides the blood circulation needed for sudden bursts of action. As the heart ages, these periods of activity become less frequent, but it is only when there is advanced deterioration of the heart that the cat gets breathless and reluctant to move at all. Heart disease is not common, but can result from old age or be due to a nutrient deficiency, such as a lack of taurine in the diet, but this only follows gross errors such as feeding a cat exclusively on dog food.

Listening in
Part of any routine examination of a cat's circulatory system includes listening to the heart. A vet can usually assess heart function with a stethoscope, but other, more sophisticated techniques are also available.

THE CIRCULATORY SYSTEM

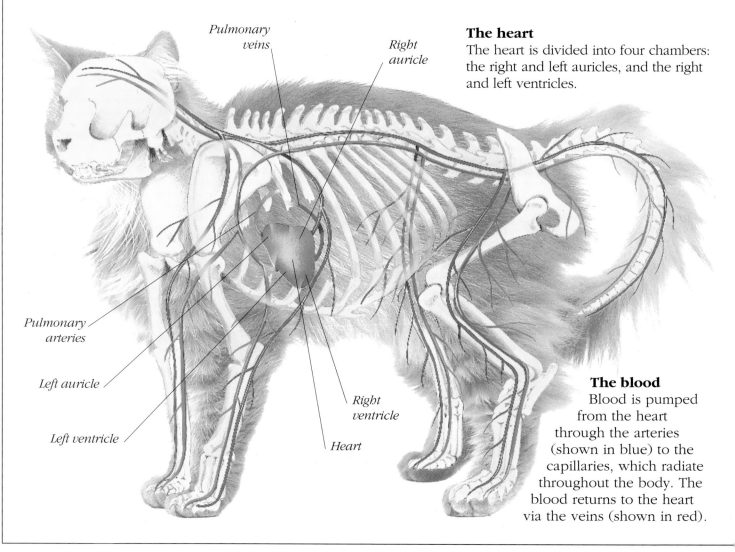

Pulmonary veins

Right auricle

Pulmonary arteries

Left auricle

Left ventricle

Right ventricle

Heart

The heart
The heart is divided into four chambers: the right and left auricles, and the right and left ventricles.

The blood
Blood is pumped from the heart through the arteries (shown in blue) to the capillaries, which radiate throughout the body. The blood returns to the heart via the veins (shown in red).

BLOOD AND HEART DISORDERS

Disorder	Description and signs	Action
Feline Leukemia Virus (FeLV)	FeLV causes cancer of the white blood cells and lymph system. It can only be spread by direct contact with an affected cat and is most common in multicat households. Symptoms of the virus are not very specific but include weight loss, vomiting, diarrhea, labored breathing, and anemia.	There is no effective treatment for FeLV. Blood tests are available to detect the virus. All cats that test positive must be isolated. A vaccine is now available.
Feline Immunodeficiency Virus (FIV)	FIV is similar to the HIV virus that affects humans, but it is specific to cats. The virus suppresses the immune system, making the cat susceptible to infection. It is not transmitted sexually but is spread through the saliva of an infected cat. A cat with FIV may seem slightly ill at first, but it may then develop secondary infections such as anemia *(see below)*.	A blood test is available to diagnose the disease, but there is no treatment or vaccine to combat the FIV virus. Humans cannot catch AIDS from cats.
Anemia	A cat suffering from anemia has a shortage of red blood cells, which reduces the amount of oxygen carried in the blood. Signs of anemia include pallor of the gums, lethargy, weakness, and loss of appetite.	Consult a vet immediately if you notice any signs of anemia. Treatment depends on the cause of the illness.
Feline Infectious Anemia (FIA)	FIA is caused by a small blood parasite that damages red blood cells and causes severe anemia *(see above)*. It is transmitted by bloodsucking parasites such as fleas and ticks.	FIA can be confirmed by a blood test. Treatment involves antibiotics, iron supplements, and blood transfusions.
Heart disease	Kittens may occasionally be born with heart abnormalities – most of them die when they are under one year old. Other problems involve a deterioration of the heart muscle, causing it to become inflamed or damaged (cardiomyopathy). The heart valves may get weaker or become blocked in an elderly cat. Signs of heart disease include heavy breathing, a bluish tinge to the gums, and a tendency to tire easily.	Consult a vet immediately if a cat shows any signs of heart disease. Treatment depends on the heart problem, but drugs can be prescribed for certain conditions.
Thrombosis	This is caused by clotted blood blocking a vessel and cutting off the blood supply. The first sign may be a sudden paralysis of the hind legs, which will feel cold to the touch.	Urgent veterinary treatment is essential. Surgery may sometimes be possible, but the recovery rate is low.
Heartworm	This uncommon feline disease usually occurs only in hot, humid parts of the world. Signs include breathing difficulties, weight loss, and a buildup of fluid in the abdomen.	If detected early, a vet can prescribe drugs to prevent the heartworm larvae from developing into adult worms.

HEARTWORM

In hot, humid countries, the heartworm *(Dirofilaria immitis)* can infest cats, although it more commonly parasitizes dogs. Preventive drugs are given in high-risk areas, but treatment is difficult, since killing the adult worm can cause fatal blockage of a blood vessel. The microscopic larvae, meanwhile, are often difficult to detect in a cat's blood, since they are not very numerous. However they can be prevented from developing into the harmful adult worms with a course of drug treatment.

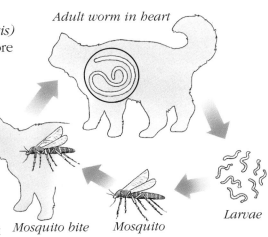

Adult worm in heart

Mosquito bite *Mosquito* *Larvae*

Life of a heartworm (above)
The worm's microscopic offspring are transmitted via a mosquito bite and develop in the heart.

BLOOD TESTING

Infectious anemia is due to tiny organisms that can inhabit the red blood cells and destroy them. A vet can identify these parasites by taking a blood sample. Other serious feline blood disorders are cancer of the white blood cells due to Feline Leukemia Virus, and the suppression of a cat's immune system as a result of Feline Immunodeficiency Virus, a relative of the AIDS virus. There are blood tests available for the detection of these different, lethal viruses and isolation procedures to prevent infection spreading. Consult a vet if any of these conditions is likely.

DISEASES TRANSMISSIBLE TO HUMANS

The infectious diseases that can be passed between humans and other animals are called zoonoses. As far as cats are concerned, however, the risk to humans is small, mainly because cats are very clean animals. In addition, infectious microorganisms tend to thrive only in particular species. For example, swine fever only affects pigs, and the common cold is confined to humans. There are a few diseases that can be passed from animals to humans. The most important feline zoonoses include rabies, toxoplasmosis, and skin irritations. However, the risk of catching any disease from your cat is minimal.

Rabies
Rabies can be passed from wild animals to pets, and then to humans.

RABIES WORLDWIDE

Map of vectors
The map shows the main vectors of rabies in different parts of the world.

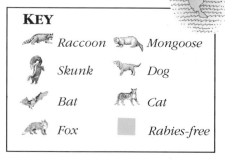

KEY

🦝	Raccoon	🦡	Mongoose
🦨	Skunk	🐕	Dog
🦇	Bat	🐈	Cat
🦊	Fox	▨	Rabies-free

VECTORS OF RABIES

The most serious disease that man can get from animals is rabies. All warm-blooded animals can be victims of rabies, but only a few animals are vectors, or carriers, of the disease. The main vectors are animals such as foxes, wolves, raccoons, skunks, bats, dogs, and mongooses. Only parts of Europe (including Great Britain), Iceland, Japan, Hawaii, the West Indies, Australia, New Zealand, and Antarctica are free of rabies. These countries must take strict quarantine measures to safeguard their status (see page 170).

DISEASES TRANSMISSIBLE TO HUMANS

Disease	Description and signs	Action
Rabies	Rabies is the most dangerous disease that can be passed from animals to humans. It is highly contagious and is transmitted through the saliva of an infected animal. There are three stages to the disease. The first stage is marked by a change in behavior. A normally friendly cat may become nervous and try to hide itself away. The cat may become increasingly aggressive and excited in the second stage, and may try to bite and scratch anyone who approaches it. The final stage is paralysis and coma, which ends in death.	There is no known treatment for rabies once the cat (or human) is showing clinical signs of the disease. Routine preventive vaccination is required by law in some parts of the United States where rabies is present. A cat suspected of having rabies must be isolated and immediate veterinary treatment should be sought.
Bacterial enteritis	A cat may occasionally eat contaminated or badly cooked meat containing bacteria and suffer from enteritis (inflammation of the intestine). *Salmonella* bacteria are a rare cause of enteritis but can be transmitted to humans. Signs of infection are fever, vomiting and diarrhea, and excessive drinking to replace lost fluids.	Consult a vet if vomiting or diarrhea are severe or persist. The cat may require antibiotics to treat the bacterial infection. Good hygiene is essential, as an affected cat may be a potential human health risk.
Tuberculosis	Tuberculosis can infect cats and other domestic animals as well as man, but it is now uncommon in most countries. The disease is usually transmitted by a cat drinking infected milk, but it can also be passed on by owners to their pets. The lungs and abdomen are the main body systems affected. Signs include fever and severe loss of condition.	Treatment of an infected cat may be possible but the public health risks have to be considered.
Toxoplasmosis	This common disease is caused by a microscopic intestinal parasite that can infect many species of animal and can be transmitted to humans. A cat becomes infected by eating contaminated prey or raw meat. Most infected cats show no signs of illness, but signs of a severe infection may include fever, loss of appetite, weight loss, and breathing difficulties. Humans may be infected from handling contaminated cat feces or, more likely, from handling infected raw meat.	The disease can be controlled by preventing a cat from scavenging and by cooking raw meat thoroughly before feeding the cat. Pregnant women are at risk and should avoid handling soiled litter. Blood tests are available to screen those at risk.
Skin problems	Ringworm is a common fungal skin infection *(see page 221)* that is contagious to humans and other animals. It causes small, round, bald patches on a cat's head and ears and circular red patches on a human's arms and legs. Fleas, lice, and fur mites may sometimes bite humans and cause skin reactions, such as itchiness and red blotches.	Prompt veterinary treatment and disinfection of bedding and grooming equipment is advisable if your cat has ringworm. Fleas and other parasites can be controlled by treatment of animals and their environment.

TOXOPLASMOSIS

Cats are sometimes carriers of the microscopic *Toxoplasma* parasite that can also infect humans. A cat is infected by eating contaminated raw meat, and cysts are then shed in the animal's feces. The risks to humans are greatest from handling infected, raw meat. Most infections are harmless, but pregnant women are particularly at risk, since the disease may cause abnormalities in the unborn child. Although cats are very careful about burying their droppings, sensible hygiene precautions should be followed when handling soiled cat litter.

BITES AND SCRATCHES

Few cats are aggressive towards humans without provocation. Many of the bites and scratches humans experience are related to clumsy handling or action that is frightening to the cat *(see pages 160-161)*. A cat's mouth contains bacteria and a bite can become infected if it is not cleaned and treated with antiseptic. If a cat bite becomes swollen or painful, you should seek medical attention. Cat scratches can also introduce infection, and even fever (known as cat-scratch fever), and should always be washed carefully.

Teeth and claws (above)
When provoked, a cat can use its teeth and claws to defend itself.

Chapter 7
NURSING

CATS THAT are sick or injured, and those recovering after a surgical operation, need careful observation, loving support and attention, and a degree of privacy. Try to create a quiet, clean, comfortable area as the feline sick room. Keep a medicine chest well stocked with essential items such as a thermometer, syringe, and dosing gun ready in case of illness. Sick cats may need to be tempted to eat a few nourishing morsels to keep their strength up. You should administer medicines in a gentle but firm way, so that you cause the sick cat the least possible distress. Consult the vet about any special nursing or feeding requirements for your cat's condition.

RESTRAINING A CAT

Most cats are not difficult to handle and restrain, but they do have to be taken in their own time with a kindly and gentle approach. Your aim should always be less rather than more restraint. It is unwise for untrained people to attempt to restrain a cat that is not used to being handled; feral cats and most farm cats are particularly resistant to being held. A lively pet may need to be restrained when being examined by a vet.

The methods of firm restraint shown on these pages should only be carried out to control a difficult cat. It is important not to use any unnecessary force, since this will frighten the cat and could even cause it injury. You may find it easiest to wrap an uncooperative cat in a towel when administering medicines at home. It is now possible to buy "masks" and bags to use at home with an unruly cat. Talk calmly and confidently to the cat while it is being examined, in order to reassure it.

HOLDING A CAT FOR EXAMINATION

Examining the head
A veterinary technician restrains the cat by holding its fore legs gently but firmly. Her forearms hold down the cat's body, allowing the vet to examine its head.

Examining the body
A calm cat is easily restrained by holding the shoulders while the skin and coat are examined by the vet.

RESTRAINING A DIFFICULT CAT

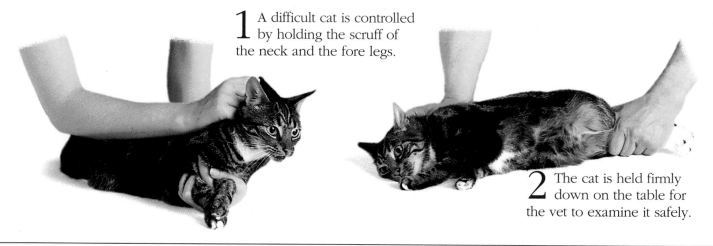

1 A difficult cat is controlled by holding the scruff of the neck and the fore legs.

2 The cat is held firmly down on the table for the vet to examine it safely.

WRAPPING A CAT IN A TOWEL

Hold the cat firmly on the towel

1 When maximum restraint is needed a large, thick towel is useful. The cat is held firmly on the towel by the scruff. It is best not to let the cat see the towel beforehand.

The paws must be wrapped in the towel

2 The cat is wrapped quickly in the towel, keeping hold of the scruff all the time.

3 A towel wrapped firmly around the cat prevents the cat from scratching when being treated or examined.

SCRUFFING A CAT

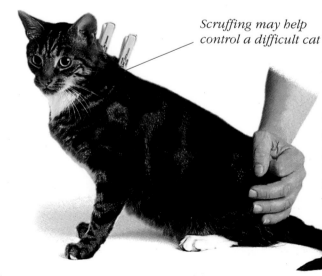

Scruffing may help control a difficult cat

Clothes pegs
One or two broad-ended clothespins placed on the scruff of the neck can immobilize a cat in the same way as lifting it up by the scruff.

HANDLE WITH CARE

Do not attempt to restrain an angry or frightened cat by holding it by the scruff or by using the "clothespin" method unless you are experienced in handling cats. You should never prolong any restraint if it is causing the animal distress. This applies to all methods of handling and restraint.

ADMINISTERING MEDICINE

You may be given some tablets or medication to administer at home after visiting the vet. Getting your cat to take the medicine it needs but does not want requires a gentle but firm approach. It is best if the cat is placed on a table or other raised surface; some cats will need to be restrained by an assistant. If the cat tries to scratch or bite, it should be wrapped in a towel *(see page 249)*. You should not try to hide medicine in food since a cat can usually detect any additions to its food bowl by smell and may refuse to eat.

GIVING A TABLET

Hold the cat's head from above

1 While an assistant holds the cat, gently enclose its head with your fingers. Do not ruffle its whiskers.

3 Place the tablet as far back as possible on the tongue at the back of the cat's mouth.

2 Grasp the head between forefinger and thumb and tip it back. Press lightly on the jaw to open the cat's mouth.

4 Close the cat's mouth and gently stroke the throat to encourage it to swallow the tablet.

GIVING A TABLET ON YOUR OWN

1 If your cat is gentle and docile, you can give it a tablet without any assistance. Grasp the cat's head with one hand and open its mouth with the other.

Tablet

2 Put the tablet on the back of the cat's tongue. Hold the mouth closed until the cat has swallowed, as shown above.

GIVING A TABLET USING A DOSING GUN

Fire the tablet into the cat's mouth

1 An alternative method of giving a tablet is to use a pill or dosing gun, which you can obtain from your vet.

2 Open the cat's mouth as shown opposite and fire the tablet with a little water to the back of the throat. Hold the mouth closed until the cat has swallowed.

GIVING MEDICINE WITH A SYRINGE

Using a plastic syringe, slowly squirt the liquid into the cat's mouth. Administer the medicine slowly so that it does not go down the wrong way.

GIVING AN INJECTION

An injection is the most effective way of administering medicine to a cat, and this is almost always done by a vet. However, when injections are required every day, for instance in the treatment of diseases such as feline diabetes, you may have to carry out this procedure yourself. Your vet will supply you with sterile syringes and discuss the procedure with you.

Draw the medicine into the syringe

1 Hold the cat firmly and make a little "tent" of loose skin at the scruff of the neck.

2 Insert the needle under the skin at the cat's neck, and slowly inject the medication.

TREATING EYES AND EARS

There are several feline eye and ear conditions that require treatment with drops or ointment prescribed by a vet. After consulting your vet you will probably be given a course of medicines to administer at home. (Never try to treat your cat with medicines intended for humans or without getting proper advice.) Your vet will be happy to demonstrate the best way to apply medication to the eyes and ears.

You should administer eye and ear drops quickly and carefully, using the minimum amount of restraint *(see pages 248–249)*. Follow the directions given by the vet and, even if the problem appears to clear up, continue the course of treatment for as long as advised to ensure that the condition does not recur.

APPLYING EYE OINTMENT

1 Hold the cat's head still with one hand. Using the other hand, gently squeeze a line of ointment onto the eyeball. Do not let the tube touch the eye.

2 Close the eyelids and hold closed for a few seconds to allow the ointment to spread over the eye.

APPLYING EYE DROPS

1 Gently clean the area around the eyes, wiping away any discharge from the corners of the eyes with a dampened cotton ball.

2 Holding the cat's head firmly with one hand, apply the required number of eye drops in both eyes.

3 Allow the eyes to bathe in the drops for a few seconds. Gently hold the eyes closed as above.

ADMINISTERING EAR DROPS

Massage the drops into the ears

1 Using a dampened cotton ball, wipe away any dirt from the inside of the ear.

2 Holding the cat's head firmly, fold the outer ear back and administer the required number of drops in both ears.

3 Be careful not to poke the dropper into the cat's ears. Gently massage the ears.

INHERITED EYE AND EAR PROBLEMS

Deaf white cat
Deafness can be associated with the gene that gives a white cat its coat color. It causes a degeneration of the inner ear.

Longhaired cat
Some pedigree longhaired cats are very prone to blocked tear ducts, which result in runny eyes.

Siamese cat
Some Siamese cats suffer from reduced binocular vision or double vision, for which they compensate by squinting. Careful breeding has reduced the number of cats affected.

Abyssinian cat (right)
Certain breeds, such as Abyssinian and Siamese cats, are prone to inherited eye problems.

SURGERY AND AFTERCARE

Most cats will need to undergo surgery under a general anesthetic at some point in their lives. Although modern techniques of surgery have reduced the dangers to a minimum, there is still a small risk involved with any type of operation. A cat makes a good surgical patient; it adapts well to cage rest and it recovers quickly after major operations.

After an operation, a cat needs to be kept warm and quiet, and its behavior should be closely observed. If the cat is restless or has a fractured limb, it may have to be confined to a pen. A cat recovering from an illness may need to be kept indoors.

Convalescence
A cat must be kept quiet and carefully watched for a week or two after an operation. Try to keep it confined to one room and prevent it from biting its stitches or removing its dressing.

SURGICAL OPERATIONS

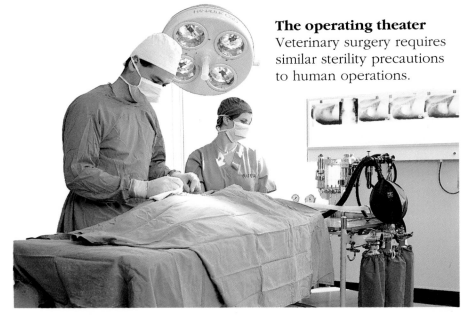

The operating theater
Veterinary surgery requires similar sterility precautions to human operations.

PRE-OPERATIVE CARE

If your cat is to undergo a routine operation, such as neutering or teeth scaling, arrange for it to be done when you have some time to care for your pet. The cat will not be allowed to eat or drink for 12 hours prior to the operation. This may seem hard, but it is important because it reduces the risk of the cat vomiting while under the anesthetic. When you deliver your cat to the clinic or hospital, you can ask when you can telephone to find out about its progress. A cat will usually be allowed to go home the same day.

ANIMAL HOSPITALS

At the animal hospital or veterinary clinic, the cat will be kept in a cage under regular supervision until it has recovered from the anesthetic. When it wakes it will be unsteady on its feet for several hours. You will be allowed to take the cat home only when the vet is satisfied that it is on the mend. The cat may be kept at the veterinary clinic for two or three days for observation following a serious operation.

Cage rest
A cat is usually put in a recovery cage after a surgical operation to allow for close observation and undisturbed rest. Some hospitals have television monitors to help watch over the animals after surgery.

POST-OPERATIVE CARE

Bandages
If a cat has a dressing covering a wound, it may do its utmost to remove it. Cover it with an elastic bandage to keep it in place for as long as possible. Keep a cat confined as directed.

RECOVERY TIMES
Most cats recover from surgical operations very quickly. Stitches may either dissolve within 7–10 days or may need to be removed by the vet. Before surgery, the fur around the site of the operation will have been shaved; this will take several weeks to grow back.

General nursing
A cat recovering from an operation must be kept warm and quiet. Make the cat comfortable by wrapping it in a large towel or blanket or by putting it in a cardboard box.

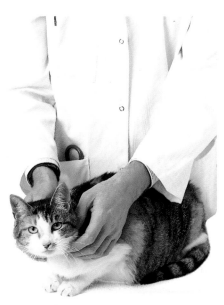

Elizabethan collar
A cat should be prevented from pulling out its stitches. An Elizabethan collar, fitted by a vet, is a simple solution that will prevent a cat from worrying a wound. Consult a vet if you notice any swelling or discharge from the wound site.

Veterinary care
If you notice any change in your cat's condition after an operation, report it immediately to a vet.

ALTERNATIVE MEDICINE

There is a growing interest and awareness in alternatives to established conventional medicine for treating cats and dogs. While homeopathic and herbal approaches can be used to treat certain ailments, you still need to consult a vet to get a proper diagnosis. Some vets even specialize in alternative medicine and can prescribe a suitable treatment for your cat. Alternative medicine cannot cure serious conditions that require surgery, but it can be used to treat many minor disorders and prevent them from recurring. For example, homeopathic creams can be used to help various common feline skin complaints.

Garlic
Garlic is reputed to act as a flea repellent and may increase a cat's resistance to infections.

NURSING A SICK CAT

A sick cat that is recovering from an operation, or that needs to be nursed at home through an illness, requires special care. For the best results, it should be cared for in familiar surroundings by people it knows and trusts. Try to make your sick cat comfortable by keeping it clean, warm, and dry. Your vet will give you instructions if your cat requires a special diet.

KEEPING WARM

The sick room
To make a sick bed for your invalid pet, cut a hole in one side of a large cardboard box. Line it with newspapers, a towel, and a lukewarm hot water bottle. The box should be placed in a quiet corner.

FEEDING A SICK CAT

Loss of appetite
A sick cat often needs to be coaxed to eat. Feed small, frequent meals, warmed to blood heat.

Spoonfeeding
If a cat refuses to eat or drink, try feeding it liquids with a spoon. Allow the cat to swallow after every few drops.

Spoonfeeding medicine
A calm cat can be spoonfed liquid medicines. This can be messy, but try to get as much of the medicine as possible into the cat's mouth.

Forcefeeding
A weak cat can be fed small amounts of liquid food with a dropper or a syringe *(see page 251)*.

GROOMING A SICK CAT

1 Clear any discharge from around the cat's eyes with a cotton ball dampened in clean, warm water. You can apply a little petroleum jelly to any sore places, but do not put it too near the cat's eyes.

2 Gently wipe away any nasal discharge and crusting around the cat's nostrils. The cat will be able to breathe more easily and will feel better with some of its sense of smell restored.

SAFE DISINFECTANTS

Disinfectants containing phenol are poisonous. Use hydrogen peroxide or a profesionally prepared product to clean the sick room.

Gently wipe the cat's mouth

3 Clean up any saliva or vomit from around the cat's mouth. Clean up the cat's behind if there is any diarrhea, and change the bedding if it becomes soiled.

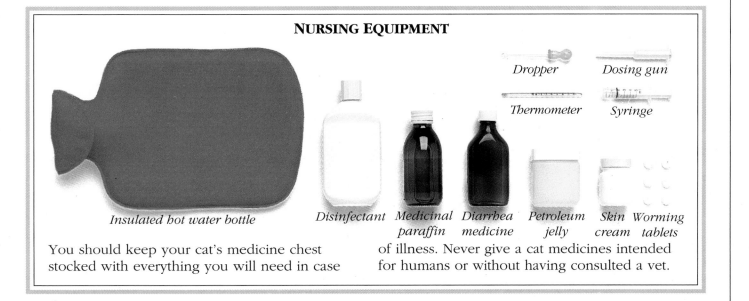

NURSING EQUIPMENT

Dropper   *Dosing gun*

Thermometer   *Syringe*

Insulated hot water bottle   *Disinfectant*   *Medicinal paraffin*   *Diarrhea medicine*   *Petroleum jelly*   *Skin cream*   *Worming tablets*

You should keep your cat's medicine chest stocked with everything you will need in case of illness. Never give a cat medicines intended for humans or without having consulted a vet.

CARING FOR AN ELDERLY CAT

Old age is not a specific disease; it comes to us all. As a cat gets older, the vital organs of its body deteriorate at different rates. Changes in the heart, brain, kidneys, and liver are the most life-threatening. Fortunately, these major organs have reasonable reserves of functional activity; more than half of the kidney function may, for example, be lost without the cat showing any signs of illness. Given plenty of loving care and close veterinary management, many cats with quite advanced kidney failure may lead fairly normal, active lives.

Regular health checkups by a vet can improve the quality of life of an elderly cat. An older cat will generally become less active and spend more time sleeping. Try not to disturb its daily routine and ensure that it has a warm bed that is kept in a cozy spot out of drafts.

SIGNS OF OLD AGE

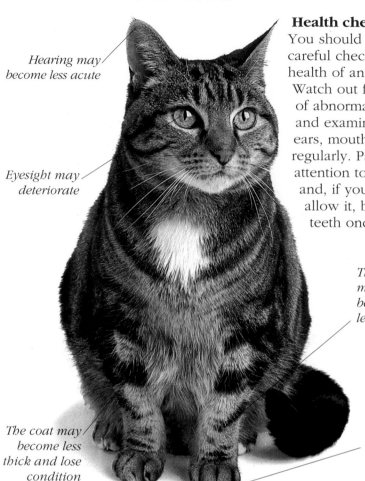

Hearing may become less acute

Eyesight may deteriorate

The coat may become less thick and lose condition

Health checks
You should keep a careful check on the health of an elderly cat. Watch out for any signs of abnormal behavior and examine its eyes, ears, mouth, and coat regularly. Pay particular attention to its mouth and, if your cat will allow it, brush its teeth once a week.

The joints and muscles may become stiff and less supple

The claws may need regular trimming if the cat is inactive

FELINE LIFE SPANS

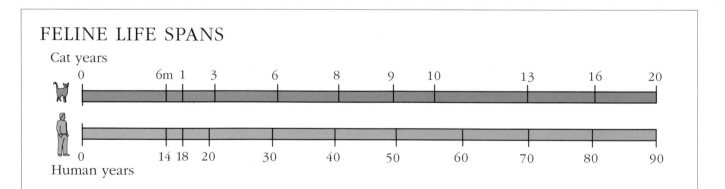

Cat years

| 0 | 6m | 1 | 3 | 6 | 8 | 9 | 10 | 13 | 16 | 20 |

Human years

| 0 | 14 | 18 | 20 | 30 | 40 | 50 | 60 | 70 | 80 | 90 |

Many people believe that cats age about seven years for every human one. In fact, their development accelerates in the early years and slows down in middle age, as shown in the life span chart above. After the age of ten, signs of old age begin to appear and the time scale is more like ours. Cats over 20 years of age can be looked upon as feline centenarians.

SPECIAL CARE

Feeding
Some cats need less food and fewer calories as they age; others may need more due to poor absorption and digestion *(see page 181).*

Weighing
If your cat loses weight while continuing to eat substantial amounts, consult your vet. On the other hand, an older cat that becomes much less active but continues to eat the same amounts of food may become obese.

Constipation
Elderly cats may become constipated. Ask your vet about a commercial feline laxative in order to relieve painful constipation.

Veterinary checkups
Regular checkups become more necessary as your cat starts to show the signs of age. They should be carried out at least every three or four months, or whenever your vet advises.

EUTHANASIA

There may come a time when your cat's life needs to be brought to a peaceful end. Any cat that has an untreatable condition, which is causing it pain or distress, can have its life ended gently and with dignity. Vets usually inject an overdose of an anesthetic into a vein, putting the cat into a deep sleep to a point where the animal will not regain consciousness. Your vet will be able to advise you and help you make the difficult decision if your pet is very sick. You may wish to plant a small rose bush or tree, or make a donation to an animal charity to perpetuate the best memories of your pet.

Pet cemeteries
You can bury your cat in a special pet cemetery.

Chapter 8

BREEDING

THE WORLD would certainly be a better place for cats if only wanted kittens were born. Consider carefully the responsibilities of breeding your cat and decide whether or not neutering is the best course of action. Unless you are active in showing your cat and helping to improve the breed, you should not breed it.

You can show your cat even if it is neutered.

Remember that kittens are demanding and need to be found caring homes. If you decide to breed your cat, advance planning is the best way to avoid problems.

HEREDITY AND BREEDING

Every cat inherits certain physical characteristics from both its parents. These characteristics are determined by genes. They represent a set of instructions that determine the cat's coat color, the length of its coat, and the color of its eyes. For every kitten in a litter, the genes are arranged in a different order, so each individual is genetically unique, no matter how similar it is in appearance.

If you wish to breed a show cat, look for a tomcat with suitable characteristics with which to mate your female.

Mother and kitten
This little kitten has a different coat color from both its parents.

A CAT FAMILY TREE

Determining coat color
Kittens with very different coat colors result from the mating of Chocolate and Blue Burmese cats. One of the kittens is the same color as the mother and one is identical to the father, but four have lighter coats. This is because the male is carrying a gene that dilutes the coat color from a silver-gray (Blue) to a lavender-gray (Lilac).

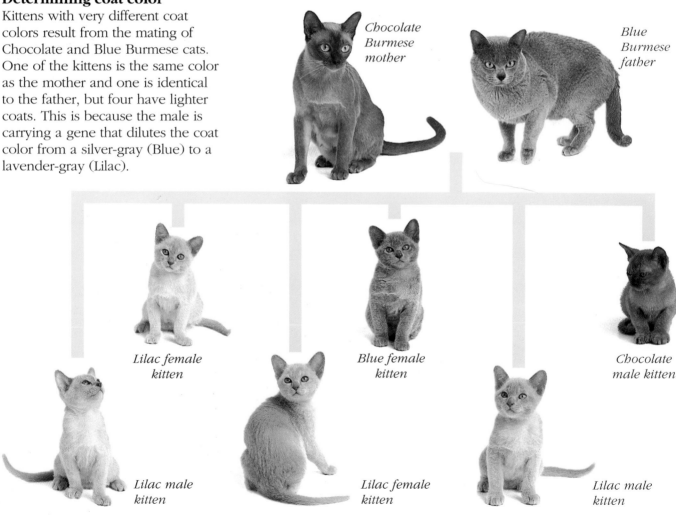

Chocolate Burmese mother

Blue Burmese father

Lilac female kitten

Blue female kitten

Chocolate male kitten

Lilac male kitten

Lilac female kitten

Lilac male kitten

INHERITED CHARACTERISTICS

*A "Stumpy"
Manx has a
residual tail*

Manx cat *(left)*
The Manx cat is a
very old breed, but if
someone applied today
for its official recognition,
this would probably not
be granted. The Manx
carries a gene that causes
the deformity of taillessness,
which is deadly if it is passed
on by both parents. The mating
of two Manx cats usually results
in the kittens dying before or
shortly after birth.

Rex cat *(right)*
Despite their similar
appearances, there
are two distinct
breeds of curly coated
Rex cat, namely the
Devon and the Cornish Rex.
Both breeds are believed to
have developed from
separate mutations.

Tortoiseshell cat *(above)*
The orange gene that results in
a tortoiseshell coat is linked to
the gene that determines the
cat's sex. This means that
nearly all tortoiseshell cats are
female. The very rare male
tortoiseshell is usually sterile.

Rogue genes *(left)*
A few genes that are passed on from
parents to offspring cause deformities.
While some inherited traits, such as a
kitten being born with extra toes
(polydactyly), are relatively
harmless, others, such as
heart defects, are fatal.

Siamese cat
The Siamese is really
a black cat with its coat
color diluted by an albino-
type gene. This is what gives
a Siamese cat its unique, pale-
colored coat with darker
markings on the head, paws,
and tail. Selective breeding has
intensified the coat color, so
that the body is darkest in
the Seal-point Siamese.

PLANNING A LITTER

Breeding your cat is an important decision that must be considered carefully. A female cat is sexually mature from about six months old and a male cat from about ten months. A queen comes into heat in two-week cycles, and each estrus lasts for two to four days. Even if you take proper precautions, an unneutered queen is almost certain to be mated. It is very difficult to confine a female cat in heat, since she will become restless and "call" or howl, attracting every local tom.

CHOOSING A SUITABLE MATE

The stud cat
If you plan to breed from your pedigree queen, you will need to find a suitable stud cat. Make inquiries at local cat shows or through the relevant breed club, which will be able to supply you with a list of reputable breeders.

COURTSHIP AND MATING

The queen may be hostile to the tom at first

1 The queen is taken to the breeder's stud cat when she comes into heat and starts to "call."

MATING A CAT
• Choose a reputable breeder.
• Cats must be vaccinated and free of STD.
• Never mate a cat that is not perfectly fit and healthy.
• Keep your cat indoors after she returns from the stud.

2 When the female begins to show an interest in the tom, the two cats are put together in the same pen. Clip both cats' claws beforehand to prevent injuries in case there is a fight.

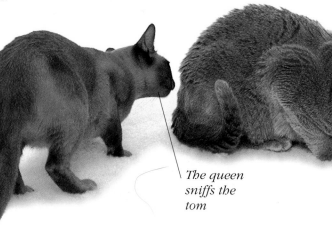

The queen sniffs the tom

3 The queen signals that she is ready for mating by rolling provocatively to attract the tom's attention.

The neck-bite immobilizes the queen

4 As part of the courtship ritual, the female rejects the first advance. The tom retreats but renews his overtures a few moments later.

5 The queen raises her rear and makes a "paddling" movement with her hind legs. As the tom mounts, he grasps her by the scruff.

6 The tom penetrates the queen and ejaculates immediately. The female cat may call out at the moment of penetration. Ovulation is stimulated by the act of mating.

Post-coital behavior
After mating, both cats separate and groom themselves. The whole mating sequence will need to be repeated several times over a period of two to three days to ensure that the queen is pregnant.

PREGNANCY AND PRE-NATAL CARE

If a mating is successsful, the queen will not come into heat as usual two or three weeks later. A pregnant cat shows the first signs of her condition soon after this. Her teats become redder and the surrounding fur may recede slightly. At around three to four weeks, a vet can confirm the pregnancy by gently palpating the cat's abdomen. A healthy cat does not require any special care other than being fed a well-balanced diet. The queen's appetite will increase, and she will gradually put on weight.

SIGNS OF PREGNANCY

The queen will put on about 2–4 lb (1–2 kg)

The teats are prominent

The abdomen is distended

A pregnant queen
A cat is noticeably fatter after the sixth week of pregnancy. Her abdomen becomes rounded and the teats redden and become very prominent.

CARING FOR A PREGNANT CAT

Feeding
A pregnant cat must be fed a nourishing, well-balanced diet, and your vet may also recommend additional feeding during the last weeks. The number of meals should be gradually increased from about the fifth week of pregnancy *(see page 181)*. Consult your vet about dosing your pregnant cat with worming tablets.

Queening box *(above)*
Provide the queen with a warm and comfortable place to give birth. Make a queening box out of a cardboard box, cut down at one side and lined with newspaper.

Active pregnancy
A healthy cat will remain lively throughout the pregnancy. She can be allowed to play with other cats and to jump, and climb, although she may slow down these activities.

A pregnant cat is still interested in playing games

DEVELOPMENT OF THE FETUS

Length of pregnancy
The average length of pregnancy is 65 days, or about nine weeks from the date of the mating. An ultrasound scan can be used six weeks into the pregnancy.

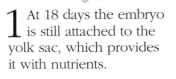

Embryo   *Placenta*

Yolk sac

Umbilical cord

2 At 22 days the embryo's head, eyes, and limbs are developing.

3 At 28 days the fetus is about 1 in (2.5 cm) long and all its internal organs have developed.

4 Between 40–45 days the bones of the skeleton form.

1 At 18 days the embryo is still attached to the yolk sac, which provides it with nutrients.

5 The fetus develops rapidly during the last three weeks before the birth. Kittens born earlier than 58 days do not usually survive. Kittens born later than 70 days are likely to be bigger than normal.

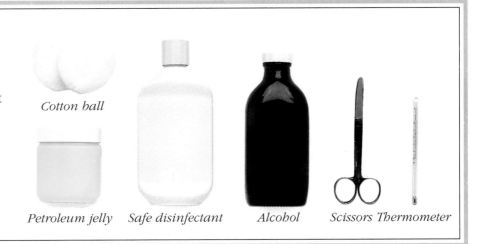

QUEENING EQUIPMENT
Prepare for the kittens' birth by making a queening box and having some essential items to hand. This equipment may be needed if you (or the vet) have to assist with the delivery *(see pages 294–295)*. A thermometer may record a drop in the cat's temperature (about 2°F/1°C) a few hours before kittening.

Cotton ball

Petroleum jelly   *Safe disinfectant*   *Alcohol*   *Scissors Thermometer*

QUEENING

GIVING BIRTH

Keep a careful watch on the queen during the last week of the pregnancy. Make sure that she is accustomed to the queening box and do not allow her to wander off or to hide herself away. The queen's behavior will warn you when the birth is imminent. She may refuse food or vomit before the labor begins. Many kittens are born at night.

1 The queen starts to breathe heavily, pant, or purr, but not in pain. A clear vaginal discharge may be seen. This first stage of labor can last as long as six hours but is usually shorter.

2 The second stage of labour begins when the queen starts "bearing down." Make a note of the time that she starts to strain, and if a kitten is not born within 30 minutes, contact a vet.

The membrane around the kitten can just be seen

3 In an ideal birth, a kitten enclosed in a bubble-like membrane will appear 15–30 minutes later. Most kittens are born headfirst, but some may be born hind legs first.

4 As soon as a kitten is born, the queen licks it to remove the membrane surrounding it and to stimulate its breathing. The third stage of labor is marked by the expulsion of the afterbirth, which the queen may eat.

HELPING AT THE BIRTH

An inexperienced mother cat may require assistance with the queening. If a queen ignores a newborn kitten or a kitten is only partially delivered, you need to take emergency action immediately or the kitten may die *(see pages 294–295)*. Make sure that your vet is on standby when the kittens are due.

5 Usually, the mother cat instinctively knows what to do. She bites through the umbilical cord with her teeth.

WHEN TO CALL THE VET

Most cats do not need any help with queening. Keep interference to a minimum. Contact a vet if the cat is distressed (*see page 294*).

6 Allow the mother cat to lick the kittens immediately. The queen may take a short rest after one or two kittens have been born and resume her straining a few moments later.

A newborn kitten looks for a teat

7 The newborn kittens may need a little help in finding a teat on which to feed. Make sure that the kittens are placed near their mother's abdomen, and encourage them to suckle as soon as possible.

8 An average litter numbers between two and six kittens and the labor may last for several hours. If the queen shows signs of weariness, she can be revived with a little milk or some of her favorite food.

Happy families
Once the queening is complete, leave the mother and kittens to rest. Make sure that the queen is provided with water, food, and a litter box. She may be reluctant to leave her kittens.

POST-NATAL CARE

Newborn kittens are totally dependent on the mother cat. The cat family should be kept in the queening box, in a warm place. Keep a watch on the kittens, particularly if the queen is inexperienced. As long as the mother is healthy, she will do all that is necessary. The queen will require at least three times more food than usual *(see page 181).*

MATERNAL CARE

Each kitten has its own preferred teat

Bonding
Shortly after a kitten is born, the mother cat will gently guide it to a teat, and it will start to suckle. The milk produced by the mother cat in the first few days after queening is called "colostrum" and is packed with nutrients and antibodies that will protect the kittens from infection.

The mother cat washes her kittens frequently

Washing
Once the kittens have finished suckling, the mother cat will wash them all over. The queen licks the kittens' bottoms to stimulate excretion of waste products. She will do this until the kittens start to eat solid food.

Suckling
By kneading its mother's body with its paws, a kitten stimulates the flow of milk. If the kittens are restless and cry a lot, this may be a sign that the queen is not producing enough milk. Consult the vet if you suspect that the kittens are not getting enough milk.

Keeping watch

The mother cat carefully guards her litter and dislikes leaving the kittens too often. If any of the kittens strays from the nest, she retrieves it by carrying it by the scruff of the neck. Do not let children pick up or handle the kittens without supervision. Try not to disturb the mother and offspring any more than is necessary.

A straying kitten is closely watched by its mother

FOSTERING KITTENS

The mother cat will not notice one or two extra mouths to feed

Foster mothers

If the mother cat has died, rejected her litter, or cannot produce milk, you will need to find a foster mother. A new queen with a small litter of her own will accept one or two orphan kittens.

Foster care

If you are raising an orphan by bottle you will need to provide the socialization it would have received from its mother and littermates.

ARTIFICIAL FEEDING

Bottle feeding

It is possible to rear orphan kittens by hand. Start by feeding the kittens every two hours with a cat milk replacer. The kittens must also be kept clean and warm. Ask your vet for guidance.

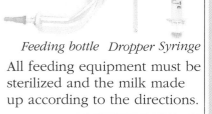

FEEDING EQUIPMENT

Feeding bottle   *Dropper*   *Syringe*

All feeding equipment must be sterilized and the milk made up according to the directions.

EARLY KITTEN CARE

For the first few weeks of their lives, kittens are at their most helpless and need a lot of attention. Up to the age of about three weeks, the mother cat will provide for their physical needs, but you will need to handle and socialize them. The kittens should gradually be weaned off their mother's milk and introduced to solid food. By the age of ten to twelve weeks, the kittens should be fully weaned and ready to leave their mother.

RAISING KITTENS

One day old
A newborn kitten is completely dependent on its mother. Its eyelids are closed and its ears are folded back, so it cannot see or hear.

The kittens instinctively huddle together to keep warm

Three weeks old
Two weeks later, the kittens are fully mobile and eager to explore. They are now ready to be given a little solid food *(see opposite).*

One week old
The kittens' eyes open at about seven days old. The litter is still very vulnerable and helpless without the mother cat, and the young sleep huddled together for security and warmth.

Four weeks old
Once the kittens are eating solids, they can be trained to use a litter box. Place the box in a quiet spot and put the kittens on it after each feed. Never rub a kitten's nose in any accidental mess that it makes.

Five weeks old

Feed the kittens a range of different foods to encourage good eating habits in later life. Finely minced cooked meat and poached white fish can be given to add a little variety to the diet as an alternative to canned kitten food.

Six weeks old

The kittens learn how to hunt by pouncing on toy prey. Boisterous games with littermates allow them to try out offensive and defensive roles.

Seven weeks old

Regular weighing and monitoring of the kittens' weights *(see page 178)* allows you to keep an eye on their development – however, you may have a problem getting them to sit still on the scales.

Nine weeks old

At eight to nine weeks of age, the kittens should be vaccinated against Feline respiratory disease and Feline Infectious Enteritis. A kitten should not go outside until it has been vaccinated.

WEANING KITTENS		
Age	**Type of food**	**Number of feeds**
3 weeks old	Powdered cat milk substitute, a little finely chopped, cooked meat or kitten food, and mother's milk.	Place in a saucer and give 4–6 times daily.
4 weeks old	Powdered cat milk substitute, finely chopped, cooked meat or kitten food, and mother's milk.	Place in a saucer and give 4–6 times daily.
5 weeks old	Finely chopped, cooked meat or kitten food as well as mother's milk.	Provide solid food 4–5 times daily.
6–8 weeks old	Increase the amount of solid food given and decrease the kittens' access to mother cat's milk.	Provide solid food 3–4 times daily.
8 weeks and older	The kittens are fully weaned. Special kitten foods are needed until they are six months old.	Provide solid food 3–4 times daily.

PREVENTING PREGNANCY

Unless you are the owner of a pedigree cat that you intend to show or breed, you should consider having it neutered to prevent unwanted kittens. Neutering is a routine operation and is normally carried out when a kitten is between four and six months old. Neutering prevents the production of the hormones that govern a cat's sex drive and the development of undesirable behavior. An unneutered tomcat marks its territory by spraying it with pungent urine. An unspayed queen comes into heat every few weeks, when she "calls" to attract males in the vicinity.

Double pregnancy
Two pregnant cats mean double the care when the kittens arrive.

MALE CATS

A castrated cat
A neutered male cat makes a very affectionate and loving pet that is less likely to stray from home or to get into fights than a tomcat.

The head, neck, and shoulders are less muscular than in an intact cat

A tomcat (below)
A tomcat is dominated by its sex drive. The secondary sexual characteristics of a tom are unpleasant for humans and make it a difficult pet to keep indoors. It marks its territory by spraying it with pungent urine.

Fight wounds around the eyes and ears are very common

NEUTERING CHECKLIST

- A cat can be castrated or spayed at any age, provided that it is healthy.
- Early castration prevents a male cat from developing undesirable behavior.
- Alternative methods of birth control are available to prevent a queen from coming into heat.

FEMALE CATS

A spayed cat
A spayed cat looks the same as an unspayed female. Contrary to popular belief, there are no benefits in letting your cat have one litter of kittens before being spayed.

A queen in heat attracts toms by her scent

Sexual behavior (*above*)
A queen in heat is restless and noisy. If she is confined indoors, she will become frustrated and do her utmost to escape.

A spayed cat looks the same as a queen

Spay wound on the flank heals quickly

The queen (*right*)
The process of giving birth and raising young will take its toll on a female cat and may cause premature aging. It is cruel to allow a cat to go through the rigours of queening, only to have the unwanted kittens destroyed.

THE NEUTERING OPERATIONS

Castration
A male cat should ideally be neutered at about six months old. Castration is a routine operation and involves the removal of the cat's testes under a general anesthetic. There are normally no stitches. A healthy cat will be back to normal a day after the operation.

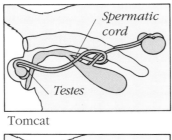

Spermatic cord

Testes

Tomcat

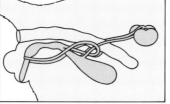

Neutered male

Spaying
A female cat should ideally be neutered at around four or five months old. A queen cannot be neutered while in heat. The operation involves the removal of the cat's uterus and ovaries under a general anesthetic. There will be a small wound on the cat's flank.

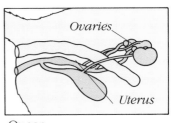

Ovaries

Uterus

Queen

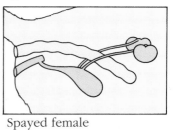

Spayed female

Chapter 9
FIRST AID

LEARN HOW to handle the most common emergencies. Prompt action in such cases as poisoning, choking, drowning, burns, bites, and stings can save life and prevent unnecessary suffering. First aid does not mean setting up a do-it-yourself veterinary practice. Your primary objectives must be to prevent further injury to the cat, to alleviate pain and distress, and to help begin the recovery process. Getting help from a vet is the highest priority. You should restrict yourself to taking only immediate necessary action to stabilize the cat's condition until veterinary assistance is available.

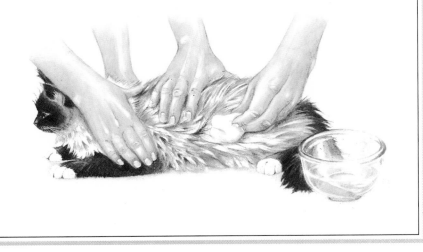

PRINCIPLES OF FIRST AID

First aid is important as an interim measure before professional veterinary help is available, and it may save your cat's life in an emergency. An injured cat may require urgent first aid to stop bleeding, treat shock, and restart or clear its breathing. The objectives of first aid should be: to prevent the cat's condition from worsening; to remove any source of harm; to alleviate pain and suffering; and to help with the recovery process. The absolute rule is to do no harm. Take essential action only and seek advice on the next course of action from a vet as soon as possible.

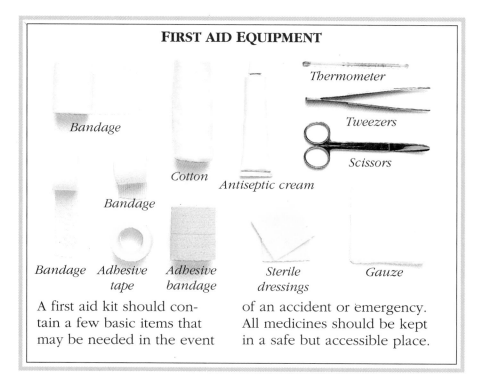

FIRST AID EQUIPMENT

Bandage

Thermometer

Tweezers

Cotton

Scissors

Antiseptic cream

Bandage

Bandage   Adhesive   Adhesive   Sterile   Gauze
           tape   bandage   dressings

A first aid kit should contain a few basic items that may be needed in the event of an accident or emergency. All medicines should be kept in a safe but accessible place.

ASSESSING AN INJURED CAT

1 Open the cat's mouth and pull the tongue forward. Clear the mouth of mucus using a piece of cotton. The head should be tilted downward so that no fluids are inhaled.

2 Count the number of breaths in or out (but not both) for one or two minutes. The rate should be 20–30 breaths per minute.

3 Feel the cat's pulse on the inside of the hind leg. Count the number of beats per minute. The rate should be 160–240 beats per minute. The heartbeat can be felt behind the cat's elbow.

Feeling the pulse

Feeling the heartbeat

CHECKING REFLEXES

Eyelid reflex

You can check the eyelid reflex by gently touching the corner of the cat's eyelid. Do not touch the eyeball itself. A cat should automatically blink if it is at all conscious.

Foot reflex

Gently pinch the web of skin between the toes. A cat should automatically react by flexing or moving its leg if it is at all conscious.

Ear reflex

Touch or gently flick the tip of the ear flap with one finger. If a cat is at all conscious, it should automatically react by twitching its ears.

FIRST AID WARNING

A semiconscious cat may feel a stimulus and be unable to react if it is in shock. Never persist with an examination longer than needed.

COLLAPSE AND SHOCK

Recognizing shock

A cat may go into a state of shock following a serious accident. It will feel cold to the touch, and its breathing and pulse will be rapid.

Conserve heat *(left)*

Make the cat as comfortable as possible. Keep it warm (unless it is suffering from heatstroke) by wrapping it loosely in a blanket or towel. Do not constrict the cat's breathing.

EMERGENCY ACTION

Do not let an unconscious cat lie on one side for more than 5–10 minutes. Do not give an unconscious cat anything by mouth.

Recovery position

If a cat is unconscious or having difficulty breathing, place it on its side with the head tilted downward. Open the mouth and ensure that the airway is clear.

ACCIDENTS

The most important thing to do in the event of an accident is to contact a vet as soon as possible. Even if a cat appears to have no external injuries, it should be given a checkup, since there may be internal damage. A vet or trained assistant can advise on immediate first aid measures. If time is critical, ask someone to telephone the clinic and alert the vet that you are on the way.

Accidental falls
A cat is unlikely to injure itself if it falls from a tree, but injuries do occur with falls from greater heights. All windows should have screens to prevent your cat from accidentally falling.

MOVING AN UNCONSCIOUS CAT

1 Move the injured cat out of any danger area. A blanket or coat will serve as an improvised stretcher. Lay the blanket out flat and then gently ease the cat onto it.

2 With the help of an assistant, gently lift the blanket up, taking care not to let the cat slip off. If the cat is conscious, you may need someone to restrain it.

3 Ensure that the airway is clear by removing any fluid from the mouth and pulling the tongue forward *(see page 278)*. Stop any severe bleeding by covering the wound with a pressure bandage or gauze pad *(see page 290)*.

4 It is advisable to transport an injured cat in a secure container. An unconscious cat can be lowered on the blanket into a large box so as not to disturb it.

MOVING AN UNCOOPERATIVE CAT

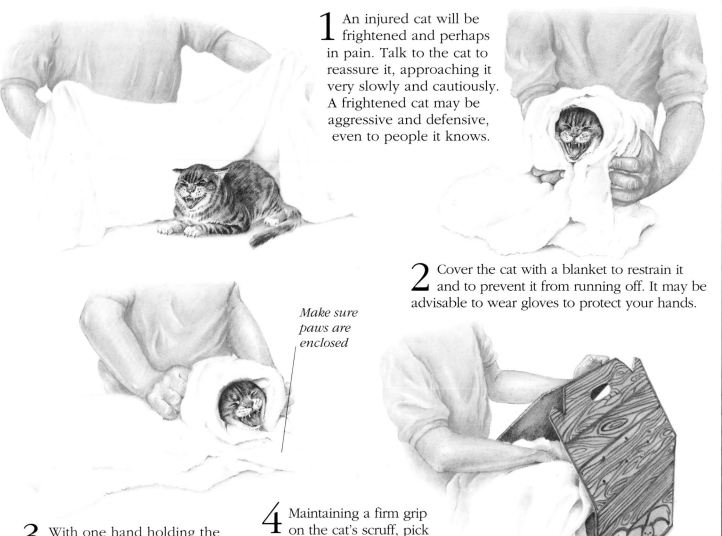

1 An injured cat will be frightened and perhaps in pain. Talk to the cat to reassure it, approaching it very slowly and cautiously. A frightened cat may be aggressive and defensive, even to people it knows.

2 Cover the cat with a blanket to restrain it and to prevent it from running off. It may be advisable to wear gloves to protect your hands.

Make sure paws are enclosed

3 With one hand holding the scruff of the neck, wrap the blanket quickly but securely around the cat's body, leaving the head exposed (*see page 249*).

4 Maintaining a firm grip on the cat's scruff, pick the cat up and put it into a carrier for transportation to the vet. Do not release your hold until you are about to fasten the carrier.

FRACTURED LIMBS

Lifting an injured cat
If you suspect that a cat has a fractured limb, handle it very carefully. Lay it on a blanket and pick it up, keeping the injured limb uppermost. Avoid twisting or bending its body. Put the cat in a carrier and get it quickly to a vet.

FIRST AID WARNING

Transport and handle a cat with a fractured limb so as to cause it the minimum disturbance. Do not attempt to apply a splint yourself, since this will distress an injured cat and probably do more harm than good.

RESUSCITATION

Prompt action taken in an emergency situation, such as a traffic accident *(see pages 280–281)*, may save your cat's life. Fortunately, emergencies are rare, but they usually occur without warning and allow little or no time to get professional help. If a cat is unconscious and its breathing and heartbeat have stopped, get someone to telephone the vet for you in order to obtain immediate advice while you try to save the animal's life.

Resuscitation must be carried out following the guidelines given opposite (or by a vet), to ensure that a cat has the best chance of recovery. A cat may suffer respiratory and heart failure following drowning, electric shock, or poisoning. For the cat to survive, its breathing or heart must be restarted within a few minutes.

ARTIFICIAL RESPIRATION

The mouth should be open to ease breathing

1 Remove the cat's collar. Lay the cat on one side in the recovery position *(see page 279)*. Open the mouth and clear the airway of any fluid *(see page 278)*.

2 If the cat has stopped breathing but the heart is still beating, proceed with artificial respiration. Using a towel, pull the tongue forward to clear the throat. This may stimulate breathing, causing the cat to regain consciousness.

3 If the cat remains unconscious, place your hands on the chest and apply gentle pressure. This expels air from the lungs, allowing them to be refilled with fresh air. Repeat every five seconds until the cat breathes.

CARDIAC MASSAGE

If a cat is unconscious and there is no sign of a heartbeat or breathing, direct stimulation of the heart may be attempted. Place your fingers on the chest at the point of the elbow and press down gently but firmly. Repeat five or six times at one-second intervals. Alternate with artificial respiration for up to ten minutes, after which the procedure is unlikely to be successful.

MOUTH-TO-MOUTH RESUSCITATION

1 If the chest cavity has been damaged, the lungs may not refill automatically, and you will have to blow air into them. Hold the unconscious cat in an upright position with its mouth closed.

2 Breathe into the nostrils for two to three seconds to inflate the lungs. The movement of the chest will be clearly visible. Pause for a two-second rest, then repeat.

Support the cat's body

3 Continue with resuscitation until the cat starts to breathe on its own. An alternative method involves breathing simultaneously into the cat's nose and open mouth.

FIRST AID WARNING

The resuscitation methods described here should only be attempted if a cat is unconscious and does not respond to normal stimuli. Do not use an excessive amount of force, since this can injure the cat.

DROWNING

1 Most cats dislike going too near water, but accidents do happen – for example, a kitten may fall into a pond or a swimming pool.

2 Take the cat out of the water and dry it quickly with a towel. If the cat is motionless, drain any water from the lungs. Hold the cat upside down by firmly gripping its hind legs above the ankle joints.

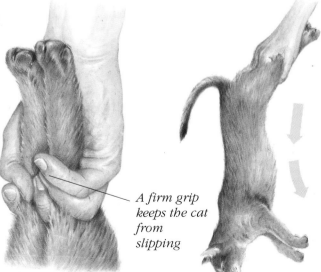

A firm grip keeps the cat from slipping

3 Swing the cat vigorously (but not violently) downward to remove water from the lungs. If there are still no signs of the cat resuming breathing, resuscitation should be started *(see opposite)*. Get the cat into warm surroundings as soon as possible.

CHOKING AND FOREIGN BODIES

Professional help from a vet is essential if a cat is having any difficulty with its breathing. However, in the unlikely event of a foreign body becoming lodged in your cat's throat, you may not have time to call a vet. You will need to take emergency action. A cat with an object such as a fish-bone lodged in its throat will be distressed and make convulsive choking noises and may paw at its mouth. This should not be confused with a cat that is coughing up a hairball.

CHOKING

1 If the cat is making coughing and choking noises and gasping for air, try to look at the back of the throat. Get someone to contact a vet for advice, meanwhile restrain the cat and open its mouth (*see page 250*) to identify the object. As with all first aid treatments, keep the cat as calm and still as possible.

FIRST AID WARNING

Do not put your fingers in a cat's mouth if it is choking, since you are likely to get bitten. It will help if the cat is restrained by being wrapped in a towel (*see page 249*).

---

2 Locate the object with a flashlight. Try to remove the object with tweezers or the handle of a teaspoon. If this does not work, try to dislodge the object by turning the cat upside down.

FOREIGN BODY IN THE MOUTH

1 A carelessly discarded fish hook can occasionally become lodged in a cat's mouth. If the hook is superficial, the barb can be carefully cut off with pliers or wire cutters.

2 The remains of the hook can then be removed safely. Do not pull on a fishing line or thread that has been swallowed. Consult a vet immediately to locate and remove the hook or needle.

FOREIGN BODY IN THE EYES

1 Grass seeds and tiny pieces of grit are the most common objects to become lodged in a cat's eyes. Hold the eyelids open and examine the eye carefully. If something has penetrated the eyeball, do not touch it.

2 If the foreign body is loose or under the eyelid, you may be able to float it out with eye drops or one or two drops of olive oil. If you are in any doubt, contact a vet.

OTHER FOREIGN BODIES

Foreign body in the ears
Similar techniques to those above can be used to remove objects such as grass seeds, from just inside the ear. Float out seeds using ear drops or one or two drops of olive oil.

FIRST AID WARNING

Never poke tweezers or anything else into a cat's ears or eyes. A great deal of damage is done this way by well-meaning owners who do more harm than good. Remember: if in doubt, it is always best to call in a vet.

Foreign body in the paws
Grass seeds and burrs can become stuck in the fur between the toes, or a cat can get a splinter in its paw. If a cat cannot remove the object with its teeth, it may need to be dislodged by hand or using tweezers. Do not try to remove any object that is embedded in the paw pad. It is advisable to consult a vet if the injury is more than a superficial scratch.

POISONING

POISONS

Poisoning is not a common occurrence, since cats are extremely careful feeders and also vomit very readily if they have eaten anything harmful. However, a cat may ingest a poison accidentally by eating either plants that have been treated with insecticides or poisoned prey. If a cat's coat becomes contaminated with chemicals, it will lick them off in an attempt to clean itself. Two common household poisons are slug killer and painkillers such as aspirin.

Treating poisoning
Contact a vet immediately and report what the cat has eaten. Signs of poisoning are usually dramatic. Do not induce vomiting unless advised to by a vet.

COAT CONTAMINATION

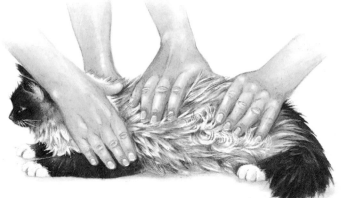

1 Soften paint or tar with petroleum jelly to help with removal. It is essential to remove any contaminant from the coat immediately to prevent the cat from licking it off while grooming.

2 Cut away any heavily contaminated fur, taking care not to cut the cat's skin. Antifreeze, bleach, and disinfectant can all be fatal if ingested.

FIRST AID WARNING

Never use solvents or paint stripper to remove paint from a cat's coat, since these are very toxic. A cat with a badly contaminated coat needs veterinary treatment. If possible, take a sample of the contaminant with you when you visit the clinic.

3 Wash as much contaminant off the coat as possible, using a dilute solution of pet shampoo and warm water. Wrap the cat in a towel, if necessary, to prevent it from licking its coat.

COMMON POISONS IN THE HOME

Poisonous plants

Many plants are toxic to cats. Most felines enjoy chewing on greenery but usually prefer grass to the leaves of plants. A cat may occasionally develop a taste for a particular plant and will need to be discouraged from eating it.

Poinsettia

Christmas cherry

Spotted dumb cane

Sweet pea

Clematis

Azalea

Oleander

Delphinium

Rhododendron

Lupin

Christmas rose

HOUSEHOLD POISONS

Poison	Signs of poisoning	Action
Rodent poisons (e.g. arsenic, strychnine, thallium, warfarin)	Restlessness, abdominal pain, vomiting, bleeding, and diarrhea. Potentially fatal.	Consult a vet immediately. Antidotes to some types of poison are available.
Antifreeze	Lack of coordination, vomiting, convulsions, followed by coma. Potentially fatal.	Consult a vet immediately. An injection may block the effect.
Alcohol, methylated spirits	Depression, vomiting, collapse, dehydration, and coma. Potentially fatal.	Consult a vet immediately. Note what type of poison has been eaten.
Painkillers (e.g. aspirin, disprin, paracetamol)	Lack of coordination, loss of balance, and vomiting. The gums will be blue if a cat has swallowed paracetamol. Potentially fatal.	Consult a vet immediately, who will induce the cat to vomit. Painkillers intended for humans are toxic to cats.
Disinfectants, household cleaners (e.g. phenols)	Severe vomiting, diarrhea, nervous signs, staggering, and coma. Potentially fatal.	Consult a vet immediately. Note what type of poison has been eaten.
Insecticides and pesticides (e.g. chlorinated hydrocarbons)	Muscle twitching, drooling, convulsions (sometimes triggered by handling), and coma. Potentially fatal.	Consult a vet immediately. There is no specific antidote.
Slug and snail poisons (e.g. metaldehyde, baysol)	Continuous salivation, muscle twitching, vomiting, diarrhea, lack of coordination, convulsions, and coma. Potentially fatal.	Consult a vet immediately. Treatment is often effective if given promptly.

BITES AND STINGS

When a cat is allowed to go outdoors, fights with other felines over territory are likely. Cat bites can quickly become infected and form abscesses, which require veterinary treatment. Insect bites and stings are rare, but can cause considerable pain and distress. In tropical countries, venomous snakes, spiders, scorpions, and toads are other hazards. Cats are usually more inquisitive than aggressive toward these creatures, but they can get too close. Kittens play-hunting are especially likely to get bitten.

INSECT BITES AND VENOM

Bee and wasp stings
Sudden swelling and pain result from stings around the face or feet. Urgent veterinary treatment is essential if a cat is unsteady or disoriented or has trouble with its breathing.

Treating stings *(right)*
A bee sting, which looks like a splinter in a red, swollen area, can be removed with tweezers. Bathe with a weak solution of sodium bicarbonate. An ice pack will help reduce swelling.

Snake and spider bites
Try to identify the type of creature that has bitten the cat, since this will help with the treatment. A snake bite will be visible as two deep puncture wounds, and the cat will keep licking the affected area.

Treating bites *(right)*
Slow the spread of the venom by applying a cold compress and then a pressure bandage just above the bite *(see page 290)*. Contact a vet immediately.

Toad venom
Some species of toad secrete a venom on their skin. If a cat picks up a toad, this venom causes the cat's mouth to become painful and inflamed.

Treating toad venom *(left)*
If the cat will allow it, flush out the mouth immediately with clean water, being careful to prevent the cat from inhaling any fluid. Wipe away excess saliva and keep the cat quiet. Seek veterinary help.

CAT BITE ABSCESS

1 When a cat bite is not detected at the time it happens, it is likely to become septic. After a few days, it will be swollen and very tender. If the cat will allow it, clean the area around the abscess and clip away surrounding fur.

2 Bathe the swollen area with lukewarm water or a weak salt solution (one teaspoonful in a glass of water). Frequent bathing should bring the abscess to a "head." Do not try to lance the abscess yourself.

Expel any remaining pus once the abscess has burst

3 After bathing for 24 hours, the abscess should burst, producing foul-smelling pus. Once the pressure has eased, the cat will feel much better.

4 Keep the wound clean and continue bathing so that the abscess does not re-form. The cat may need antibiotics to control infection.

FIGHT WOUNDS

Occasionally a cat may return home in a very disheveled state, signifying that it has been in a fight. Some of its fur may be missing, ears and eyelids may be torn, and teeth or claws broken. Any minor cuts or lacerations should be cleaned up *(see page 290)*. A bite from another cat is not normally visible at the time. In many cases, this turns septic in a few days and the wound becomes swollen and painful to the touch. If you know that your cat has been in a fight and if it seems to be distressed, it is best to take it to a vet for a thorough examination.

Ears may be torn and bleeding

Neck may be bitten

Base of the tail is a common site for abscesses

EMERGENCY ACTION

Call a vet immediately if an abscess is very large or does not rupture 24 hours after bathing. The abscess may need to be lanced and drained by a vet. Antibiotics may sometimes be required to prevent the abscess from re-forming and to eliminate bacterial infection.

Assessing an injury
Examine the cat to determine its condition. Stop any bleeding and consult a vet if an injury is serious.

BANDAGING WOUNDS

Since most cats lead quite adventurous lives, they risk an occasional injury. The most common causes of wounds are bites and scratches from other cats *(see page 289).* If your cat is injured, the main first aid aim is to control shock and minimize blood loss. The best way to stop bleeding is to cover the wound with a gauze pad and apply pressure. A handkerchief or strips of cloth can be used as a bandage in an emergency.

CUTS AND LACERATIONS

1 Examine the cat, keeping it as calm as possible. Gently wipe away any blood or dirt, using a damp cotton ball. Contact a vet if the injury is more than superficial.

2 With the help of an assistant to steady the cat, trim away any matted fur. Petroleum jelly applied around the edges of the injury will prevent hair from falling into the open wound.

3 Minor cuts and lacerations can be treated with a mild antiseptic suitable for cats, such as dilute hydrogen peroxide solution.

STOPPING BLEEDING

Apply a cold-water compress

1 Contact a vet at once if an injury is bleeding heavily. Meanwhile stanch the flow of blood with a gauze pad soaked in cold water.

2 The bleeding should stop after a minute or two. If it does not, secure the gauze with a bandage and put another pad over the top.

3 Wrap another bandage around the cat to keep the gauze pads in place. Maintain pressure on the bleeding points. Consult a vet.

APPLYING DRESSINGS

1 Simple dressings can be applied to minor wounds or to control bleeding, but bandaging of more serious injuries should be done by a vet. First cover the wound with a gauze pad.

2 Secure the gauze pad over the wound by covering with bandages. The bandage should be firm but not too tight, since this may restrict the circulation. Do not apply a tourniquet without veterinary advice.

SERIOUS INJURIES

Torso wounds
When there are very extensive injuries or bruising, a complete body bandage can be made out of a clean pillow case, in order to reduce further injury on the way to the vet. All dressings should be changed daily, or when there is evidence of blood or discharge seeping through.

BANDAGING A MINOR WOUND

FIRST AID WARNING

Never bandage a limb too tightly, since this may constrict the circulation. Do not move a limb if there is pain or swelling, since bones may be broken.

1 When bandaging a paw, first clean the site of the wound (*see opposite*). Put small tufts of cotton between the cat's toes to prevent rubbing and discomfort.

Insert cotton between the toes

2 Cover the wound with an absorbent pad $\frac{1}{2}$ in (1 cm) thick. Do not use cotton, since the fibers may stick to the wound and disturb any clot that is forming.

3 Secure the pad in position with adhesive tape, looped under the foot, then around the leg. Be careful not to restrict the blood supply. Check the wound regularly to make sure that it is healing.

BURNS AND OTHER INJURIES

E ven though cats are always getting into inaccessible places, they usually manage to avoid being burned or scalded. Their thick coats may also give them some added protection. When accidents do occur, they are usually caused by boiling water, hot grease, or open fires. Shock is associated with burns and cold-related injuries, so it is vital to consult a vet at once.

SCALDS

1 If a cat has been scalded, the affected area of its body must be swabbed with cold water as soon as possible. Do not apply any butter or skin cream to the wound.

Swab wound with cold water

2 Make an ice pack with ice cubes in a freezer bag or wrapped in a piece of clean cloth. Apply this to the burn while contacting the vet.

3 Apply petroleum jelly to the wound (if the cat will allow it). Do not cut away any surrounding fur. Do not cover the wound.

CHEMICAL BURNS

1 Wash any chemical off the coat at once. Weak solutions of sodium bicarbonate or vinegar may help neutralize the effects of acid and alkali, respectively.

2 Put an ice pack on the injured area while contacting the vet. An affected limb can be placed under cold running water for several minutes. It may be advisable to wear rubber gloves when touching any chemicals.

Use only water where chemical is unknown

ELECTRICAL BURNS AND SHOCK

1 Kittens are most likely to chew or bite through electrical wiring. Even if a cat only suffers mild burns to the tongue and to the corners of its mouth, it needs to be examined by a vet, since there may be other injuries or complications.

SUNBURN

Apply sunblock cream to ears

Sunburn on the ear tips
Cats in hot, tropical regions are prone to sunburn on their ears. As a precaution, cats with pale-colored coats should be kept indoors during the sunniest part of the day and their ears protected with a sunblock cream.

2 Switch off the current before touching the injured cat. If this is not possible, use a broom handle to move the live wire away from the cat. Contact a vet.

EMERGENCY ACTION

Severe electrical shock can be fatal or result in heart failure. The cat may require emergency resuscitation (*see pages 282–283*). Contact your vet immediately for further advice.

FROSTBITE AND HYPOTHERMIA

Frostbite
The parts of a cat's body that can be affected by frostbite in severe weather are the paws, tail, and ears. Paws can be gently warmed by immersing in warm water.

Hypothermia
This involves a cooling down of the whole body and can result in death. The cat should be placed in a warm, sheltered place and covered with blankets. Warm the cat up gradually.

OTHER EMERGENCIES

Even though most cats have no trouble giving birth, problems do sometimes occur. You should contact a vet if your cat seems to be distressed or in pain, or has been straining for more than half an hour without producing a kitten. A mother cat and newborn kittens may occasionally need immediate first aid while a vet is on the way or if veterinary help is not available. This may mean the difference between life and death. Other emergencies needing urgent first aid treatment include heatstroke and asphyxia.

LABOR PROBLEMS

When to call a vet

Keep a close but discreet watch on your cat as she goes into labor. If she seems distressed and has not delivered a kitten within 30 minutes after she has started straining, you should contact a vet.

QUEENING PROBLEMS

Disorder	Description and signs	Action
Miscarriage	Premature labor is rare in cats but can be caused by an accident, infection, stress, or an abnormal fetus. Symptoms may include straining, vomiting, diarrhea, and bleeding from the vulva.	If you know the kittens are not due, contact a vet immediately. Keep the cat warm and quiet. There is not much that can be done to prevent miscarriage once it begins.
Uterine rupture	This may occur as the result of an accident in late pregnancy, or just before or during the delivery. The queen may show signs of shock or abdominal discomfort, or she may fail to go into labor. If the queen is in shock, she may collapse, breathe rapidly, and have a racing pulse and diluted pupils.	Contact a vet immediately. Shock requires urgent veterinary treatment. Keep the cat warm and calm, reassuring it by gently speaking to it until it can be treated by a vet.
Vulval discharge and hemorrhage	Some vulval discharge is normal for a few days after the birth, but if it is brown or foul-smelling, it may indicate an infection or retained fetal membranes. Bleeding from the vulva signifies internal hemorrhage and can be life-threatening.	Consult a vet immediately. Keep the queen warm and quiet to prevent her from going into shock. Put a pad of gauze against the vulva to soak up any discharge or blood.
Fading Kitten Syndrome	Sometimes kittens may be born underweight or deformed or fail to suckle. In some cases, apparently normal kittens will fade away and die after a few days or weeks.	There is often not much that can be done to save affected kittens, although you may be able to feed them by hand. Severely deformed kittens may need to be humanely destroyed by a vet.
Rejected kittens	Occasionally, a queen may not be able to produce sufficient milk or be unable to nurse her litter. She may reject the kittens shortly after the birth, or the runt of the litter may be ousted by its siblings. Like many animals, a cat produces several offspring to allow for some not surviving to adulthood in the wild. Rejected kittens may be fostered by another queen or reared by hand (see page 271).	Consult a vet for advice. Orphan kittens must be kept warm, well fed, and clean. To begin with, they must be fed every two hours with special replacement cat milk. After feeding, the anal area of a kitten needs to be gently wiped with a piece of damp cotton to encourage elimination of waste products. The mother cat may accept the kittens back when they are partially weaned.

HELPING WITH QUEENING

1 If a kitten is stuck partly out of the vulva and the queen seems to be in difficulty, you need to act immediately. Wash your hands, then lubricate the vulva with petroleum jelly. Firmly grasp the kitten and gently ease it out as the queen bears down.

2 If the queen ignores the kitten, you must pull off the membrane covering it and clear its mouth and nostrils of mucus. Rub it dry with a towel. When it is breathing, soak some cotton and scissors in antiseptic. Tie the cotton around the umbilical cord about 1 in (2.5 cm) from the navel.

3 Cut the umbilical cord on the side attached to the placenta. Alternatively the cord can be separated by hand. Do not pull on the cord, since this may damage the kitten. Encourage the kitten to suckle.

FIRST AID WARNING

If a kitten's head or one of its limbs is held up inside the birth passage, do not attempt to force it out. Seek veterinary help immediately.

HEATSTROKE AND ASPHYXIA

Heatstroke
A cat suffering from heatstroke may collapse. Lower its temperature by wrapping it in towels soaked in cool (but not ice-cold) water.

Asphyxia
A cat may collapse if it inhales carbon monoxide fumes. It must be allowed to breathe fresh air as soon as possible and encouraged to move about to stimulate circulation.

Chapter 10

SHOWING

BREEDERS WHO exhibit pedigree cats at shows are striving to achieve perfection within the standards of their chosen breed. Competition among entrants to have their feline judged to be the best of a breed or best in a category is always intense. The formalities for entering a cat in a competition and the ways in which different types of cat show are organized vary around the world. Shows often have classes for household pets, and this is probably a good place for a beginner to start. The competitive drive of showing your cat can become totally absorbing, so be warned!

CAT SHOWS

Breeders constantly strive to produce the finest cats for exhibition, so visiting a show can be a rewarding and educational experience. Almost every familiar breed is likely to be present at a large cat show, as well as a few rare ones not generally seen. Shows are run by the controlling authority for all cat clubs and societies in a particular country. In the United States, the Cat Fanciers' Association (CFA) and other cat organizations establish breed standards, register pedigrees, and approve the dates of major shows. In Great Britain, the Governing Council of the Cat Fancy (GCCF) is responsible for the show rules and has approved standards for all the pedigree cat breeds.

THE HISTORY OF CAT SHOWS

First pedigree breeder
An early North American breeder, Mrs. Clinton Locke, pictured with her two Siamese cats.

The first modern cat show *(below)*
Crystal Palace in London was the venue for the first large cat show, which took place in 1871. Longhairs and British Shorthairs were among the cats exhibited. The first North American cat show was held in New England for the Maine Coon breed at about the same time.

HOW A SHOW IS ORGANIZED

Kitten class
Cats under nine months of age have separate open classes for all breeds. Kittens compete with others of the same breed, sex, and color. At a large show, kitten classes for popular breeds may be divided by sex or by age.

Open class
The most important of all the classes. At a large cat show there will be open classes for all the breeds represented. To become a champion, a cat must win three open classes at different shows.

Neuter class
Pedigree cats that are castrated males or spayed females have separate open classes of their own. They compete against other neuters of the same breed and are judged according to the same breed standards as intact cats.

Household pet class
Neutered cats of unknown or unregistered parentage can be entered in the class for household pets. There is no written standard for nonpedigree cats. They are judged for their uniqueness, any unusual markings, and temperament.

BRITISH AND AMERICAN SHOWS

Shows in Great Britain
All cat shows operate under the Governing Council of the Cat Fancy. After a veterinary inspection, cats are given a number. Pens are numbered but carry no other distinguishing marks. Judging takes place on a table that is wheeled from pen to pen *(see page 303)*.

Shows in the United States
The Cat Fanciers' Association is the largest of the eight cat authorities in the United States. Classes are divided into "allbreed" or "specialty," with a separate household pet competition. Judging takes place on tables set up in full view of the public attending the show.

JUDGING SHOW CATS

Over the past century, interest in pedigree cats has played a central role in creating the rich spectrum of breeds we see today. Selective breeding programs have been used to enhance particular physical characteristics and to create cats that look attractive to the human eye. Fortunately, in contrast to dog breeding, there have been few instances of this having harmful effects. A pedigree cat is judged against a standard that specifies how a perfect example of its type should look. Points are awarded for the appearance of the cat's head, eyes, body, and coat.

Registering a kitten
Register your pedigree kitten with the appropriate cat association.

EXAMPLES OF HOW CATS ARE JUDGED

Head (20 points)
Round face, with full cheeks and a strong chin.

Body (25 points)
"Cobby" type, low on legs, with a broad, deep chest.

Tail (10 points)
Thick and of medium length.

British Blue Shorthair *(left)*
The British Shorthair is a compact and powerful cat, with a strong, muscular body on short legs. It has a broad head, with round eyes, and ears set well apart.

Eyes (10 points)
Copper, orange, or deep gold in color.

Coat (35 points)
Short and dense (not too long or fluffy). Color should be light to medium blue, with no tabby markings or silver tipping.

Tail (10 points)
Short and bushy, but in proportion to body length.

Head (25 points)
Round and broad, with a short nose and a strong chin.

Eyes (10 points)
Deep orange or brilliant copper.

Cream Shaded Cameo Longhair *(right)*
This classic Pedigree Longhair cat has a "cobby" build, with a sturdy, rounded body and short, thick legs. It has a broad head, with round eyes and small ears.

Coat (40 points)
Long and thick, and fine in texture. Color should be white with cream tipping, with no tabby markings.

Body (15 points)
Stocky or "cobby" in build, with short, thick legs.

Head (20 points)
Wedge-shaped face, long and narrow, with pricked ears.

Eyes (20 points)
Clear, bright, vivid blue. A squint is a fault.

Tail (5 points)
Long and tapering, with no kink at the end.

Red-point Siamese *(left)*
The Siamese has a unique, pale-colored coat and darker markings on its face, paws, and tail. It has a long, slim, oriental build, with slanted eyes, and elegant legs and feet.

Body (20 points)
Long, svelte, oriental build, with slim legs.

Coat (35 Points)
Very short and fine. Color should be white, shading to apricot on the body and reddish-gold on the points (barring is permissible).

Usual Abyssinian *(right)*
The Abyssinian's ticked coat, in which each hair has several different-colored bands, is very distinctive. The build of this cat is muscular and lithe, and the head is less elongated than that of the Siamese.

Head (15 points)
Round and gently wedge-shaped, with large, preferably tufted, ears.

Eyes (10 points)
Amber, hazel, or green. A light eye color is undesirable.

Coat (45 points)
Short, fine, and close-lying, with double or preferably treble ticking. Color should be a ruddy brown ticked with black. A pale overall color is a fault and so are black or gray base hairs.

Body (30 points)
Medium in length, and lithe and muscular in appearance. A "cobby" build is not permissible.

Head (20 points)
Medium, wedge-shaped head, with a distinct nose break.

Eyes (25 points)
Golden-yellow eyes preferred. Green eyes are a serious fault in Brown Burmese, but Blue Burmese may show a slight fading of color.

Coat (20 points)
Short and glossy, with a satin finish. Color should be a mixture of blue and cream, with no obvious barring.

Body (35 points)
Medium in size, feeling muscular and heavier than it appears.

Blue Tortoiseshell Burmese *(left)*
The Burmese cat is prized for its smooth and glossy coat. Its build is more round-bodied and muscular than that of the Siamese. The British Burmese is more oriental in appearance than the sturdier North American variety.

TAKING PART IN A CAT SHOW

The preparations for showing your cat should begin several weeks, or even months, beforehand. If your cat has not been shown before, you will have to get it accustomed to being confined in a pen and to being handled. Maintaining a show cat involves good feeding and daily grooming.

GROOMING FOR SHOWING

A cat's eyes and ears must be spotlessly clean

1 A longhaired cat needs to be bathed before a show to ensure that its coat is in perfect condition *(see pages 196–197)*. On the show day, remove any staining around the eyes with a damp cotton ball.

2 Final grooming takes place in the pen. Carefully brush the shorter hairs on the cat's face with a small toothbrush. Do not put the toothbrush too close to the eyes.

3 As a finishing touch, use a slicker brush to make the cat's fur stand out fully from its body. The fur around the cat's neck should frame the face.

SHOWING EQUIPMENT
The only items allowed in a cat's pen are a litter box, blanket, and water bowl. You will also require the following: cat food; a white ribbon or elastic collar on which the cat's entry number can be pinned; vaccination certificates; show documentation; and brushes and combs.

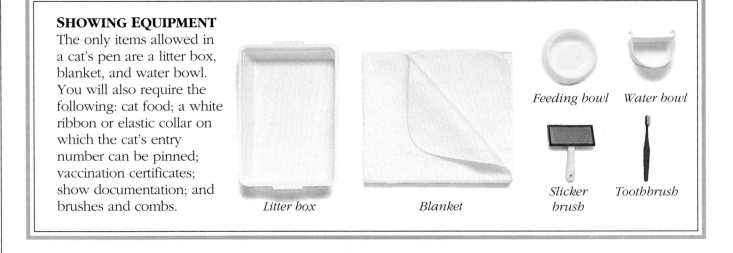

Litter box *Blanket* *Feeding bowl* *Water bowl* *Slicker brush* *Toothbrush*

THE DAY OF THE SHOW

Examining (left)
Any cat entered for competition should be in good health. In some countries every cat entered is examined by a vet. A sick animal is not allowed to take part in the competition.

A cat is scrutinized by a judge

Judging (right)
Cats are judged at a movable table near their pens. In North American shows, cats are examined in public.

Awarding points (below)
A pedigree cat is judged against its breed standard. A maximum of 100 points is awarded for its head, eyes, condition, and coat *(see pages 300–301)*.

Prizewinning cat
A well-trained show cat sits proudly in its pen and enjoys all the attention that it receives. Rosettes are pinned on the pens of the winners.

Best in show (below)
The climax of a cat show comes when all the entries have been judged. This is when the best cat in the show is announced.

GLOSSARY

Abscess Collection of pus forming painful swelling. Usually the result of a cat bite.
Ailurophile Cat lover.
Ailurophobe Cat hater.
Albino Lack of pigment melanin, causing white fur and pink eyes.
Angora Breed of cat with long hair and slim, long body. Lacks woolly undercoat of true longhaired cats.
Awn hairs Bristly hairs of undercoat with thickened tips.

Back-cross Offspring of mating between adult cat and its own kitten.
Bicolor Coats consisting of white hair mixed with one other color.
Breed A type of cat, named for its color, size, and shape.
Breed standard A description of ideal characteristics against which each breed of cat is measured. This is determined by the national cat society of each country.

Calico American name for Tortoiseshell-and-White cat.
Canker See Otitis.
Carpal pad Extra fleshy pad above others on front paws, thought to help stop skidding when a cat lands after jumping.
Castrate To remove testicles to prevent reproduction and sexual behavior.
Cat flap Hinged flap set in a door that enables a cat to come and go as it wants.
Cat flu See Feline respiratory disease.
Catnip The herb Nepeta cataria, which gives off a scent that most cats find irresistible. Used in some cat toys.
Cattery Establishment that boards cats while owners are away.
Chinchilla Longhaired cat whose white fur is tipped with black.
Chlamydial disease Affects cat's eyes and the respiratory system.
Chromosomes Tiny strands of DNA that store genetic information.
Cobby A stocky, rounded body shape, with short legs and long fur.
Coccidiosis Caused by protozoan parasite that affects the digestive system.
Colorpoint A cat whose face, ears, legs, feet, and tail are of a different color than the rest of its body.
Conjunctivitis Inflammation of the thin outer layer of the eye, causing watering and soreness. Associated with Feline respiratory disease.

Dermatitis An inflammation of the skin.
Dew claw Extra toe on hind leg above paw. Its function is not known.
DNA Chemical substance that makes up chromosomes, from which all life begins.
Dominant gene The gene that overrides a recessive gene in a pairing of chromosomes, so that its characteristics are always evident in the offspring.
Down hairs Soft hairs under guard hairs that insulate body.

Ear mites Tiny parasites living in ear canal, causing irritation.
Elizabethan collar Cardboard or plastic funnel fitted over head to prevent cat interfering with wounds.
Estrus Periods during which a female cat is sexually responsive to a male, commonly known as heat or season.

Feline Calici Virus (FCV) One of the two common viruses causing Feline respiratory disease. Signs include coughing, sneezing, watery eyes, and runny nose. See also Feline respiratory disease and Feline Viral Rhinotracheitis.
Feline Dysautonomia Nervous disorder causing persistent pupil dilation, regurgitation, and rapid weight loss. Once known as Key-Gaskell Syndrome.
Feline Infectious Anaemia Disease caused by parasite in blood. Signs are fever, weight loss, and lethargy.
Feline Immunodeficiency Virus (FIV) A relative of the HIV virus, which weakens the immune system, eventually causing death. Highly contagious to other cats, but not to humans or other animals.
Feline Infectious Enteritis (FIE) Virus causing loss of white blood cells, and fatal in most cases. Signs include depression, severe diarrhea, vomiting, and abdominal pain. Also called Feline Panleukopenia.
Feline Infectious Peritonitis (FIP) Usually fatal virus disease. Signs include fluid accumulation in the abdomen, jaundice, and anemia.
Feline Leukemia Virus (FeLV) Virus affecting lymphatic system, suppressing immunity to disease. Usually fatal. Signs include weight loss, vomiting, diarrhea, and difficulty in breathing.
Feline Panleukopenia See Feline Infectious Enteritis.
Feline respiratory disease Sometimes known as "cat flu". See Feline Viral Rhinotracheitis and Feline Calici Virus.
Feline Urological Syndrome (FUS) Inflammation of bladder and urethra. Sandy deposits in bladder and urethra can lead to blood in urine and difficulty in urination. Obstruction is a real emergency.
Feline Viral Rhinotracheitis (FVR) The more serious of the two common viruses that cause Feline respiratory disease. Signs include high fever, and a discharge from the eyes and nose. May sometimes be fatal, especially in kittens and elderly cats. See also Feline respiratory disease and Feline Calici Virus.
Feral Domestic animals that have reverted to a wild state.
Flea collar Special collar with chemical impregnated to kill fleas.
Fleas The most common parasite found on a cat's skin. Live by feeding on blood. Cats may be sensitive to bites or flea dirt.
Flehming Grimacing and lifting the upper lip to bring a scent into contact with the Jacobson's organ for sensory analysis. Usually related to sexual behavior of tomcats.
Flukes Parasites found in intestine and liver, causing diarrhea and anemia.
Foreign Another term for a cat of oriental appearance, such as a Siamese cat.

Gastritis Inflammation of the stomach walls causing vomiting and lack of appetite.
Gene Tiny bead of DNA on chromosomes that carries information on physical characteristics such as coat color, eye color, length of coat, and many others.
Gene pool The total number of genes available within a breed.
Glaucoma Enlargement of eyeball caused by increased pressure from within.
Groom To brush or comb a cat's coat.

Guard hairs Thick, coarse hairs that protect softer down hairs underneath, in some cats providing a waterproof layer.

Hematoma Blood blister in ear flap usually due to scratching and bursting of a blood vessel.

Harvest mites Parasites that appear in the autumn and can cause skin irritation. Also known as chiggers.

Haw See Third eyelid.

Heat See Estrus.

Heartworms Parasite found in tropical areas of the world. Transmitted by mosquitoes and lives in heart.

Hock A cat's ankle.

Hookworms Bloodsucking worms that live in small intestine. Can cause weight loss, diarrhea, and anemia.

Intact An unneutered cat.

Jacobson's organ A sensory organ above the roof of the mouth that analyzes smells and tastes, and sends a signal to the brain.

Keratitis Inflammation of cornea, resulting in eye becoming cloudy.

Key-Gaskell Syndrome See Feline Dysautonomia.

Kitten pen Wire cage in which a new cat or kitten can live briefly while being introduced to a household.

Lactational Tetany Due to inadequate calcium levels in blood during nursing. Causes vomiting and staggering. Also known as Milk Fever.

Lice Parasites that suck blood, causing anemia in a severe infestation.

Litter The absorbent granules used in a cat's toilet box. Also a family of kittens.

Litter box Shallow box filled with litter.

Longhaired Cat whose coat has long top hairs, with a thick, woolly undercoat.

Mange mite Minute parasites that burrow into a cat's skin, causing chronic hair loss, irritation, and inflammation.

Manx Tailless breed of cat, caused by mutant gene that can be associated with lethal characteristics.

Mastitis Infection of milk glands.

Metacarpal pads Thick pads of tissue on paws to keep a cat from slipping.

Middle ear disease Infection of inner ear. Signs include tilting of head to one side, staggering, and partial deafness.

Milk Fever See Lactational Tetany.

Neuter To castrate males or spay females to prevent reproduction and unwanted sexual behaviour.

Nictitating membrane See Third eyelid.

Odd-eyed Cat with one blue eye and the other orange. Blue eyes in white cats may be associated with deafness.

Oriental Foreign breeds with almond-shaped eyes, wedge-shaped heads, and long limbs. Examples are the Abyssinian, Siamese, and Burmese.

Otitis A term for inflammation of outer ear, caused by mites, bacteria, or foreign bodies. Also known as canker.

Pedigree A record of ancestry, showing a cat's family tree over several generations.

Pedigree Longhair Pedigree cat with a long outer coat. Also known as Persian.

Peritonitis An inflammation of the peritoneum in the abdomen. See also Feline Infectious Peritonitis.

Persian See Pedigree Longhair.

Points The face, ears, legs, feet, and tail, which may be a different color than the rest of the body, as in a Siamese cat.

Polydactyly Having extra number of toes.

Prolapse Condition in which internal organs such as uterus or rectum are pushed outside body by straining.

Quarantine Period of isolation in which animals entering certain countries from abroad must be kept to prevent the spread of rabies.

Queen Unspayed female cat.

Queening Giving birth.

Rabies Serious virus disease affecting nervous system. Transmission is by bite from an infected animal.

Recessive gene One whose characteristics are overridden by a dominant gene in each pairing of chromosomes, so that it is not evident in the resulting offspring.

Register List of pedigree cats. In order to be allowed to enter cat shows, each purebred cat must be registered upon birth with the national cat authority.

Ringworm Form of fungal infection that causes scaly skin and irritation.

Roundworms Parasites found in cat's digestive tract, feeding on digesting food. Can cause diarrhea, especially in kittens.

Scent marking A cat marks its territory with urine, or with scent from glands on the head, sending a clear message to any intruding cats. It may also scratch furniture and trees, sharpening its claws and leaving a scent from glands on its paw pads.

Scratching post A covered post upon which a cat can exercise its claws without damaging furniture. It will also mark the post with scent to denote its territory.

Scratching See Scent marking.

Season See Estrus.

Selective breeding Breeding of pedigree cats by planned matings to enhance certain physical characteristics, such as eye color.

Siamese Oriental, shorthaired cat, with pale-colored coat and points of a different color.

Spay Operation to remove ovaries and uterus to prevent estrus and pregnancy.

Stud Uncastrated tomcat used specifically for breeding purposes.

Tabby Cat with striped, blotched, or spotted markings. Pattern used in the wild for breaking up the body shape so that the cat can hide itself in the undergrowth.

Tapeworms Intestinal parasites that feed on cat's partly digested food. Fleas are needed to complete the life cycle.

Territory Area patrolled by a cat, which it considers to be its own. A cat will fiercely defend its territory against intruders.

Third eyelid Eyelid that is sometimes visible at corners of a cat's eyes.

Ticks Parasites that burrow into a cat's skin to feed on blood. Some types of tick can transmit diseases.

Tipped Coat whose top hairs are tipped with a different color than the undercoat.

Tomcat An uncastrated male cat.

Topcoat Outer layer of hair that forms overall color of cat.

Tortoiseshell Coat resulting from linkage of dominant and recessive orange genes, both carried by female chromosome. Tortoiseshell cats are usually female.

Toxoplasmosis Disease caused by parasite, often in raw meat, which affects digestive system. Causes diarrhea. Can sometimes be transmitted to humans.

Tumor Swelling on or beneath skin due to abnormal growth. Can be cancerous.

Undercoat Thick layer of insulating fur under topcoat.

Vetting in Examination by a vet upon entry into a British cat show. No longer required in American cat shows.

Weaning Gradual change in a kitten's diet from mother's milk to solid food.

Zoonoses Diseases that can be passed between vertebrate species including man.

Additional Information

USEFUL ADDRESSES

American Cat Association
8101 Katherine Avenue,
Panorama City, CA 91402
(818) 782-6080

**American Cat Fanciers'
Association, Inc**
Highway 248
Branson, MO 65616
(417) 334-5430
Cat registry; sponsors cat clubs throughout
the country and internationally.

**American Society for the
Prevention of Cruelty
to Animals (ASPCA)**
441 East 92nd Street,
New York, New York 10028
(212) 876-7700
Nonprofit animal advocacy group;
America's oldest humane society.
Educational information, publications,
audiovisual materials, legislative support
and activities nationwide, behavior hotline
for NYC area.

**American Veterinary
Medical Association**
1931 North Meacham Road,
Schaumburg, Illinois 60173

Canadian Cat Association
83 Kennedy Road South,
Unit 1805,
Brampton, Ontario
Canada L6W 3P3
(416) 459-1481

Cat Fanciers' Association, Inc.
1805 Atlantic Avenue,
Manasquan, New Jersey 08736
(908) 528-9797
The largest cat registry in North America.
Sponsors cat showsthroughout the country
and internationally. Produces educational
information and audiovisual materials.

Cat Fancier's Federation
9509 Montgomery Road,
Cincinnati, Ohio 45242
(513) 984-1841
Cat Registry; sponsors cat shows.

**Humane Society of
the United States**
2100 L Street, NW,
Washington, DC 20037
Nonprofit animal advocacy organization.
Publications, specialty items, audiovisual
materials, and legislative and
investigative activity.

International Cat Association
PO Box 2684,
Harlingen, Texas 78551
(512) 428-8046
Cat registry; sponsors cat clubs around the
United States and internationally.

PERIODICALS

The Cat Fancier's Newsletter
304 Hastings St.
Redlands, CA 92373
(714) 793-5061

Cat World International
P.O. Box 35635
Phoenix, AZ 85069
(602) 995-1822

Cat Fancy
PO Box 6050,
Mission Viejo, CA 92690
(714) 855-8822

Cats Magazine
PO Box 290037,
Port Orange, FL 32129
(904) 788-2770

I Love Cats
950 Third Avenue, 16th Floor,
New York, New York 10022
(212) 888-1855

FURTHER READING

Anderson, Robert, & Wrede, Barbara,
Caring for Older Cats & Dogs,
Williamson Pub. Co., 1990

Behrend, Katrin & Wegler, Monica,
How to Raise a Happy & Healthy Cat,
Barron's, 1991

Caras, Roger, *The Cat Is Watching,*
Simon & Schuster, 1990

Caras, Roger, *A Celebration of Cats,*
Simon & Schuster, 1987

Gerstenfeld, Sheldon, *The Cat Care
Book,* Addison Wesley, 1990

Hawcroft, Tim, *The Howell Book of
Cat Care,* Howell Book House, 1991

Martyn, Elizabeth, & Taylor, David,
The Little Cat Behavior Book, Dorling
Kindersley Inc., 1991

Martyn, Elizabeth, & Taylor, David,
The Little Cat Care Book, Dorling
Kindersley Inc., 1991

Morris, Desmond, *Catwatching,*
Crown, 1987

Taylor, David, *The Ultimate Cat Book,*
Simon & Schuster, 1989

Thies, Dagmar, *Cat Care,* T.F.H.
Publications, 1989

Viner, Bradley, *The Cat Care Manual,*
Barron's, 1986

Index

Acknowledgements

SECTION ONE

Author's acknowledgments

Almost all of my professional hours are spent in clinical practice but when I need a little writing time Jenny Berry and Amanda Topp, two exceptionally good veterinary nurses, hold the fort. Many thanks. The same applies to my family, especially my wife Julia, who lets me disappear into the country each weekend to concentrate on writing. I did not know it at the time, and I am sure that he did not realize it either, but my father, through his collection of animals, primed me from childhood to have an interest in animal behavior. As I write this he remains a healthy octogenarian, proud as Punch of what his youngest son does. I hope he enjoys showing this book to his friends.

Publisher's acknowledgments

For book design and illustration Cooper•Wilson; for computer graphics Salvo Tomasselli; for editorial assistance Corinne Hall, Charyn Jones, Stephanie Jackson, Jackie Douglas and Vicky Davenport; for the index Karin Woodruff; for design assistance Juliet Cooke; for picture research Diana Morris; for providing cats for photography on location Natasha Guttmann, Esther Bruml, Karen Tanner, Carolyn Stephenson, Blackie Merrifield, Jenny Berry, Jane Burton, Heather Creasey, Liz Button, Lynn Medcalf and Margaret Correia; for location photography Steve Gorton and Tim Ridley; for providing props John Palmer Ltd. (cat brush) and Steetley Minerals Ltd. (cat-litter basket).

Jane Burton would like to thank:

For help to find, handle and feed cats Hazel Taylor, Sue Hall, Di Everet, Les Tolley and Janet Tedder; for lending cats for photography Carolyn Woods; for modelling Arabella Grinstead and Louisa Hall.

Photographic credits

Key: l = left, r = right, t = top, b = bottom, c = center.
All photography by Jane Burton except for:
Steve Gorton: **p.5** all pictures, **p.9** bl, br, **p.11** br, **p.15** tl, bl, **p.16** t, **p.45** b, **p. 107** bl, **p.111** bl, **p.117** t, b, **p.118** both pictures, **p.121** b. *Tim Ridley:* **p.25** br, **p.27** bl, **pp.40-41** all pictures except for **40** br, **41** tr; **p.42** br, **p.46** l, **p.95** br, **p.107** tr. *Dave King:* **p.95** cr, **p.110** br, **p.112** t, **p.120** tr, **p.122** t. *Kim Taylor:* **p.22** cl, **pp. 92-93** c. *Animals Unlimited:* **p.111** br, **p.119** bc, br. *Bruce Coleman Ltd:* **p.24** cl, **p.25** tl, **p.112** b; **p.113** tl; *Jane Burton* **p.19** br; *Hans Reinhard* **p.119** t, c. *Marc Henrie:* **p.114** t. *David Keith Jones:* **p.114** br. *Natural History Photographic Agency:* *M. Savonius* **p.90** c.

SECTION TWO

Author's acknowledgments

Any work of this kind requires an enormous effort from a large number of people. All of these deserve my sincere gratitude. The team at Dorling Kindersley is unsurpassed. In the forefront of this admirable group are Project Editor Alison Melvin, Art Editor Lee Griffiths, and Managing Editor Krystyna Mayer. It is these tireless people who create the book. The author is only one of the team. The photographs produced by Dorling Kindersley set the highest standards. Steve Gorton and Tim Ridley approached the notoriously difficult task of capturing cats in every pose with humanity, immense skill, and inextinguishable good humor.

My former colleagues at the Waltham Centre for Pet Nutrition, especially Dr. Helen Nott, Dr. Jo Wills, Dr. Ivan Burger, Dr. Kay Earle, Helen Munday, and Dr. Ian Robinson have been most helpful, as have Pedigree Petfoods, the Pedigree Education Centre, and Denise Reed. Many veterinarians and the BSAVA have given help and encouragement, particularly Dr. Bruce Fogle. The Royal Veterinary College, my own *alma mater*, was very helpful. I am grateful to the Principal, Professor Lance Lanyon, and the staff of the Queen Mother Hospital and its Director, Professor Roger Batt. Polly Curds and Liz Ravenor of the RVC Animal Care Trust provided much cheerfully given assistance. Professor Oswald Jarrett and Dr. Helen Laird of Glasgow University Veterinary School kindly sent information on feline viruses.

Among the countless individuals who I must thank are Betty Thomas and Sophie Hamilton-Moore of the Feline Advisory Bureau, Peter Neville, everyone at the Wood Green Animal Shelter, and Benita Horder, librarian at the Royal College of Veterinary Surgeons.

Publisher's acknowledgments

For providing animals for photography: Ben and Vicky Adams *(Ferret)*; Rosemary Alger *(Champion Typha Plush Velvat, also known as "The Toy Boy")*; Stacey Berenson *(Tammy)*; Jenny Berry *(Hamster and Puffin)*; Maria Dorey *(Bella)*; Moyra Flynn *(Sydney, Bianca, Bill, and Ben)*; Janice Hall *(Seamus)*; Pat Heller *(Phoebe)*; Intellectual Animals *(Jules, Wilma, Cherry, and Glynis)*; Sue Kempster *(Harry and Melissa)*; Krystyna Mayer *(Mruczek)*; Alison Melvin *(Nelson and Winston)*; Christina Oates *(Cloud)*; Eunice Paterson *(Soames and Fleur)*; Sally Powell *(Violet)*; Sue Roberts *(Blue Boy and Hoppy)*; Pauline Rogers *(Misty, Lulu, and Ollie)*; Di Sanderson *(Billy)*; Celia Slack *(Bluey and kittens)*; Katy Slack *(Chockie*

and kittens); Karen Tanner *(Cherami, Fortune Cookie, and kittens)*; Hazel Taylor *(Maisie)*; Amanda Topp *(Tiddles)*; Alison Trehorne *(Lollipop and Humbug)*; RVC Animal Care Trust *(Chloe)*; Beany Smith *(Smudge)*.
For modeling: "Cookie" Baran and Stacey Berenson. For handling cats: Kate Forey, Jenny Berry, Etta Rumsey, and Di Sanderson. For supplying equipment and materials: Animal Fair, Kensington, London W8.
For design assistance: Colette Cheng. For editorial assistance: Lynn Parr. For page make-up and computer assistance: Patrizio Semproni. For picture research: Diana Morris.
Dorling Kindersley wish to thank Terence C. Bate BVSc, LLB, MRCVS of the RSPCA for his valuable advice on the text.

ASPCA acknowledgments

Numerous staff provided special assistance, helping to research and review material for this publication, most especially Gordon Robinson, VMD, Micky Niego, Jacque Schultz, and Liz Teal.

Illustrations

Angelica Elsebach: 277, 278-279, 280-281, 282-283, 284-285, 286, 288-289, 290-291, 292-293, 294-295 Chris Forsey: 133, 165, 167, 171, 218, 219, 220, 222, 224, 226, 228, 229, 230, 232, 234, 236, 238, 240, 242, 244.

Photography

KEY: t *top*, b *bottom*, c *center*, l *left*, r *right*
All photography by Steve Gorton and Tim Ridley except for:
Animals Unlimited: 166bl, 190t, 191bl, 179bl Ardea: 133c Bodleian Library, Oxford: 132t
Jane Burton: 128tl, 130, 136t, 137r, 138t, 138b, 139cr, 141cr, 145b 147b, 154c, 156r, 162b, 164c, 164b, 166t, 176t, 178t, 191br, 198-199, 200-201, 202-203, 204-205, 206-207, 218b, 220t, 225bl, 230b, 234t, 239b, 240t, 241b, 244t, 245b, 253cl, 263bl, 274b, 299tl Bruce Coleman Ltd: 133tr, 164t Hans Reinhard Eric Crichton: 287cl, 287cr, 287brc Tom Dobbie: 287t E.T. Archive: 132br John Glover: 287crc, 287blc Jerry Harpur: 287clc, 287bl, 287br Marc Henrie: 221b Michael Holford: 132c, 132bl Larry Johnson: 299br Dave King: 127tr, 129b, 131cl, 131b, 139cl, 141t, 142-143, 146t, 146c, 147t, 190b, 191c, 191c, 208, 209t, 209c, 212-213, 214, 253bl, 263t, 263c, 263cr, 274c, 299c, 300c, 300b, 301 Oxford Scientific Films: 133tl Frank Schneidemeyer, 170b London Scientific Films David Ward: 254b Matthew Ward: 250t, 251, 253cr, 253br.